Colección Támesis

SERIE A: MONOGRAFÍAS, 303

GENDER, RACE AND PATRIOTISM
IN THE WORKS OF NÍSIA FLORESTA

CHARLOTTE HAMMOND MATTHEWS

GENDER, RACE AND PATRIOTISM IN THE WORKS OF NÍSIA FLORESTA

TAMESIS

First published 2012 by Tamesis, Woodbridge

ISBN 978 1 85566 235 3

Tamesis is an imprint of Boydell & Brewer Ltd
PO Box 9, Woodbridge, Suffolk IP12 3DF, UK
and of Boydell & Brewer Inc.
668 Mt Hope Avenue, Rochester, NY 14620, USA
website: www.boydellandbrewer.com

A CIP catalogue record for this book is available
from the British Library

The publisher has no responsibility for the continued existence or accuracy
of URLs for external or third-party internet websites referred to in this book,
and does not guarantee that any content on such websites is, or will remain,
accurate or appropriate

Papers used by Boydell & Brewer Ltd are natural, recyclable products
made from wood grown in sustainable forests

MIX
Paper from
responsible sources
FSC® C013604

Printed and bound in Great Britain by
CPI Group (UK) Ltd, Croydon, CR0 4YY

CONTENTS

ACKNOWLEDGEMENTS

This study was funded by the Arts and Humanities Research Council (AHRC) in conjunction with the research project 'Gendering Latin American Independence: Women's Political Culture and the Textual Construction of Gender' (2002–5).

I wish to thank Catherine Davies, Iona Macintyre, Jill Liddell, Nathalie Bernardo da Câmara, Peggy Sharpe, and Steve Matthews, as well as the many Brazilian archivists and librarians, in particular Maria das Graças Gonçalves da Silva and her colleagues in the Biblioteca Nacional in Rio, for all their invaluable support and assistance. Above all I would like to offer the warmest thanks to Hilary Owen for her guidance and encouragement over many years, and for the conversation that first set me on this path.

Elements of Chapters 3, 4 and 5 were first published as 'Nature, Nurture and Nation: Nísia Floresta's engagement in the breast-feeding debate in Brazil and France', Feminist Review, 79 (2005), reproduced with permission of Palgrave Macmillan. Part of Chapter 2 appears as 'Teaching, Preaching and Practice: Nísia Floresta's shifting vision of women's education in nine-teenth-century Brazil', in Dominant Culture and the Education of Women, edited by Julia Paulk (Cambridge: Cambridge Scholars Publishing, 2008). A modified version of Chapter 1 appears as 'Between "founding text" and "literary prank": reasoning the roots of Nísia Floresta's Direitos das Mulheres e Injustiça dos Homens', Ellipsis, 8 (2010). I am very grateful to all the publishers for permission to reproduce this material.

LIST OF ABBREVIATIONS

Works by Floresta

Direitos	*Direitos das Mulheres e Injustiça dos Homens*
Conselhos	'Conselhos à Minha Filha, com 40 Pensamentos em Versos'
Fany	'Fany ou o Modelo das Donzelas'
Discurso	*Discurso que as suas educandas dirigio N F B Augusta, em 18 de dezembro de 1847*
Lágrima	*A Lágrima de um Caheté*
Opúsculo	*Opúsculo Humanitário*
'Paginas'	'Paginas de uma vida obscura'
'Passeio'	'Passeio ao Aqueducto da Carioca'
'Pranto'	'O Pranto Filial'
Itinerário	*Itinerário de uma Viagem à Alemanha*
Cintilações	*Cintilações de uma Alma Brasileira*
'Abismo'	'O abismo sob as flores da civilização'
'Viagem'	'Viagem Magnética'
'Luxemburgo'	'Um passeio no jardim de Luxemburgo'
Três Anos	*Três anos na Itália seguidos de uma viagem à Grécia,* Vol. 1
Fragmentos	*Fragmentos de uma Obra Inédita*

Other Abbreviations

Woman Not Inferior	Sophia, A Person of Quality, *Woman Not Inferior to Man: or, A short and modest Vindication of the Natural Right of the Fair-Sex to a Perfect Equality of Power, Dignity and Esteem, with the Men*, facsimile edn (London: Brentham Press, 1975)
Vindication	Mary Wollstonecraft, *A Vindication of the Rights of Woman* (Oxford: Oxford University Press, 1999)
'Diálogos'	Ana Euridice Eufrosina de Barandas, 'Diálogos', in *O Ramalhete, ou flores escolhidas no jardim da imaginação*, 2nd edn (Porto Alegre: Nova Dimensão, 1990), pp. 97–111

Notes on Quotations
I have chosen to maintain the original orthography in all quotations.

When referring to the ideas expressed in *Woman Not Inferior*, I will in all instances quote and/or give the relevant page numbers from *Direitos*, Floresta's translation of that text. The corresponding page(s) in the original English text will then be given in square brackets, in order to facilitate comparisons.

Introduction

Nísia Floresta Brasileira Augusta is unquestionably one of the most significant women writers of the early and mid-nineteenth century in Brazil, if not the most significant. Her output was prolific, including eight publications in Brazil, some running to several editions and subsequently translated into French and Italian, a further five publications in Europe, and a number of collaborations in newspapers in Rio de Janeiro and possibly elsewhere. Yet despite leaving this considerable literary legacy, even before her death in France in 1885 Floresta's life and work was surrounded by myth and misinformation. Although much has been done to reveal the details of her biography, the hagiographic construction of the writer and her work, which still persists even within the more recent scholarly context of the 'rediscovery' of nineteenth-century women's literature, has continued to foster some of the most fundamental myths upon which her position in the Brazilian canon is founded. Moreover, this hagiographical approach has hindered an objective analysis of Floresta's work, and it is essentially this imbalance that I wish to address in this study, by instigating a disinterested re-evaluation of the place the writer occupies in the Brazilian canon and of the many claims that are made for her work.

Floresta was born Dionísia Gonçalves Pinto on 12 October 1810 in Papari, in the north-eastern province of Rio Grande do Norte. The pseudonym by which she was known in Brazil and Europe throughout her adult life was of her own making, although it was not employed with a view to literary anonymity. Rather, it was a determined act of self-construction (the first of many), under which Floresta not only wrote, but also taught and lived: 'Floresta' after her parents' *sítio* where she was born; 'Brasileira' as a statement of patriotic identification with her newly independent nation; 'Augusta' in homage to the father of her children, Manuel Augusto de Faria Rocha. Thus Floresta defines herself by her *pátria*, both in the traditional sense of one's birthplace, and in the developing sense of national loyalty, and by her family, and these parallel discursive spaces also govern much of her work.

Although a large number of studies and articles have been written about Floresta, considerably more than about most of her female contemporaries, her life and work have only been subject to one extensive study until now: the doctoral research of Constância Lima Duarte, which was published in 1995.[1] Duarte's excellent and thorough research, through which she has collated and corrected pre-existing details regarding Floresta's biography, as well as unearthing new information and locating a number of texts which were unknown or thought lost, is of great value, and an important source of reference in this study. However, as the perceived 'definitive' work on Floresta to date, and a work which does not escape the hagiographic traditions of Floresta's earlier biographies, it is also the starting point for many of the contentions and challenges I shall be making to Floresta's canonicity.

Floresta has certainly not always enjoyed the elevated position she now occupies. Even before her death, the uncertain details of her private life were leading to defamatory accusations not only of adultery in her youth, but also that her interaction with famous European intellectuals, and in particular Auguste Comte, was more intimate than intellectual, and even that a number of her publications were not her own work. Although widely contested, the echo of these intimations was to survive until recent decades, as Duarte observes, recounting that in the 1970s chains were still to be found around Floresta's tomb in the town of Papari, renamed Nísia Floresta in 1948, to prevent her ghost from accosting lone men at night.[2]

However, an alternative, positive construction began to take shape at the end of the nineteenth century, and it is interesting to note that it is also through her association with Comte that this rehabilitation first took place. Duarte observes that it was the Brazilian positivists 'que mais se empenharam em torná-la conhecida', celebrating her friendship with Comte, and focusing particularly on her condemnation of slavery.[3] Moreover, perhaps with a specific view to countering suggestions of a sexual relationship, more than one early twentieth-century biographer presented Floresta's friendship with Comte as evidence of her moral integrity as well as her intellectual superiority.[4] More importantly, the emphasis given by early biographers to her interaction with Comte and other leading European intellectuals of the day no doubt reflects the value and authority that this male endorsement was seen to provide.

The notoriety that had been thrust upon Floresta in the early days of the

---

[1]   Constância Lima Duarte, *Nísia Floresta: Vida e Obra* (Natal: EDUFRN, 1995). A second edition of this text was published in 2008, again by EDUFRN. All quotations in this study are taken from the first edition. This study contains a comprehensive bibliography on Floresta.

[2]   Duarte, *Vida e Obra*, p. 72.

[3]   Duarte, *Vida e Obra*, p. 183.

[4]   For example, Joaquim de Meiroz Grillo, 'Conferencia proferida na então vila de Goianinha, em 1924', appendix to João Medeiros Filho, *Nísia Floresta*, Separata do livro em preparo *Um advogado na Academia de Letras* (Natal: [n. pub.], 1981); and Oliveira Lima, 'Nísia Floresta: discurso pronunciado na Escola Doméstica do Natal' (manuscript, 1919).

myth-making process may go some way to explaining the idealisation that has followed. In an impassioned attempt to redress the balance, a genuinely objective analysis of her work has often been neglected in favour of a simplistic construction as feminist, abolitionist and federal-republican, as an enlightened and 'ultraliberal' spirit and 'o exemplo vivo [...] [das] virtudes domésticas e cívicas'.[5] Even now, when her reputation and her place in the canon are secure, her work continues to be read with a view to further confirming and expanding on her almost mythological status in the world of Brazilian women's writing. For example, Duarte states that 'em sua militância literária, a autora mostrar-se-á sempre coerente com os princípios liberais, assumindo o discurso progressista em defesa do oprimido, seja ele o índio, o negro ou a mulher', whilst Maria Helena Mendonça observes Floresta's empathy and identification with the 'other' in her work.[6] Yet, as I will outline through the course of this book, her white, middle-class positioning in fact tends to make such an identification extremely problematic, if not impossible.

The details of Floresta's own biography are certainly not the focus of this study. However, a brief consideration of certain events in her life, and of incidents emphasised by those who have studied her, is essential to an understanding of her work and of the claims subsequently made for her.[7] Floresta's early life was repeatedly disrupted by regional, nativist revolts, which eventually forced her family to definitively abandon the *sítio* Floresta and establish themselves in Olinda. Before this departure, in 1823 Floresta married at the age of thirteen, but this union was clearly unsuccessful and she quickly returned to her family. In 1828 Floresta's father was assassinated, at the order of a powerful member of the Pernambucan elite, according to the writer herself.[8]

In the same year, she began to live with a young student at the Olinda law faculty, Manuel Augusto de Faria Rocha, with whom she went on to have two children in 1830 and 1833. In 1832 Floresta's first work was published in Recife, and shortly afterwards the family moved to Porto Alegre. Only seven months after the birth of their son, Manuel Augusto died, leaving Floresta to support herself and two very young children, which she did by teaching. Once again, regionalist, republican rebellion disrupted her life, this time in the guise of the Guerra Farroupilha (1835–45), the most sustained assault on national unity during the unsettled early years of independence. In 1837

---

5   Lima, pp. 5 and 9.
6   Duarte, *Vida e Obra*, p. 111; Maria Helena Mendonça, 'Nísia Floresta: romantismo e consciência reformadora', in *Desafiando o Cânone (2): ecos de vozes femininas na literatura brasileira do século XIX*, ed. Helena Parente Cunha (Rio de Janeiro: Faculdade de Letras da UFRJ, 2001), pp. 27–40 (p. 32).
7   Except where otherwise stated, information is taken from Duarte, *Vida e Obra*, pp. 16–74.
8   *Fragmentos de uma Obra Inédita*, pp. 51–2.

Floresta and her family (which appears to have included her mother, sister and half-sister) moved to Rio where she established the Collegio Augusto school for girls, teaching and publishing for more than ten years.

In 1849 she travelled to France with her children. The reason Floresta herself gives for this departure is a medical one: her daughter's health had been severely affected by a bad fall from a horse and she was advised that the European air might aid recovery.[9] It has inevitably been suggested that Floresta felt obliged to leave Rio to escape the criticisms of her advanced, liberal notions on education, and perhaps other subjects, although Hilda Hübner Flores condemns as 'línguas felinas' those who talk of exile.[10] Whilst she cannot have been forced to leave, it is certainly easy to imagine that Floresta would not have found the stifling conservatism of the Rio *corte* conducive, and the intellectual appeal of Paris must have been great. Whatever her reasons, this first visit to Europe was certainly an immensely important learning experience for Floresta, and its influence is immediately apparent in her work.

She returned to Rio in 1852, where she continued to teach and published in the press and in book form, but remained for only four years before returning to establish permanent residence in Europe. She was to return to Brazil only once more in her lifetime, in 1872, for a visit of a little over two years. In Europe, where she was accompanied at all times by her daughter, whilst her son remained in Brazil, she began her short-lived friendship with Auguste Comte, who died the following year. She travelled extensively in Italy, Greece, Germany, Belgium, Portugal and England, and published a number of works. In fact the majority of her work by volume was produced in Europe, in French and Italian, including some seven hundred pages on the three years she spent in Italy. Nísia Floresta died and was buried in Bonsecour near Rouen in the April of 1885, and in 1954 she made her final journey back to Brazil for reburial in the place of her birth. Despite her much-proclaimed patriotism, having chosen to live out her days in the country she considered to be her 'segunda pátria', it is doubtful whether this was a journey she would have wished for.

Despite the recent valuable research on Floresta's life, which has uncovered many previously uncertain details, much remains unclear. The most intriguing lacuna surrounds the circumstances of her first marriage. Not only do the reasons for its failure lie in the realm of speculation, more significantly, neither is it known how, or whether, the marriage was legally terminated, a question which in turn affects the status of her second partnership. Hilda Hübner Flores, observing the extreme rarity of annulments and the fact that

---

[9]   *Fragmentos*, p. 65.
[10]   Hilda Agnes Hübner Flores, 'Nísia Floresta Brasileira Augusta', *Letras de Hoje*, 89 (Sept. 1992), 101–13 (p. 105).

'divorce' represented only legal separation, concludes that it is unlikely that Floresta was able to marry the father of her children,[11] although some earlier biographers state that she did.[12] Since few registry documents survive from that period, it is impossible to draw a definitive conclusion. What is certain is that the couple lived as man and wife, and the move to Porto Alegre would have allowed them to escape any lingering scandal. Their son's birth certificate states that he is legitimate,[13] indicating that their union was considered to be legal by the Porto Alegre authorities, and for simplicity I shall refer to Manuel Augusto as Floresta's husband, as she herself does in the frequent references she makes to him throughout her work.

Another interesting question is how Floresta continued to support herself after the end of her teaching career. Once in Europe she travelled constantly, staying in comfortable hotels and apparently living amongst the elite of society wherever she settled, with little evidence of a means of income. Her published work cannot account for this lifestyle. The most likely explanation, put forward by Adauto da Câmara, is that upon her mother's death Floresta inherited the proceeds of land belonging to her mother's wealthy family in Rio Grande do Norte.[14] What is most interesting, however, is that financial independence would have given Floresta the freedom to publish without the constraints of conservative market forces. The fact that her later work does not express the more radical ideas which were now an option for her suggests that Floresta's conservatism reflects her own opinions and cannot be entirely explained by a need to appeal to and engage with her readers' attitudes.

A further small but extremely significant aspect of Floresta's biography, which is unlikely ever to be clarified, is the assertion that she gave *conferências* in Rio in 1842 in which she preached, amongst other things, the abolition of slavery and the benefits of a federal republic. The first reference to this event appears in Ignez Sabino's account of her life, published more than a decade after Floresta's death.[15] These meetings are not mentioned by Innocencio da Silva in his influential *Diccionario Bibliographico Portuguez*, of 1862, which is widely considered to be an accurate and reliable source, and Sabino does not indicate her own sources, meaning that the origins of this assertion are unknown. Moreover, despite stating that the *conferências* were

11 Flores, 'Nísia Floresta', p. 102.
12 E.g. Henrique Castriciano, writing in the 1920s (cited in Flores, 'Nísia Floresta', p. 102); and Adauto da Câmara, *História de Nísia Floresta*, 2nd edn (1st edn 1941) (Natal: Departamento Estadual de Imprensa, 1997), p. 27.
13 Duarte, *Vida e Obra*, p. 25.
14 Câmara, *História*, p. 82. It is possible, however, that this source of income was not endless, since Floresta appears to have lived out her final years in modest circumstances. See Duarte, *Vida e Obra*, p. 63.
15 Ignez Sabino, *Mulheres Illustres do Brazil* (Rio de Janeiro and Paris: H Garnier, 1899), pp. 171–7.

published,[16] no contemporary documentary evidence has survived to record their occurrence or content. Although it seems unlikely that there is no truth behind the claim, her reputation as an abolitionist and a republican has been based to a considerable extent on a historical moment that cannot be verified, whilst evidence of which we can be quite confident, that is to say the content of her published writing, is often overlooked.

That said, even the full extent of her published work is not known. Some of her texts have been lost, including a short piece of didactic fiction entitled *Daciz, ou a jovem perfeita*, published in Rio in 1847, an extensive (apparently unfinished) work of fiction, *Dedicação de uma amiga* (Rio, 1850), and a further novel, *Parsis* (Paris, 1867), about which nothing is known.[17] Furthermore, studies of her work have all included the information that she published many articles in the *Jornal do Comércio*, the *Mercantil*, the *Diário do Rio de Janeiro*, *O Liberal* and the *Brasil Illustrado* in Rio as well as in the Paris and Florence press, once again apparently taking Innocencio da Silva as their primary source. Yet her European articles have never been located, and only four pieces published in the *Brasil Illustrado* have been identified as examples of her work in the Carioca press, together with the serialisation of a text also published in book form, *Opúsculo Humanitário*, in *O Liberal* and the *Diário* in 1853 to 1854. Duarte suggests that an anonymous article entitled 'A Mulher', which appeared in the *Diário* on 2 February 1854, might be of Floresta's authorship.[18] In the information given on Floresta in the dictionary of Brazilian women published in 2000, it is stated quite categorically that a series of articles published in *O Liberal* with the title 'A emancipação da mulher' are Floresta's work,[19] but the source of this assertion is unclear and neither suggestion can be confidently confirmed.

The difficulty in assuming the authorship of articles relating to Floresta's area of interest becomes apparent when assessing further claims made by Duarte regarding articles published in Recife and Porto Alegre. In the first instance, she suggests that Floresta wrote for the *Espelho das Brasileiras*, which ran for a short time in 1831, a paper which, although edited by a man, was the first in Pernambuco, and one of the first in the country, to be dedicated to women. Duarte writes: 'durante os trinta números do jornal, [...], Nísia vai colaborar com artigos em que trata da condição feminina em diversas culturas antigas'.[20] However, only one example remains in the Archivo Público in Recife, the issue dating from 8 April 1831, and it was not

---

16   Sabino, p. 172.
17   See Innocencio Francisco da Silva, *Diccionario Bibliographico Portuguez*, Tomo 6 (Lisbon: Imprensa Nacional, 1862), p. 296; and Duarte, *Vida e Obra*, p. 54.
18   Duarte, *Vida e Obra*, p. 41.
19   Érico Vital Brazil and Schuma Schumaher (eds), *Dicionário Mulheres do Brasil* (Rio de Janeiro: Jorge Zahar, 2000), p. 452.
20   Duarte, *Vida e Obra*, p. 23.

possible to locate examples of the paper elsewhere. It is from this same issue that Duarte quotes, and it is not made clear whether she consulted any other numbers. This example alone is certainly not sufficient to justify the conclusion that it is of Floresta's authorship. On the other hand, the article's content is indeed reminiscent of Floresta's later writing, so neither is it possible to deny the suggestion.

Somewhat more problematic is the suggestion that articles, including one entitled 'Pernambuco', which were published in the Porto Alegre paper *O Recopilador Liberal*, might well have been written by Floresta.[21] This paper frequently carried articles from newspapers from other parts of Brazil, and the article identified by Duarte is just such a reproduction. In reality, 'Quotidiana Fidedigna' is not a pseudonym but the name of the Recife-based paper from which the article originated. However, what appears only as a suggested possibility in Duarte's text is converted into hard fact in the *Dicionário Mulheres do Brasil*, which contains the following confident assertion: 'encontram-se artigos seus assinados com o pseudônimo de "Quotidiana Fidedigna" nos jornais *O Recopilador Liberal* e *O Campeão da Legalidade*'.[22] This sort of appropriation and concretisation of speculative material is one of the ways in which the myth of Nísia Floresta continues to be elaborated and expanded. In order to guarantee a historically accurate study, I shall therefore limit myself to those texts about which there appears to be no doubt of Floresta's authorship.

Through the course of this book I will look in turn at the principal discursive areas with which Floresta is associated, and upon which her canonicity has been established. First and most fundamental to her reputation is, of course, her writing on women, and this will be dealt with in the first three chapters. The starting point for a fresh analysis of Floresta's feminism must be her first publication, *Direitos das Mulheres e Injustiça dos Homens*, a text which has always been central to her construction as pioneering feminist. However, its relatively recent identification as a direct translation of an obscure eighteenth-century text, rather than the free translation of Wollstonecraft that it was previously believed to be, challenges much of what has been claimed for this text and I will consider how this new knowledge affects Floresta's position in the Brazilian canon and a reading of her own subsequent work.

The question of women's education is also central to an analysis of Floresta's writing and her life since it is her first and most enduring concern, reflected throughout her published work and in the school for girls she oper-

---

21 Duarte, *Vida e Obra*, p. 28.
22 Brazil and Schumaher, p. 451. The second paper mentioned is in fact unrelated to the 'Quotidiana Fidedigna' articles, instead carrying an article on education in Brazil which Duarte also suggests bears Floresta's hallmark (*Vida e Obra*, p. 29).

ated in Rio. The second chapter will therefore look at both Floresta's own teaching career and the vision of women's education to emerge from her writing, drawing conclusions from the prominent gap between what she 'practised' and what she 'preached'. Finally, in Chapter 3, I will look at Floresta's own writings on women's wider condition and role in society, since it is here that we must now look to test the limits of her feminism. I will chart her final move away from the baseline of intellectual and spiritual equality to be found in the text she translated, towards the profoundly differentiating, and delineating discourses of moral superiority and patriotic motherhood, and consider the various factors which may have shaped her thinking.

I shall then move on to look at some of the other big questions of post-independence Brazil that Floresta addresses in her work, beginning, in Chapter 4, with constructions of the native Indian. I will look primarily at one particular text, the 1849 poem *A Lágrima de um Caheté*, which has earned Floresta the title of 'Indianist' and indeed 'Indigenist', and which occupies an extremely unusual position within the body of her work. I will assess the Indianist credentials of this work and evaluate some of the claims made for it. Through references drawn from several of her other publications I will then go on to outline Floresta's discussion of the Brazilian Indian in a non-fiction context, and consider what a comparison of these very different interventions simultaneously reveals about her engagement with romantic literary discourse and her perception of the indigenous population within Brazilian society.

In the fifth chapter I will turn my attention to Floresta's discussions of black slavery, which have earned her the title of abolitionist, second only to her feminist reputation. I will re-evaluate this title through a close analysis of all her various writings on slavery in Brazil and Europe, evaluating the influence of the prevailing discourses of the day on her thinking. I will conclude the chapter with a discussion of her limited engagement with gender issues in slavery and consider why Floresta never attempts to draw a parallel between the oppression of women and the oppression of slaves, or to unite these two powerful critical discourses.

In the final chapter I shall in part attempt to reassess Floresta's construction as a political idealist, by looking beyond her one obviously pro-federalist publication to the sporadic and varied references to political ideology found in the remainder of her writing. However, the question of national governance will constitute only one part of a wider discussion of the writer's very different constructions of Brazil for her Brazilian and European readers and the profound influence that Floresta's travels to Europe have on her concept of the Brazilian nation. In the preceding chapters I will have observed how Floresta employs the rhetoric of patriotism to add momentum to her arguments on a range of social issues; in Chapter 6, I will discuss how patriotic motivations come to dominate her later works, shaping and limiting her discussion of, and engagement with, the world around her.

The purpose of this study is not to deny Floresta's immensely important position within the development of women's writing and feminist writing in Brazil. Rather it is an attempt to look beyond the idealised image of the woman and her work, which the need to recover and valorise women's participation in nineteenth-century Brazil has inevitably produced. By establishing the true nature of Floresta's participation in the varied social discourses she engaged with and testing the extent of her much-lauded 'pioneirismo' in these discourses, by which she has been consistently defined, I hope that this study will serve to secure Floresta's place in the Brazilian canon, with some inevitable modifications, on a more impartial and solid foundation.

1

The 'Translator of Wollstonecraft'

Floresta's literary career, her engagement with the discourse of women's emancipation, and her subsequent canonisation as Brazil's first feminist, begins in Recife in 1832, and it begins with a bang. Her first published text, which appeared under the full title of *Direitos das Mulheres e Injustiça dos Homens, por Mistriss Godwin. Tradusido livremente do Francez para Portuguez, e offerecido às Brasileiras e Academicos Brasileiros por Nisia Floresta Brasileira Augusta*, is the first known work to be published in Brazil dealing directly with the issues of women's intellectual equality and their capacity, and right, to be educated and participate in the active processes of society on an equal footing with men. Moreover, it is without doubt amongst the most radical and forceful in the claims it makes for women of any such text published throughout the nineteenth century, original or in translation. The title alone is direct and combative and its contents amount to a firm and succinct deconstruction of the traditional arguments for male supremacy and female submission, concluding that women possess all the attributes necessary to play a full and equal role to men in spheres as diverse and elevated as the teaching of the sciences, government and military employment. Furthermore, the text maintains a consistently caustic tone, belittling men's actions and ridiculing their irrational thought processes. With her name attached to such a revolutionary piece of writing, it is not surprising that Floresta has been hailed by many of her commentators as the precursor of women's emancipation in Brazil. Roberto Seidl, for example, concluded that, 'lendo-se este folheto conclui-se logo que a Nísia Floresta cabe, sem favor algum, o título de precursora do feminismo no Brasil e quiçá na America do Sul'.[1]

Yet its surprising content is only the beginning of the significance of *Direitos* in the history of scholarly commentary on Floresta and her work. In fact, it is the question of the text's origins, and of Floresta's motivations for translating and publishing such a radical work, which offer the most valuable insight into the writer's intellectual development. It is also through the continuing tension surrounding its history that *Direitos* has become synonymous with the misinformation and mythologisation which continues to surround

---

[1]   Roberto Seidl, *Nisia Floresta, 1810–1885* (Rio de Janeiro: [n. pub.], 1933), p. 9.

Floresta, her life and her work. It is therefore to the question of textual origin that I must turn first, as any commentary on this and Floresta's subsequent works is inevitably predicated on the claims made for *Direitos*.

Ironically, the root cause of the myth that has shaped discussion of *Direitos* for most of the text's history, originates from Floresta's own hand. It is the writer herself who states that the text is translated from the work of 'Mistriss Godwin', who is, of course, none other than Mary Wollstonecraft under her husband William Godwin's name. Due, presumably to the partial similarity in titles, it has therefore always been assumed that the text Floresta translated was Wollstonecraft's most famous work, *A Vindication of the Rights of Woman*. For many years, studies of Floresta's work made the mistake of describing *Direitos* as a direct translation, an error that appears to have originated in Innocencio da Silva's early bibliography, in which the essential word 'livremente' is omitted from the title.[2] This assumption passed unnoticed and without investigation for a hundred and fifty years, despite the fact that only a superficial familiarity with Wollstonecraft's work would have immediately revealed striking differences between the two books both in content, style and length.

After the apparent loss of all surviving copies some time after 1940, this mistake might have passed unchallenged into the history books, but in the late 1980s the text was relocated and re-edited by Constância Lima Duarte. In the course of preparing the 1989 re-edition, Duarte made the first real comparison of Floresta's text with its purported original, revealing the massive differences between the two works. She therefore concluded that 'escapando com ousadia da mera tradução literal', Floresta had assimilated Mary Wollstonecraft's ideas and rewritten them, shaped by her own experiences and motivations and by the specifically Brazilian context which she was addressing.[3] *Direitos* was in fact, Duarte wrote, '*um outro* texto, o *seu* texto sobre os direitos das mulheres', in which 'nossa autora se [coloca] em pé de igualdade com Wollstonecraft e até com o pensamento europeu'.[4] It is not difficult to see the significance of this reappraisal of Floresta's first publication. Whilst the very fact that she had translated the work of the famous English feminist had earned her the title of 'precursora do feminismo no Brasil', noted above, as the original author of such an early and radical text, Floresta's place was secure, not only in the Brazilian canon, but alongside any of the great feminist writers of the period. As a 'nova escritura', Duarte could justifiably claim, 'temos sim, nesta "tradução livre", talvez o texto fundante do feminismo brasileiro'.[5]

---

2   Silva, *Diccionario*, p. 295.
3   See Duarte's foreword to *Direitos*, p. 19.
4   Constância Lima Duarte, 'Posfácio: Nos primórdios do feminismo brasileiro', in *Direitos*, pp. 97–134 (pp. 107–8).
5   Duarte, 'Posfácio', p. 108.

Then, in 1995, a startling new discovery turned all previous comment on *Direitos* upside down and 'pôs fim definitivo à busca das origens do livro'.[6] The Brazilian scholar Maria Lúcia Pallares-Burke observed striking similarities between *Direitos* and a little known work entitled *De l'Égalité des Deux Sexes*, published in 1673 by an obscure French writer and thinker, François Poulain de la Barre.[7] In this seventeenth-century French text she found '*ipsis litteris*, muitos dos trechos mais incisivos da obra [de Floresta], traduzidos, diga-se de passagem, com grande talento e mestria por Nísia Floresta'.[8] Poulain de la Barre employed Cartesian rationalism to assess women's status, concluding an absolute equality with men in all but reproductive biology and producing a feminism that is 'elegant in its simplicity and radical in its conclusions'.[9] Despite, or perhaps because of, its revolutionary content, *De l'Égalité des Deux Sexes* was all but ignored at the time of its publication and sank into rapid oblivion.[10]

Poulain de la Barre's arguments were not to be entirely silenced, however. In 1739, an English writer, who remains hidden behind the pseudonym 'Sophia, A Person of Quality',[11] published a sixty-two-page feminist pamphlet: *Woman not Inferior to Man: or A Short and Modest Vindication of the Natural Right of the Fair-Sex to a Perfect Equality of Power, Dignity and Esteem, with the Men* in which (s)he reproduced, without credit, large parts of *De l'Égalité des Deux Sexes*. Thus, Pallares-Burke discovered, it was not through direct contact with the work of Poulain de la Barre that the Frenchman's Cartesian defence of equality had found a new audience a hundred and sixty years later on the other side of the Atlantic. The true origins of *Direitos* were finally revealed: Floresta had in fact translated '*literalmente* e na sua *totalidade*' Sophia's eighteenth-century English tract.[12]

However, this remarkable information, which fundamentally refashions

6   Maria Lúcia Garcia Pallares-Burke, 'A Mary Wollstonecraft que o Brasil conheceu, ou a travessura literária de Nísia Floresta', in *Nísia Floresta, O Carapuceiro e outros ensaios de tradução cultural* (São Paulo: Editora HUCITEC, 1996), pp. 167–92 (p. 177). This article first appeared in the *Caderno Mais* of the *Folha de São Paulo*, 10 September 1995.

7   Pallares-Burke, 'A Mary Wollstonecraft', p. 175–6.

8   Pallares-Burke, 'A Mary Wollstonecraft', p. 176.

9   Clarke, 'Introduction' in François Poulain de la Barre, *The Equality of the Sexes*, trans. Desmond M. Clarke (Manchester and New York: Manchester University Press, 1990), pp. 1–39 (p. 21).

10   Clarke, p. 31.

11   Lady Sophia Fermor and Lady Mary Wortley Montagu have both been proposed as likely candidates. See Pallares-Burke, 'A Mary Wollstonecraft', p. 178, and the foreword to the facsimile reproduction of *Woman not Inferior*.

12   Pallares-Burke, 'A Mary Wollstonecraft', p. 177. It is important to note that when referring to Sophia's arguments, as I will do through the course of this and subsequent chapters, many are in fact the arguments of Poulain de la Barre. For simplicity, however, I will take the English writer as my usual point of reference.

the conclusions to be drawn from Floresta's text, was not well received in Brazil. In fact, to all intents and purposes, it was simply not received at all. Three years after Pallares-Burke's research appeared, Duarte published a response in which she stated that it was not Pallares-Burke's discoveries, but 'o tratamento e a utilização dados a essas mesmas descobertas' that she wished to contest.[13] It is perhaps not surprising that Pallares-Burke's description of *Direitos* as a 'plágio-tradução de outro plágio' and an 'ousada travessura literária'[14] should have caused dismay, and Duarte sets out to challenge these polemical accusations, questioning whether a contemporary definition of plagiarism can be applied to the literary practices and authorial conventions of another age, and dismissing, quite rightly I would suggest, the notion of deliberate trickery implicit in the word 'travessura'.

It is not the case, however, that Duarte did not seek to contest Pallares-Burke's fundamental discovery. On the contrary, she reiterates the claims she had previously made for Floresta's text (discussed above), focusing only on the influence of Poulain de la Barre's work on the text and apparently treating Sophia's work as nothing more than an additional source of influence, thus tacitly denying Pallares-Burke's identification of *Direitos* as a direct translation of *Woman not Inferior*.[15] In her 2005 publication *Nísia Floresta: a primeira feminista do Brasil*, which contains a short analysis of Floresta's writings on women alongside extracts of her work, Duarte continues to claim *Direitos* as an essentially original text, stating that as well as Wollstonecraft, Floresta 'buscou inspiração [...] em outros autores europeus, como Poulain de la Barre, Sophie, e mesmo [...] Olympe de Gouges'.[16]

Aside from Duarte's article, Pallares-Burke's extremely significant discovery has provoked virtually no response and, knowingly or otherwise, references to Floresta in other recent historical and literary studies also continue to propagate the myth.[17] It is clear that Pallares-Burke's article has not received the coverage or led to the kind of re-evaluation that might have been expected.[18]

---

13   Constância Lima Duarte, 'Nísia Floresta: Incompreensão em relação à sua Genialidade', *Ciência e Trópico*, 26 (July/Dec 1998), 253–60 (p. 253).

14   Pallares-Burke, 'A Mary Wollstonecraft', pp. 178 and 184.

15   Duarte, 'Nísia Floresta: Incompreensão', p. 253.

16   Constância Lima Duarte, *Nísia Floresta: a primeira feminista do Brasil* (Florianópolis: Editora Mulheres; EDUNISC, 2005), pp. 17–18.

17   Two such examples can be found in Emilia Viotti da Costa, 'Patriarchalism and the Myth of the Helpless Woman', in *The Brazilian Empire: Myths and Histories*, revised edn (London: University of North Carolina Press, 2000), p. 257; and in Mendonça, p. 29.

18   Very few other references and/or responses to Pallares-Burke's research are to be found in the decade following the publication of her article. Those I have located are: 1. A review of Pallares-Burkes's work (Fraya Frehse, 'Review of *Nísia Floresta, O Carapuceiro e outros ensaios de traduçao cultural*, by Maria Lúcia Pallares-Burke', *Revista da Antropologia*, 40: 2 (1997), 235–45. 2. A very short pamphlet on Floresta's life and work, aimed at a general reader, in which Pallares-Burke's discovery is mentioned (Nathalie Bernardo da Câmara, *Da Aurora ao*

On the contrary, Floresta's 'free translation of Mary Wollstonecraft' remains absolutely central to her construction and reputation within Brazil and beyond. More than that, it has become a sort of epithet from which she seems unable to escape, and the translating of Wollstonecraft is unquestionably, and reductively, the act of writing by which she has come to be known and defined.

Whilst the limited academic response to Pallares-Burke's discovery means that many in the field of women's literature and history in Brazil no doubt remain unaware of its existence, it seems possible that the ongoing lack of critical engagement with such a valuable piece of research may also reflect resentment of the implied accusations of plagiarism or deceit contained in Pallares-Burke's article, and more importantly, a reluctance to see Floresta's contribution reduced once more to that of mere translator. As faithful translator of another writer's work, Floresta can no longer be credited with the touches of rhetorical magic Duarte identified in *Direitos*,[19] nor can she be positioned on an equal footing with great European feminists such as Wollstonecraft (at least with reference to her first publication).

The effect is even more far-reaching than that, however. As a straightforward translation, *Direitos* can no longer be identified as the 'texto fundante' of Brazilian feminism. In 1837 the *gaúcha* Ana de Barandas wrote a short Cartesian dialogue, which was published as part of a collection in 1845. This text, entitled 'Diálogos', in which de Barandas defends women's right to political participation, reveals the influence of Floresta's translation, and it is almost certain that the two women were acquainted, and probably friends, since they lived close to each other in Porto Alegre and were related by marriage.[20] However, Hilary Owen notes that, based on the notion of a nativist refashioning of European feminist thinking as the marker of the founding of Brazilian feminism, as has been claimed for Floresta's *Direitos*, it is in fact de Barandas's text which initiates this reworking. Therefore it is de Barandas

---

Crepúsculo (Natal: Fundação José Augusto, 1997)). 3. A short and for the most part extremely critical commentary on the process of 'rediscovering' nineteenth-century women writers, in which the author refers to Pallares-Burke's research but draws attention exclusively to the notion of *Direitos* as a plagiarism (Wilson Martins, 'Cidade das Mulheres', *Jornal de Poesia/O Globo On Line – Prosa e Verso*, 20 November 1999). 4. An article looking at the subversive practices of women translators, which suggests, taking its lead from Duarte, that *Direitos* reveals the influence of Wollstonecraft, Sophia and Poulain de la Barre, and is therefore 'uma montagem toda pessoal' (Marie France Dépêche, 'As traduções subversivas feministas ontem e hoje', *Labrys, Estudos Feministas*, 1–2 (2002)). To date, the only study to take Pallares-Burke's findings as a starting point for a wider re-evaluation of Floresta's work and position in the Brazilian canon is Owen's discussion of Floresta's contemporary Ana de Barandas (discussed later in this chapter).

19   Duarte, 'Posfácio', p. 118.

20   Hilda Agnes Hübner Flores, 'Ana Euridice Eufrosina de Barandas: Vida e Obra', in Ana de Barandas, *O Ramalhete, ou flores escolhidas no jardim da imaginação* (Porto Alegre: Nova Dimensão, 1990), pp. 11–50 (pp. 40–2).

who has the strongest claim to the title of 'Brazil's first feminist'.[21] As such, the effect on Floresta's status in the feminist canon is unquestionably significant, and could go some way to explaining why Pallares-Burke's research appears to have been allowed to sink without trace, leaving only the faintest of ripples on the calm waters of Floresta's 'first feminist' credentials.

Regardless of this problematic ongoing canonisation of Floresta's early literary contribution, the fact remains that at the age of twenty-two Floresta encountered, translated and, for whatever reason, misattributed the anonymous Sophia's *Woman Not Inferior to Man*. This act, remarkable in its own right, brings an entirely new set of challenges and implications to an analysis of *Direitos*. Moreover, Floresta would not have made her translation from the English original, but from a French translation, a fact we can be sure of, not only because Floresta states as much in the full title of her text, but also because she was fluent in French, and possibly Italian, at this time, but not English.[22] That Floresta knew the text only in its French version is extremely significant and must influence any consideration of *Direitos*. It is not something that Pallares-Burke takes into account in her aforementioned article, and this omission undermines a number of the conclusions she draws regarding both the quality of the translation and the circumstances surrounding its publication as the work of 'Mistriss Godwin'.

In terms of the translation itself, a reading of the French version serves to both enhance and diminish Floresta's reputation as represented by Pallares-Burke. On the one hand, she identifies two of the most serious errors of translation, in which the original meaning is completely lost, but a comparison with the French version reveals that both these mistakes originated there, and that Floresta faithfully translated the text she had before her.[23] However, Pallares-Burke also points out several instances in which the Brazilian text differs in some small but significant way from the English original, drawing certain conclusions about Floresta's motivations from these alterations. Whilst a few minor moderations are indeed of Floresta's making, the majority are once again revealed to be the work of the French translator.[24]

---

[21]   Hilary Owen, 'Gender and Revolution in Southern Brazil: Restitching the Farroupilha War in the Works of Delfina Benigna da Cunha and Ana de Barandas', in Catherine Davies, Claire Brewster and Hilary Owen, *Latin American Independence: Gender, Politics, Text* (Liverpool: Liverpool University Press, 2006), pp. 210–40 (p. 235).

[22]   *Woman Not Inferior to Man* was translated into French in 1750 with the title *La Femme n'est pas Inférieure à l'Homme* and the same edition was republished the following year, this time bearing the title *Le Triomphe des Dames*. See Camille Garnier, '"La Femme n'est pas inférieure à l'homme" (1750): oeuvre de Madeleine Darsant de Puisieux ou simple traduction français?', *Revue d'Histoire Littéraire de la France*, 4 (1987), 709–13 (p. 709). I have consulted an example of *Le Triomphe des Dames*.

[23]   See Pallares-Burke, 'A Mary Wollstonecraft', p. 179 (note 28).

[24]   See my article 'Between "founding text" and "literary prank": reasoning the roots of

In fact, a comparison of *Direitos* with the French text known to Floresta reveals her to be an even more faithful and precise translator than Pallares-Burke would like to suggest. Whilst this excuses Floresta from some glaring mistranslations, it also denies her almost any meaningful input into the text, definitively ending the claim that Floresta moderated her translation to better fit the national context or her own particular concerns and motivations. However, once *Direitos* is acknowledged as a direct translation, the content of the text ceases to be of primary concern in a study of this publication. Instead, together with a consideration of how Sophia's ideas influenced her own work, which I will address in subsequent chapters, what must take precedence is the fascinating and challenging question of why Floresta claimed that her direct translation of *Woman not Inferior* was a free translation of Mary Wollstonecraft. It is primarily to this thorny issue that Pallares-Burke turns her attention in her essay. Once again, though, the mediatory effect of the French translation, missing from the conclusions drawn by the Brazilian scholar, has an important part to play in addressing this question.

Pallares-Burke begins by noting that, above all else, it is clear that Floresta did not seek to claim personal credit as the original author of *Direitos*, something which, it is observed, she could easily have attempted, considering the obscurity of the text. Neither, Pallares-Burke adds, can it be realistically suggested that Floresta was seeking to pass Wollstonecraft off as a plagiariser of Sophia's text (a notion which, it is suggested, might have occurred to a reader familiar with *Woman not Inferior* but not with *Vindication*).[25] However, beyond clearing Floresta of these two unlikely potential accusations, the conclusions Pallares-Burke goes on to draw are themselves fundamentally accusatory in their tone and nature. This posture is firmly established in the following sentence, which serves as introduction to her discussion of Floresta's motivations: 'Se, como diz o ditado popular, "ladrão que rouba ladrão tem cem anos de perdão", então Nísia, que já foi beneficiada com mais de sesenta anos de lambuja, pode ser interpelada sobre os motives que a levaram a forjar, de certo sentido, uma tradução para difundir idéias emancipatórias femininas'.[26]

As mentioned previously, Pallares-Burke refers to *Direitos* as a trick, or fraud, and a plagiarism. The starting point for all these accusations is, of course, the belief that Floresta knowingly and deliberately misled her readers in attributing her translation to 'Mistriss Godwin'. Her position is also dependent on the assumption that Floresta had encountered and read Wollstonecraft's *Vindication of the Rights of Woman*. In fact this assumption

Nísia Floresta's *Direitos das Mulheres e Injustiça dos Homens'*, *Ellipsis*, 8 (2010), 9–36, for a closer discussion of these variations between the three texts.
25   Pallares-Burke, 'A Mary Wollstonecraft', p. 184.
26   Pallares-Burke, 'A Mary Wollstonecraft', p. 184.

is as central to Pallares-Burke's argument as it is to Duarte's. Pallares-Burke suggests that Floresta chose not to translate Wollstonecraft's text because its arguments were not radical enough for her at that time, stating that, in light of her personal circumstances, Floresta would not have been attracted to a text which, 'não obstante negar a inferioridade natural da mulher e exigir-lhe educação igual à do homem, ainda considerava que os papéis centrais da mulher em sociedade eram os de esposa e mãe'.[27] Observing the striking parallels between the unconventional, at times scandalous, lives of Floresta and Wollstonecraft,[28] Pallares-Burke concludes that despite rejecting her arguments in favour of Sophia's, the Brazilian writer would have felt a profound connection with Wollstonecraft, and therefore attributed *Direitos* to the great feminist writer in homage to and recognition of this fellow independent woman who, like Floresta herself, had challenged the conventions of her time and borne the brunt of public disapproval.[29]

It is, of course, the notion that Floresta read and rejected the work of Mary Wollstonecraft more than any other factor, which underlies Pallares-Burke's belief that she was attracted to the more radical aspects of *Woman not Inferior*. It is this assumption that I now wish to question. Floresta was clearly familiar with Mary Wollstonecraft as a literary figure; she would not have attributed her translation to her if she were not. However, it is worth noting that Floresta uses Wollstonecraft's married name, yet she was only to become William Godwin's wife in 1797, five years after the publication of *Vindication* and of its French translation, which was also published in 1792. Had Floresta seen a copy of *Vindication* in English or French (the language in which she would have read it), its author is unlikely to have been named as Mistress, or Mrs, Godwin. It therefore seems more likely that the Brazilian writer claimed her translation to be of 'Mistriss Godwin' because that was the name by which she knew the writer, through second-hand reference to her life and work. This idea would appear to be confirmed by references to Wollstonecraft that appear in Floresta's

---

[27] Pallares-Burke, 'A Mary Wollstonecraft', p. 187.

[28] Wollstonecraft had an illegitimate daughter by her first relationship with Gilbert Imlay, twice attempted suicide and contracted an extremely unorthodox marriage to William Godwin, when already pregnant with their daughter. See Janet Todd, 'Introduction and notes', in Mary Wollstonecraft, *A Vindication of the Rights of Woman* (Oxford: Oxford University Press, 1999), pp. vii–xxxvi (p. xxxvi). As discussed in the introduction, Floresta had apparently abandoned her first husband, a scandal which appears to have followed her for many years.

[29] Pallares-Burke, 'A Mary Wollstonecraft', pp. 185–6. She even goes so far as to suggest that by attributing Sophia's book to Wollstonecraft, 'Nísia estava, de certo modo, a dizer que esta era a obra que mais condizia com alguém que desafiara tão arrojada e revolucionáriamente as convenções sociais' (p. 187). Pallares-Burke is not the only scholar to observe the similarities in the writers' lives. Adauto da Câmara also suggests that Floresta related intimately with Wollstonecraft's circumstances (and those of her daughter) and, believing *Direitos* to be a translation of *Vindication*, concluded that this personal connection led Floresta to translate her English counterpart's work (p. 86).

later publications, by which time it is clear that she was familiar with her work, in which she uses the maiden name by which Wollstonecraft was, and is, generally known as a writer. In truth, there is no evidence to indicate that Floresta had read *Vindication* or indeed any of Wollstonecraft's work at this early time, and the use of her name certainly cannot be taken as confirmation that she had. There is no reason to think that Floresta did not simply happen upon the French translation of Sophia's long-forgotten text in the motley collection of European publications which were shipped across the Atlantic for consumption by an avid and insatiable Brazilian readership.

Even embracing the assumption that Floresta had read *Vindication*, there remains another, more obvious explanation for her decision not to translate it, which must be at least considered alongside the notion that its arguments were too conservative. From a purely practical viewpoint, a translation of Wollstonecraft's text would not have been an easy task. It is a far larger work than Sophia's pamphlet, and much less coherently structured and argued. It was written in just six weeks, and as a result is disjointed and repetitive, making it difficult to read in comparison with the succinct and well-ordered *Woman not Inferior*.[30] Moreover, in terms of content, Wollstonecraft looks in detail at a specifically British context, dedicating considerable space to a consideration of the relative states of women in different social classes. Sophia, on the other hand, takes a loftier, more universal overview of women, their abilities and their general state of subjection. It is easy to see why Floresta might have seen *Woman not Inferior*, with its simple, clearly expressed ideas, as a more accessible text both to translate and to read, and therefore likely to have a greater impact.

Whatever her reasons for translating Sophia, either in preference to or, very likely, in the absence of Wollstonecraft's *Vindication*, we are left with the question of why Floresta then attributed the text to Wollstonecraft. It is here that the significance of the French translation of *Woman not Inferior* returns to the fore: the most important factor that must be understood when considering her motivations in this regard is that Floresta did not know who the author of the text was. She could not have attributed her work to 'Sophia', because neither edition of the French translation gives the original pseudonym. If the edition to which she had access was that of 1750, all she would have known was that it was 'traduit de l'Anglois'; if it was the 1751 edition this information would have been expanded to 'traduit de l'Anglois de Miledi P***'.[31]

---

[30] Janet Todd suggests that this disorganised, hurried style was one favoured by polemicists at the time to convey the impression that their opinions came straight from the heart, forced into print by the strength of their convictions and indignation at the publication of those arguments to which they were opposed (p. xix).

[31] Garnier, p. 709. In fact it is unclear who this 'Miledi P***' is meant to refer to, for although the P appears to reflect the translator, Puisieux, Garnier concludes that the translator is more likely to have been Philippe-Florent de Puisieux than his wife Madeleine Darsant de

It seems unlikely that Floresta would have genuinely believed the text to be the work of Mary Wollstonecraft, since it would have shown the date of publication as 1750/51 and Wollstonecraft was only born in 1759. However, we cannot be sure of the extent of Floresta's knowledge regarding the English writer and a genuine mistake of this kind cannot be ruled out, as it is possible the still very young Floresta may have been aware of little more than Wollstonecraft's name as the author of a famous defence of women's rights. It is also important to note that it is Floresta's subsequent biographers who assumed that *Direitos* was specifically a translation of *Vindication*. In truth the titles differ markedly in their implication, and if Floresta had, in all innocence, believed the text before her to be Wollstonecraft's most famous work, it seems likely that she would have reproduced the title more accurately in order to attract attention and identify the work clearly.

What is more probable is that, keen to attribute the text to an original author and lacking any indication of who that might have been, Floresta shrewdly opted for a name that would be well-known to her readers, thus enhancing the appeal of the book. As described above, Pallares-Burke observes that Floresta clearly did not wish to pass *Direitos* off as her own work, and naming an original author would certainly have emphasised the fact that the text was a translation.[32] Pallares-Burke makes this observation only to credit Floresta with some literary honesty (before going on to accuse her of a sort of plagiarism by proxy), but it may, in fact, have suited Floresta very well at that time to highlight the non-originality of her publication. By using a translation to air her own opinions and concerns, Floresta's secondary position as translator would have offered her a degree of protection from the criticisms which she knew would be levelled against her. She was clearly well aware that even to translate another's, and a foreigner's, radical views would be considered inappropriate, writing in the dedication with which she introduces the translation that she hopes her readers will not criticise her 'temeridade' (*Direitos*, p. 22). More specifically, by naming the already scandalous English writer as author, Floresta may have hoped to further deflect disapproval away from her own role as messenger. It is possible that the absence of contemporary critical comment on *Direitos*, discussed below, may reflect the success of this ploy. Furthermore, by stressing the European origins of the text, Floresta would have tapped into the lucrative market produced by the obsession

---

Puisieux, to whom the text has traditionally been accredited (p. 711). Moreover, 'miledi' was a term of address for upper-class English women and therefore seems to be referring to the original author.

[32] It is no doubt in large part due to the absence of an original author in the French translation of *Woman not Inferior* that as recently as 1984 it was still being credited as the original work of Madame de Puisieux (see Garnier, p. 710).

with French and English products, fashions and ideas which had gripped the educated sections of Brazilian society since the opening of the nation's ports in 1808.

Pallares-Burke suggests that it was not only the famous name but also the infamous details of Wollstonecraft's private life which would have attracted readers to a translation of her work,[33] and it is certainly likely that the intimacies of the English writer's life would have been well known in Brazil; perhaps rather better known than her literary production. It is also undeniable that certain clear similarities can be observed between these incidents and Floresta's early life. However, it is for this very reason that I would challenge the suggestion that Floresta's motivation for attributing *Direitos* to Wollstonecraft lay in her recognition of these similarities.

At a time when a woman's worth was entirely dependent on her reputation, and more particularly on her sexual reputation, Wollstonecraft's life would have been viewed with horror, and it is very probable that this would have biased people's opinion of her writings. In fact this attitude is still alive and well more than a century later in Adauto da Câmara's *História de Nísia Floresta*, in which he not only refers to the scandals surrounding Wollstonecraft herself, due to her 'aventuras amorosas', but also describes the continuing immorality of her family: her husband William Godwin, rearing his children 'na pouca vergonha de seus princípios licenciosos', and her daughter Mary, 'contaminada das teorias dos pais', eloping with Shelley. He goes on to observe that this infamous behaviour 'eriçava o pudor da sociedade européia, tendo chegado até aqui. Nísia, por certo, conhecia aquelas agitações sentimentais'.[34]

Whilst Floresta had certainly had scandal in her young life, and may well have empathised with the circumstances of Wollstonecraft's private life, it seems extraordinary to suggest that she would have wished to pay homage to these parallels and thus draw the reader's attention to her own history. Her reputation as an adulteress is one from which she would surely have been desperate to escape as she began her new life with Manuel Augusto and their daughter, particularly if we believe that she was seeking work as a teacher in Recife, as Duarte suggests.[35] Moreover, she carried *Direitos* with her to Porto Alegre and then again to Rio, republishing the text each time. Floresta certainly would not have wished to encourage rumours regarding her unsuccessful and unsatisfactorily terminated first marriage as she set out to establish herself in these new cities. It therefore seems far more likely that, assuming Floresta was aware that the text she had translated was not Wollstonecraft's work, her decision to falsely attribute *Direitos* to her stems from an astute awareness of the success which such a polemical author would secure her translation, and not a conscious desire to link her own name and reputation with Wollstonecraft's.

There is also a further possible explanation for the confusion regarding the identity of the text and its author, one which would absolve Floresta of any real part in the mystery. Bearing in mind that the French translation of *Woman not Inferior* which somehow made its way across the Atlantic and into Floresta's hands was already eighty years old, it is highly likely that the original title page would have been damaged, perhaps to the point of illegibility, or even missing altogether. It is even possible to imagine that a bookseller, either in France or Brazil, keen to enhance the saleability of his stock, might have produced a new cover stating the original author to be Wollstonecraft. In this case Floresta could have translated a text which had been presented to her as the work of the famous English writer.[36]

What the above discussion reveals, above all else, is that the possible explanations for Floresta's surprising act of authorial mis-appropriation are all but endless. Moreover, none escape the realm of speculation and it is unlikely that evidence will ever come to light to change this unstable, malleable situation. In a moment of unintentional irony, having resolutely ignored and denied the slip in Floresta's status which inevitably accompanies Pallares-Burke's revelation of the true origins of *Direitos*, Duarte concludes 'sem dúvida, teria sido bem diferente e mais simples, se [Floresta] tivesse realizado simplesmente uma tradução literal e se colocasse como porta-voz servil de discursos alheios'.[37] This is, in fact, precisely what Floresta did do, yet this knowledge has done nothing to simplify an analysis of *Direitos*. On the contrary, it has given rise to a series of intriguing and unanswerable questions, which make Floresta's first venture into the world of letters all the more complex and challenging.

The only enlightening features of Floresta's publication, from which it is possible to draw clear and firm conclusions about her own intentions, are the title and the brief foreword in the form of a dedication, both of which are Floresta's own creations. Her choice of title is interesting because it seems to present a more open challenge, containing a direct criticism of men's treatment of women, something not found in the main or sub-titles of either Wollstonecraft's or Sophia's texts. At first glance it appears to be a surprising move, as a more radical and combative title might have been expected to

---

[36]   The practice of booksellers adding to or altering the information provided by a title page has been recorded. See, for example, David Finkelstein and Alistair McCleery, *An Introduction to Book History* (New York and London: Routledge, 2005), p. 70; Rietje van Vliet, 'Print and Public in Europe 1600–1800', in *A Companion to the History of the Book*, ed. Simon Eliot and Jonathon Rose (Oxford: Blackwell, 2007), pp. 247–58 (p. 256); G. L. Brook, *Books and Book-Collecting* (Aldershot: Gower, 1982), p. 143.

[37]   Duarte, 'Nísia Floresta: Incompreensão', p. 259.

provoke more immediate criticism, but Floresta may have hoped that by making the text's controversial content more apparent in the title, she would attract a greater number of readers. Or perhaps it reflects a little bit of that revolutionary young spirit which Pallares-Burke and Duarte are both so keen to identify in Floresta, despite their very different claims.

The dedication, however, provides a genuine, valuable insight into Floresta's motivations for publishing *Direitos* and the effects she hoped the book might produce on the 'brasileiras e acadêmicos brasileiros' to whom it is dedicated (*Direitos*, pp. 21–2). First addressing her female readers, whom she refers to as 'caras Patrícias' (p. 21), she urges them to educate themselves and endeavour to remain virtuous at all times, such that, 'sobresaindo essas qualidades amáveis e naturais ao nosso sexo, que até o presente têm sido abatidas pela desprezível ignorância em que os homens, parece de propósito, têm nos conservado, eles reconheçam que o Céu nos há destinado para merecer na Sociedade uma mais alta consideração' (p. 21).

Here we find convincing evidence that Floresta was already expressly concerned with the dual issues of education and feminine virtue – the dominant themes of her early writing, as I will discuss in Chapter 2 – a fact which also contradicts the notion that she might have been prepared to draw attention to her own less than virtuous parallels with Wollstonecraft. Moreover, the suggestion that women deserve a 'mais alta consideração' in society is markedly different from the radical claims made by Sophia. After all, a higher regard is by no means synonymous with the higher position demanded by Sophia in her declaration of women's equal ability to be professors, lawyers, generals, politicians etc. However, Floresta goes on to observe the miserable condition of women 'que até em pequenos empregos não podemos desenvolver nossos talentos naturais' (p. 22), indicating that she was not opposed to the notion of women participating in the public sphere of paid employment. Such a timid appeal is a far cry from the demands made by the English text and no doubt reflects her realistic expectations and a desire not to alienate her male readers.

Floresta's appeal to Brazil's academics is equally significant and revealing of her thinking. She clearly specifies that it is to the new generation of young academics, the 'mocidade Acadêmica' (p. 21), that she directs her translation. In them, she says, the nation's greatest expectations are invested, because they are the statesmen and legislators of tomorrow. Her hopes for these young men are clear: 'algum dia nas vagas horas de vossos altos ministérios, lançareis vistas de justiça sobre o nosso sexo em geral' (p. 22). In addressing the young men who were expected to take responsibility for the direction of the newly independent nation, it becomes clear that Floresta saw in the publication of *Direitos* a possible means of influencing the way they saw the female condition, and thus in turn influencing the future of the laws and norms which maintained that condition. However, Floresta is not seduced by impossible dreams of revolution. She immediately goes on to qualify the changes she hopes to see: '... se não para empreender uma metamorfose na ordem presente das coisas, ao menos para conseguirmos uma melhor sorte' (p. 22).

This statement, a clear attempt to lessen the challenge posed by the text and reassure her male readers, is in fact a reiteration of a stronger and more surprising disclaimer issued by the English original (and translated via the French by Floresta): 'De quanto tenho dito até o presente não tem sido com a intenção de revoltar pessoa alguma de meu sexo contra os homens, nem de transformar a ordem presente das coisas, relativamente ao Governo e auto-ridade. Não, fiquem as coisas no seu mesmo estado' (*Direitos*, p. 89 [56]). Moreover, Floresta's own focus on virtue and education, observed above, and her call for women to be afforded a higher consideration, also find an echo in the text she translated. Sophia suggests that she means only to show 'que meu sexo não é tão desprezível como os homens querem fazer crer' (p. 89 [56]), and discusses at length the relative tendency to virtue in men and women, at all times emphasising that any lack of virtue in her own sex is due to their exclusion from education (pp. 49–52 [25–7]). It is extremely significant that it should be the rhetorical climb-down of the conclusion to *Woman not Inferior* which finds its way into Floresta's foreword, rather than the forceful, revolutionary arguments which characterise the majority of the text. What Floresta's own contribution appears to indicate, then, is that it was the more conservative foundational elements of *Woman not Inferior* which attracted her to the text, and these elements remain in place throughout her own subsequent literary career.

Direitos has been described as the most interesting Recife publication of the period,[38] and with such a radical subject matter, its appearance would certainly be expected to have provoked a considerable degree of comment, if not scandal. A society which still considered it unnecessary, if not actu-ally pernicious, to educate girls in anything more than basic reading and writing, would have struggled to accept such a resounding attack on the deeply conservative heart of Brazil's patriarchal social system. It is therefore surprising that no direct criticism of or reference to this work has ever been located in the Recife press (nor indeed in Porto Alegre or Rio de Janeiro where the book was subsequently also put on sale). Hilda Flores suggests that this silence is explained by the fact that the only way to maintain the status quo of male superiority was to ignore such challenges.[39] However, this would seem to fly in the face of a strong trend for political and social criticism visible in the early nineteenth century press, flexing its new-found muscles after the establishment of a national printing press in 1808, and may

---

38   Laurence Hallewell, *Books in Brazil: A History of the Publishing Trade* (Metuchen, NJ and London: Scarecrow, 1982), p. 87.
39   Flores, 'Nísia Floresta', p. 103.

also have much to do with the fact that it was a translation and, as such, would have been perceived as part of the tide of European and in particular English and French texts (some more welcome than others),[40] which were flowing into the country.

In fact, *Direitos* appears to have enjoyed a considerable popular success at the time, running certainly to two editions, in Recife and Porto Alegre, and possibly a third in Rio, where the work is known to have been put on sale.[41] Most significantly, we can be certain that the text was widely circulated in the capital following its appearance there in 1839, thanks to a delightful literary occurrence which is cited in a number of studies of Floresta and her work.[42] In 1844, Joaquim Manuel de Macedo published the novel *A Moreninha*, generally considered to be the first romantic novel of Brazilian literature. In it the reader is informed that the vivacious and argumentative 'Moreninha' of the title, D. Carolina, had read 'Mary de Wollstonecraft', and further details in the passage clearly indicate that it must be *Direitos* to which Macedo is referring. The student Leopoldo is clearly echoing Sophia's radical notions of equality in public life, not Wollstonecraft's defence of equal education, when he sarcastically observes: 'a bela senhora é filósofa! ... faze idéia! Já leu Mary de Wollstonecraft e, como esta defende os direitos das mulheres, agastou-se comigo, porque lhe pedi uma comenda para quando fosse ministra do Estado, e a patente de cirugião de exército, no caso de chegar a ser General.'[43]

As Duarte observes, the inclusion of this reference in a popular novel, with no clarification from the author, shows not only that Macedo himself had read *Direitos*, but also that he fully expected his readers to be, at the very least, familiar with the name and ideas of 'Mary Wollstonecraft', if not with the actual text of her work, as he would have believed *Direitos* to be.[44] Duarte, of course, maintains that it is Floresta's own arguments that inspire the heroine of the novel; Pallares-Burke, on the other hand, observes the curious irony by which the radical arguments of the 'dupla Poulain-Sophia' should have come to shape Macedo's character and the generations of real-life 'moreninhas' who might have been inspired by her.[45]

---

[40] New ideas from France, which had been reaching Brazilian shores from even before the French Revolution, were commonly referred to as the 'abominable French principles', see Maria Lúcia Pallares-Burke, 'A Spectator in the Tropics: A Case Study in the Production and Reproduction of Culture', *Comparative Studies in Society and History*, 36: 4 (1994), 676–701 (p. 691).

[41] See Duarte's introduction to *Direitos*, pp. 15–16.

[42] Including Duarte, 'Posfácio', pp. 128–30; Pallares-Burke, 'A Mary Wollstonecraft', pp. 191–2; June Hahner, *Emancipating the Female Sex: The Struggle for Women's Rights in Brazil, 1850–1940* (Durham, NC and London: Duke University Press, 1990), p. 15.

[43] J.M. de Macedo, *A Moreninha*, 34th edn (São Paulo: Editora Ática, 2001), p. 69.

[44] Duarte, 'Posfácio', p. 129.

[45] Pallares-Burke, 'A Mary Wollstonecraft', pp. 191–2.

This appearance in *A Moreninha* is the only concrete example of the influence *Direitos* had on Floresta's fellow writers, and June Hahner is right in observing that 'we cannot easily measure the direct impact of this translation'.[46] However, it seems likely that the repercussions of the text extend beyond this one instance. In her postscript to *Direitos*, Duarte observes the increasing engagement with notions of female emancipation in the press and other publications during the decades following the appearance of *Direitos*, quoting various examples and suggesting that 'aqui e ali, encontram-se ressonâncias do mesmo pensamento expressado por Nísia'.[47] By far the most important of these resonances is to be found in Ana de Barandas's 'Diálogos', discussed above.

The significance of this probable influence lies in the fact that, in reality, it was not 'as idéias nisianas', as Duarte suggests,[48] or even the ideas of Mary Wollstonecraft, but the Cartesian logic of the little known Poulain de la Barre, transmitted via Sophia, that inspired de Barandas's text. Moreover, as discussed above, now that *Direitos* cannot be considered a separate, original piece of writing by Floresta, 'Diálogos' takes on a new importance. Thus, whilst no longer able to claim the title for herself, Floresta and her translation played a central role in the birth of original feminist writing in Brazil, and through this connection, the text which could well be Brazilian feminism's new 'texto fundante', de Barandas's 'Diálogos', also reveals its unusual and unexpected intellectual influences. In fact, since the two women appear to have been acquainted, this influence is unlikely to have been one-sided, and Floresta's own ideas may also have been influenced by de Barandas's thinking and writing.[49]

Floresta's own part in these events has inevitably suffered as the truth about the origins of *Direitos* has emerged, yet her contribution must still be afforded the value it deserves. Pallares-Burke observes that even to translate such a radical text 'era, por si só, um ato revolucionário',[50] and even as a translation, *Direitos* remains the first rallying-cry in the fight for Brazilian women's emancipation. Furthermore, although always considerably less radical in tone than 'Diálogos', unlike her *gaúcha* contemporary (or indeed any other woman writing in mid-nineteenth-century Brazil), Floresta continued to write at length on the subject of women's education and their value to society, eventually producing a body of work that represents a concerted appeal for an improvement in women's condition and status and reflects the writer's very genuine and passionate concern for the subject.

---

[46] Hahner, *Emancipating the Female Sex*, p. 15.

[47] Duarte, 'Posfácio', p. 132.

[48] Duarte, 'Posfácio', p. 126.

[49] Hilda Flores also hints at this possible ongoing, mutual influence. Flores, 'Ana Euridice', p. 42.

[50] Pallares-Burke, 'A Mary Wollstonecraft', p. 189.

As mentioned above, a number of the core arguments of *Woman not Inferior* can be traced through Floresta's subsequent work, but the use these arguments are put to, and the conclusions she draws from them, differ massively from the English text. A consideration of these similarities and differences, which I will make in Chapters 2 and 3, is central to an analysis of Floresta's work since, as a direct translation, *Direitos/Woman not Inferior*, and the Cartesian rationalism of Poulain de la Barre they carry, must be viewed as an early influence, as well as an early production. Whether Floresta was primarily attracted to the most conservative or most militant aspects of Sophia's work, it might be assumed that she did not fundamentally disagree with any of the core claims made by the text, including women's ability to fulfil the most difficult and elevated public offices. Her willingness to translate these ideas, taken in conjunction with the details of her own life, in which she published extensively, provided for herself and her family, travelled independently, and interacted with some of the most eminent thinkers and writers of her day, certainly indicates that she did not believe public life to be beyond the capabilities of a woman.

In a study of Floresta's own writing and the increasingly private role she advocates for her fellow women, this valuable insight into her underlying convictions helps us to understand the process by which she arrived at her final position regarding women's place in society. It clearly demonstrates that Floresta does not exclude women from the public sphere because she believes they lack the ability, but because such activity does not fit with the vision of idealised womanhood that she comes to advocate. In turn, this knowledge helps to demonstrate the force of the various intellectual influences which shape her work, from Enlightenment thought to contemporary European liberalism, the predominantly Catholic discourse of maternalism in Brazil and Europe, and the growing influence of Positivism through her friendship with Auguste Comte. To a certain extent, therefore, it is through this widening gap between ability and appropriateness that Floresta's feminism must now be evaluated.

Maria Lúcia Pallares-Burke's identification of the true origins of *Direitos* overturns one of the cornerstones upon which Floresta's position in the feminist and wider Brazilian canon has always been constructed. As such, it could and should have cleared the way for a concerted re-reading and reappraisal of Floresta's work and reputation. That this has not happened in the years following the publication of that research is a shame, and not only in terms of scholarly accuracy. The seemingly inescapable epithet of 'translator of Mary Wollstonecraft' in fact does Floresta no favours. Rather, this association with one of the most famous names in the historiography of liberal feminist discourse serves to keep Floresta's own work in the shadows, bringing a disproportionate focus to her first, and it must be said unrepresentative, publication. Meanwhile much of her own intellectual output, unique in its scope and volume amongst nineteenth-century Brazilian women's writing, remains largely uncommented upon. It is this imbalance which I hope to go some way towards addressing in the chapters that follow.

2

The Educator

Throughout her work, Floresta's discussion of women's rights and responsibilities, condition and role in society is invariably founded on the question
of education. In fact, it is on the subject of women's education that Floresta's
participation and place in Brazilian Letters should first be established: her
early works are almost exclusively devoted to the education of girls, and
whilst later publications address a wide range of social issues, the question
of education continues to pervade her work. In fact, Floresta's entire opus
might be said to be didactic in its purpose, although for most of her writing
career her 'pupils' are adult and by no means only women. In her discussion
of the 1857 essay 'A Mulher', Duarte observes the text's 'caráter nitidamente
formativo, pois, mais que *informar*, pretende *formar* consciências',[1] and this
claim can easily be extended to Floresta's writing as a whole. Moreover – and
of immense significance in an analysis of Floresta's positioning regarding
female education and for a wider evaluation of her vision of useful womanhood – she also transcribed thought into action through the Collegio Augusto,
the school for girls that she ran for eighteen years in the Brazilian capital.

In this chapter I will therefore look at both Floresta's teaching career and
the education she prescribed for women in her writing, and the prominent
discrepancies between the two. I will also briefly identify the arguments
used to defend women's equal education in Sophia's *Woman Not Inferior*
and trace the influence of Floresta's translation through her own work. These
points of contact and divergences between the text she translated, Floresta's
own writing, and her active involvement in teaching will help to reveal her
motivations, the development of her ideas and the influences, national and
international, at work upon them. First, however, I will briefly outline the
historical reality of women's education in Brazil at the time and more specifically the prevailing discourses employed against and increasingly in favour
of an improvement in the situation. By contextualising Floresta's engagement
with this national scenario as teacher and writer, I hope to show how her position both challenged and was influenced by the growing and shifting debate
on female education, as well as the impact that, as an early contributor, her

---

[1] Duarte, *Vida e Obra*, p. 252; author's italics.

own writing may have had on the arguments that were consistently used to defend the education of women until well after the end of the Empire.

Under colonial rule, female education had focused on domestic arts and moral, Christian doctrine, whilst the daughters of the colonial elite were also taught the social graces of music, singing and dance. Reading and writing were never a priority.[2] This focus was to remain largely unchallenged for much of the nineteenth century and it is this failure, not only of the post-independence government but also of the population as a whole, to bring about any real change in policy or attitudes that provokes the strongest criticism in Floresta's writing. Throughout the nineteenth century neither the arguments employed, with limited success, by those in favour of improved female education, nor those used to discourage such an improvement, were to change much. Whilst female education was consistently defended in terms of the benefit to the family and the nation, traditional fears regarding the corrupting effect of knowledge also persisted, and popular prejudices often spoke louder than liberal social and political rhetoric. One of the greatest barriers to improved female education throughout the Imperial period was the suspicion and general lack of interest with which many parents viewed the subject. Parents often removed daughters from school before they had acquired a good knowledge of the three Rs, concerned only that they should learn the domestic skills and social graces deemed necessary for a woman.[3] This emphasis is something Floresta identifies frequently in her work, and she criticises parents for valuing such superficial lessons.

Later in the century some schools attempted to widen their curriculum but such moves frequently met with strong social resistance and these schools were often forced to close through lack of pupils or change their curriculum to suit conservative and suspicious parents.[4] The pressure of parental demands is also something Floresta comments on in *Opúsculo*, suggesting that she may have had first-hand experience of the problem. In fact, within such a conservative and repressive context it seems surprising that Floresta's own school, in which she taught a relatively wide range of subjects, remained open and successful for nearly two decades. The Collegio Augusto closed its doors definitively in 1856 when Floresta left for Europe, having received surprisingly few documented criticisms of its extensive curriculum in the Carioca press. This scarcity of critical notices, coupled with certain positive reports, indicates that there must have been some limited support for a more progressive approach to female education in the capital at that time.

***

[2]   *Mulher Brasileira – Bibliografia Anotada*, vol. 2 (São Paulo: Fundação Carlos Chagas; Brasiliense, 1981), pp. 213–14.

[3]   Heleieth Saffioti, *Women in Class Society*, trans. Michael Vale (New York and London: Monthly Review Press, 1978), p. 147; and Hahner, *Emancipating the Femal Sex*, p. 14.

[4]   *Mulher Brasileira*, p. 218.

Parents were not the only sector of society that remained critical of expanding education for girls. Drawing on popular fears, social and religious commentators also defended limited female education as a social necessity in order to preserve the family, and in the second half of the century critics employed 'fashionable' biological arguments, claiming that the relative weight of male and female brains proved women's intellectual inferiority and that women's weak constitution made study impossible, as it could result in a wide range of ailments.[5] The latter is one of several notions debunked by Floresta in *Opúsculo*.

These negative arguments by no means dominated the debate on the education of women. Particularly in the second half of the century, philosophers, moralists, journalists, politicians and doctors all began to defend an improvement in women's education,[6] usually emphasising the immense benefits to the nation to be had from such a move. However, these arguments were constructed within an ideological framework that was no less patriarchal than the arguments employed against women's education: the benefits described were invariably for the nation and the family, that is to say, for the white male citizens by whom the nation was discursively configured. Through her focus on national interest, in many ways Floresta also adopts this male-centred discourse. However, by suggesting that education is women's only route to happiness, social status and spiritual autonomy, she also presents education as offering some personal benefits to women's own social and psychological well-being.

Female education was generally seen as being necessary to equip women to educate their sons and produce good citizens. This emphasis on maternal influence was in fact central to political discourse on education after independence. The 1827 law on public schooling stated that: 'As mulheres carecem tanto mais de instrução, porquanto são elas que dão a primeira educação aos seus filhos. São elas que fazem os homens bons e maus; são as origens das grandes desordens, como dos grandes bens; os homens moldam a sua conduta aos sentimentos delas.'[7] However, it is only in the second half of the century that criticism of women's poor education begins to mount and this rhetoric of the educated mother contributing to national progress through her children finds a popular voice. Hahner quotes from two influential studies, published in

---

5   Costa, 'Patriarchalism', pp. 263–4; *Mulher Brasileira*, pp. 220–1.

6   Duarte, *Vida e Obra*, p. 203. In fact Duarte suggests that a virtual consensus was reached that society could not progress without the education of women (p. 202).

7   Quoted in Eliane Marta Santos Teixeira Lopes, 'A Educação da mulher: A feminização do magistério', *Teoria & Educação*, 4 (1991), 22–40 (p. 26). This law was written by the Senator José Lino Coutinho, whose name would be forever linked with female education after the publication in 1849 of *Cartas sobre a educação de Cora*, a collection of letters which he had written some twenty years earlier to his daughter's guardian/governess and later to Cora herself, covering a wide range of issues concerning her physical, moral and intellectual formation.

1867 and 1874, that rely heavily on this discourse.[8] Whilst Floresta's employment of this argument in *Opúsculo* (1853) may partly reflect the influence
of the first moves towards this nationalist revaluation of female education, it
also positions her at the forefront of the movement and as a source of inspiration to later writers. In fact, not only Floresta's argument, but one of the core
ideas from *Woman Not Inferior* can be identified in the defence of women's
education given by Tobias Barreto in the Pernambucan Provincial Assembly
in 1879, in which he noted with regard to men's greater intellectual development that 'we take as an effect of nature, what is only an effect of society'.[9]
Like Floresta before him, he is quick to add that he does not favour equal
rights or political emancipation for women.

Central to almost all definitions of female education was a solid formation in the Catholic faith. Guacira Lopes Louro notes how Catholic doctrine
constructed an idealised femininity through the dichotomy of Eve and
Mary.[10] Floresta, herself devoutly Catholic, repeatedly asserts the importance
of a sound religious education for girls, employs Mary as evidence of God's
higher plans for women and constructs women's domestic and maternal
duties as sacred. The profound influence of Catholic conservatism is also
clearly apparent in her work through the constant valuation of feminine virtue
and modesty.

Although most of those writing about female education in the nineteenth
century were men, some women did begin to discuss the subject in print,
particularly in the second half of the century when women's education became
a popular subject for debate in the burgeoning female press.[11] Women writing
on the subject always identified education as the key to female emancipation,
discussing the need to redefine women's status in society. However, this small
but gradually expanding minority of literate women continued to emphasise
women's role as wife and mother and stress above all the improvements such
changes would bring to society and the nation, calling only for better treatment
within the family for themselves.[12] In this, Floresta was typical, and as one of
the earliest female voices to join the debate on women's education, may well
have helped to shape the arguments which women were to use in defence
of education throughout the remainder of the century. Emília Viotti da Costa
quotes from various women who contributed to the magazine *A Mensageira*,
published from 1897 to 1900, employing arguments that echo Floresta's, and
indeed Sophia's, writing, such as: 'Men scorn women's ignorance, but forget

[8]   Hahner, *Emancipating the Femal Sex*, pp. 48–9.
[9]   Quoted in Costa, 'Patriarchalism', p. 264.
[10]   Guacira Lopes Louro, 'Mulheres na sala de aula', in *História das mulheres no Brasil*,
ed. Mary del Priore, 2nd edn (São Paulo: Contexto, 1997), pp. 443–81 (p. 447).
[11]   Costa, 'Patriarchalism', p. 257; *Mulher Brasileira*, p. 220.
[12]   Hahner, *Emancipating the Female Sex*, pp. xiv and 42.

that they educated them to be slaves.'[13] Costa ends her discussion with the conclusion that 'by the end of the century, women's education had been tied to the idea of national destiny' (p. 264), a connection which Floresta had drawn explicitly and repeatedly almost fifty years earlier.

However, it is also important to note that she was not unique in addressing these issues at mid-century, even as a woman. Two Argentinian women based in Rio, Maria Benedita de Oliveira e Silva (using the pseudonym Zaira Americana), and Joana Paula Manso de Noronha, the founder and editor of the *Jornal das Senhoras*, were producing very similar writing on women's education in the early 1850s, and, in the latter case, even a more radical defence of women's emancipation.[14] Where Floresta differs from these contemporaries, however, is that she put theory into practice by running her own school.

As the above discussion begins to suggest, an analysis of Floresta's writing on education reveals the influence of prevailing discourses and attitudes of the day, both in the arguments she adopts and in the positions and prejudices she challenges, as well as revealing the possible input her own thinking contributed to the debate. Moreover, it is possible to trace a clear development in the writer's defence of education away from the ideas she translated from *Woman Not Inferior* in 1832, towards a fundamentally limiting definition of education within an explicitly patriotic discourse of national construction and progress. However, it is not only from Floresta's written work that we unveil her vision of women's education; the curriculum she offered to her own pupils in the Collegio Augusto, unhampered by the conventions and restrictions of the published word, arguably provides a more honest insight into the level of instruction Floresta considered appropriate and advantageous to her sex. It is therefore one of the most intriguing aspects of Floresta's intervention in this debate that the focus she adopts in her writing, on virtue and domestic duty, appears to be at odds with the education she put into practice for well over a decade in her Rio school. This active involvement in teaching girls, and the curriculum she chose to teach, must also be taken into consideration in an analysis of her approach to female education. It is Floresta's teaching career that I shall therefore consider first, since she in fact began to teach several years before publishing any work of her own, and her pedagogic practices must inevitably contextualise her writing on education.

---

13 Costa, 'Patriarchalism', p. 262.
14 *Zaira Americana Mostra as Imensas Vantagens que a Sociedade inteira obtém da Ilustração, Virtudes e Perfeita Educação da Mulher, como Mãe e Esposa do Homem* (Rio de Janeiro: Typ. Dois de Dezembro de Paula Brito, 1853); *A Jornal das Senhoras*, 1 January 1852 to 1855.

Education in practice in the Collegio Augusto

Floresta's teaching career began early; in fact it has been implied that she may have begun to teach as early as 1829, at the age of nineteen, whilst still living in Pernambuco. Constância Lima Duarte suggests that it may have been Floresta who placed an announcement which appeared in the *Diário de Pernambuco* in April and May of that year advertising the teaching of reading, writing, simple arithmetic, Christian doctrine and 'os elementos de civilidade' to girls. She states that this teacher could be 'a própria Nísia que, dizem, ensinava a meninas na própria casa no tempo em que residiu em Olinda'.[15] Unfortunately she does not clarify who, in fact, had previously made such an assertion, and without proper documentary evidence it is impossible to verify whether Floresta was teaching at this time.

However, it does seem clear that Floresta worked as a teacher whilst living in Porto Alegre, and this certainly makes sense, given the premature death of her husband in 1833 and the subsequent need to support her family. More than one scholar mentions a school run by Floresta in the Rua Nova,[16] and it is to a school on this same street that the slave Domingos takes his master's child in Floresta's 'Paginas de uma vida obscura' (1855), a text which includes certain biographical details. Floresta herself also states that she had already been teaching for four years when she arrived in Rio de Janeiro,[17] giving weight to the idea that she began to seek paid teaching work only after she was widowed.

Almost immediately on arrival in the capital Floresta established the Collegio Augusto and it is interesting to compare the advertisement which she placed with similar ones for other girls' schools at the time. For example, an establishment operating in 1846 is advertised as follows: 'onde se continúa a ensinar a ler, escrever, contar, grammatica nacional, francez, dansa, coser, bordar, marcar e tudo quanto é proprio para a educação de uma menina'.[18] The reader is led to understand that what is fitting in a girl's education is a continuation of the list of domestic skills which the advertisement begins. In contrast, Floresta advertises her school as 'hum collegio de educação para meninas, no qual, além de ler, escrever, contar, coser, bordar, marcar, e tudo o mais que toca à educação domestica de huma menina, ensinar-se-ha a grammatica da língua nacional por hum methodo fácil, o francez, o italiano, e os princípios mais geraes da geographia'.[19]

Whilst Floresta still highlights the teaching of domestic skills, a necessary focus in order to attract most parents at that time, the use of the expression

---

15 Duarte, *Vida e Obra*, p. 24.
16 For example, Duarte, *Vida e Obra*, p. 27; Seidl, p. 18.
17 See Floresta's advertisement in the *Jornal do Commercio*, 31 January 1838.
18 *Jornal do Commercio*, 18 December 1846.
19 *Jornal do Commercio*, 31 January 1838.

'além de' reveals her desire to emphasise the ways in which her curriculum extended beyond this domestic focus. More significantly, in the first advertisement, domestic skills constitute a large part of what is seen as a girl's education per se. Floresta, on the other hand, sees such skills only as part of 'a educação domestica'. What is also interesting about Floresta's choice of wording is that she includes the basic skills of literacy and numeracy in her definition of domestic education, apparently equating them with needlework. At a time when only a very small minority of elite women could read and write, this suggestion would have been surprising and it reveals Floresta's advanced thinking regarding both women's education and their role within the family. A literate and numerate woman could play a much more significant, administrative role in the general management and economy of her household. Moreover, whilst Floresta saw the three Rs as being fundamental to even the most basic female instruction, she saw *education* for women as being something distinct from the mere acquisition of domestic skills. This notion of a more profound education is also central to Floresta's writing, but whilst her written work primarily suggests that this extension beyond the teaching of domestic skills should take the form of a sound moral and religious education, the nature of the curriculum she taught indicates that she favoured a genuine broadening of intellectual, abstract knowledge for her own pupils.

The curriculum taught at the Collegio Augusto was in fact considerably broader even than that advertised when the school opened in 1838. In 1846 Floresta published the results of the school's examinations in the *Jornal do Commercio* and the subjects examined included literature, poetry, translation and grammar in French and Italian, geography and cosmography, ancient and modern history and Latin.[20] At the time, Floresta's own daughter, who won one of the prizes, was just short of her seventeenth birthday, indicating that the Collegio Augusto taught girls well beyond the usual age of twelve or thirteen. The school received praise and support from some sources. For example, ten gentlemen of standing, whose names were published in the above article, assessed the examinations and awarded the prizes, indicating that they were happy to be associated with such a forward-thinking establishment. The school also appears to have received praise from the papal nuncio, an event which several biographers and historians mention.[21] It is in fact Floresta herself who provides this information, recalling the occasion in her Italian travel journal when she meets the man again in Rome. She describes his surprise and pleasure on hearing the pupils recite poetry and prose in Italian, but, she informs her readers, he is most amazed to hear a girl reciting from the *Æneid* and translating Horace (*Três Anos*, p. 97). Very few

---

[20] *Jornal do Commercio*, 18 December 1846.
[21] For example, Câmara, *História*, p. 44; Costa, 'Patriarchalism', pp. 257–8.

women indeed would have learnt Latin at this time and teaching it to girls is likely to have been considered by many to be highly subversive since it allowed, amongst other things, an understanding of the Catholic liturgy. It is interesting to note that her decision to teach Latin was apparently supported by an official source of papal authority. However, since it is Floresta herself who recounts the event, a certain bias must be allowed for and it is possible that the nuncio's surprise was in fact rather greater than his pleasure. It is certainly little wonder that he remembers Floresta when he meets her again some ten years later in Rome.

Alongside this (apparent) support from high places, Floresta and her school also suffered harsh and vindictive criticism in the Carioca press, some of it apparently provoked by her decision to publish her examination results (something she had not done before 1846). This move to publicise her school's extensive curriculum appears to have been too much of a challenge for at least one critic to bear. A brief comment which appeared only two weeks after Floresta's results were published, describes her as 'quem toma o maior interesse pelo adiantamento de suas discípulas. *Trabalhos de língua não faltaram; os de agulha ficaram no escuro. Os maridos precisam de mulher que trabalhe mais e fale menos.*'[22] Two weeks on, a similar tone can be found in the following attack, possibly written by the same critic, in which the teaching of Latin clearly causes particular outrage:

> há casas de educação que têm o mau gosto de ensinar às meninas a fazer vestidos ou camisas. Mas parece que D. Augusta acha isso muito prosaico. Ensina-lhes latim. E porque não grego ou hebraico? Pobre directora! [...] Notaremos apenas a D. Floresta que se esquece um tanto do verdadeiro fim da educação, que é adquirir conhecimentos úteis e não vencer dificuldades, sem nenhuma utilidade real.[23]

Such condemnations exemplify the patriarchal prejudices which Floresta and like-minded educators of girls would have encountered frequently, reflecting the continuing, widespread belief that the instruction of girls should prepare them only for the practicalities of marriage.

What is most interesting in an appraisal of Floresta's participation in education in the broadest sense is that whilst she was prepared to face public criticism and slanderous insults to offer a broad and enlightened curriculum to her own pupils, she was clearly not interested in defending, or willing to risk a similar attack on her written work by defending such a challenging position for the wider female population.

---

[22] *O Mercantil*, 2 January 1847; author's italics.

[23] *O Mercantil*, 17 January 1847. At times these snide criticisms became extremely personal, apparently alluding to Floresta's first, unsuccessful marriage (see Duarte, *Vida e Obra*, p. 34).

Education in theory in Floresta's writing

A consideration of the discursive, social and personal factors that contributed to this considerable toning-down of her published prescriptions for
women's education must begin where Floresta began: with her translation of *Woman Not Inferior*. Floresta's decision to translate Sophia's text
would suggest that she sympathised with the arguments voiced in it, yet,
as discussed in the next chapter, the radical stance adopted by *Woman Not
Inferior* is clearly contradictory to Floresta's own position as expressed in her
subsequent works. Where Floresta's own views and those of the anonymous
Sophia clearly do coincide is in the identification of poor education as the
root cause of women's condition and their repression and I would suggest
that it may have been the English text's core assertion of women's right to,
and need for, education that appealed to Floresta, rather than its flamboyant
claims regarding women's superior suitability for public office. Indeed, many
aspects of Sophia's defence of education, which I will briefly outline, remain
central to Floresta's own discussion of women's education. However, the
Brazilian writer also adopts a number of very different tactics from those of
her English predecessor, and these similarities and divergences tell us a great
deal about her motivations for translating Sophia, about the development of
her own concept of the purpose and nature of female education, and about
the external influences which challenged and essentially deposed Sophia's
rational, Cartesian humanism.

There are several key arguments regarding women's education which are
reiterated many times in *Woman Not Inferior*. The starting point for the text's
appeal for equal education is the assertion that women are rational creatures
(*Direitos*, pp. 41, 64, 71 [16, 36, 42]), who are at least as able to control their
passions and operate according to reason as men are.[24] From this position it is
argued that women therefore have a natural right to equal education with men
(pp. 49, 52, 56 [24, 27, 30]) and, being physically and spiritually identical to
them in every way except with regard to reproduction (p. 47 [23]), women
are capable of everything that men are, providing they are given the same
opportunities and access to equal education (p. 49 [24]).

Sophia also sets out to refute the notion that education has a negative effect
on women's behaviour. Men's suggestion that education makes women proud
and vicious is condemned as a 'pretexto [...] desprezível e extravagente' (p.
49 [24]). Instead the writer seeks to establish a clear link between education
and virtue, stating that 'o verdadeiro e sólido conhecimento não pode tornar
as mulheres, assim como os homens, senão mais submissas e mais virtuosas'

---

24 This foundational importance of reason in all the text's arguments originates from
the Cartesian principle which Sophia 'inherited' from Poulain de la Barre's seventeenth-
century work.

(p. 49 [25]) and describing exactly how knowledge facilitates virtue through a better understanding of oneself and the wider world (pp. 50 and 52 [25–6 and 27]). By a logical extension, she therefore concludes that all women's faults can be attributed to their lack of education.

It is precisely with regard to this association with virtue that we find the passage that most closely reflects the position Floresta later adopts for herself in defence of female education:

> É um grande absurdo pretender que as ciências são inúteis às mulheres, pela razão de que elas são excluídas dos cargos públicos, único fim a que os homens se aplicam. A virtude e felicidade são tão indispensáveis na vida privada, como na pública, e a ciência é um meio necessário para se alcançar uma e outra. (p. 51 [27])

It is this implication that education can be equally beneficial within the private sphere that dominates Floresta's own engagement in the debate on the subject, as indeed it dominated the rhetoric of those (mostly male) contemporaries who also defended an improvement in women's education.

Woman Not Inferior adopts a very hard line against men, repeatedly accusing them of deliberately depriving women of education in order to prevent them from progressing in public life and to maintain their own position of mastery over them, and thus concluding that, since a lack of education is the root cause of women's faults, it is men who must take the blame for those faults (p. 56 [30]). This is a posture Floresta echoes in her own works, although rarely with the vehemence of the text she translated.

Finally, Sophia stresses that the education of women would in fact be in the best interests of men as well as women, suggesting that life for all would be much happier and more harmonious without conflicts generated by the distrust and disregard for the opposite sex which the current situation results in (pp. 89–90 [56–7]). The text concludes by exhorting women to put aside idle pursuits and 'aplicar-se à cultura de suas almas, a fim de se tornarem capazes de obrar com tanta dignidade a que a Natureza nos destinou' (p. 94 [61]). The sentiment behind this appeal can be found throughout Floresta's work, in particular the importance of dignity, although for Floresta this comes not directly from knowledge, but from a woman's virtue, awakened and nourished by proper education.

All the ideas outlined above can be found, to a greater or lesser extent, in Floresta's own works, although she employs some more whole-heartedly than others. Her own ideas coincide most closely with the text she translated in the identification of education as the means to virtue, and the corresponding belief that women cannot be held responsible for faults which are born out of a lack of education. It is interesting to observe that in her own works Floresta does not explain the link between education and virtue as explicitly as it is outlined in *Woman Not Inferior*, nor does she make a clear argument for broad and complete knowledge as an aid to virtue, something which is described clearly and at some length by Sophia. Instead she focuses on the need for moral and religious education, implying that virtue should be taught directly, rather than being acquired through knowledge and an understanding of the world. Floresta's emphasis on feminine virtue and propriety no doubt reflects the influence of her own strong Catholic faith and the powerful rhetoric of Catholic conservatism in Brazilian society, in contrast to Sophia's, and more specifically (as a Huguenot ex-priest), Poulain's enlightened Protestantism.

However, beyond the similarities identified above, the discussion of female education in *Woman Not Inferior* differs very significantly from Floresta's own works in a number of ways; in fact Sophia's basic focus and aims in defending women's education are clearly distinct from Floresta's. Firstly, we do not find Floresta's focus on motherhood in the English text and although Sophia begins by highlighting the supreme value to society of women's ability to bear and rear children (pp. 35–7 [11–14]), she establishes no specific link between education and the fulfilment of maternal duties, an association upon which Floresta's own appeals for women's education are increasingly founded.

In fact, Sophia is not really interested in women's actions in the private sphere at all. The text as a whole clearly reveals the belief that women are not only able, but also have the right, to participate in every kind of activity open to men.[25] With this aim in mind *Woman Not Inferior* extends the argument for women's education to its rational Cartesian conclusion: that equal ability and education should mean equal participation and power (pp. 77 and 86 [48 and 55]). It is here, of course, that the most fundamental, irreconcilable difference with Floresta's own writings becomes apparent. Whether restricted by her own conservatism or by the need to get her work published in a deeply conservative society, Floresta was unable to make any such claims, instead limiting herself to an appeal for education as a route to female value through domestic, familial duty.

As discussed in the previous chapter, Floresta's own brief prologue to her translation clearly indicates that it is women's education that governs her agenda, lending weight to the idea that it was predominantly *Woman Not Inferior*'s appeal for equal education that attracted Floresta to the text. Women's poor education and its detrimental effects are referred to twice in the two short paragraphs (*Direitos*, pp. 21 and 22). Floresta reiterates the English text's appeal to women to educate themselves: 'espero, que longe de conceberdes qualquer sentimento de vaidade em vossos corações com a leitura deste pequeno livro, procureis ilustrar o vosso espírito […] unindo

---

[25]   The only exception to this which is acknowledged in the text is with regard to the clergy, from which women are prohibited by God; a distinction which, in a particularly deft rhetorical move, is attributed to men's lack of moral fortitude (*Direitos*, p. 74 [45–6]).

sempre a este proveitoso exercício a prática da virtude' (p. 21). This passage
not only makes clear her specific interest in education but also her concern
for feminine virtue. Already we see the two being inexorably tied in her
vision of improved womanhood, as indeed they remain throughout her work.
In fact, in her early work Floresta's focus lies exclusively with the personal
dignity and social esteem that virtue, through education, affords to women.
It is to these early texts that I shall now turn my attention.

Writing in Brazil

After the publication of the first edition of *Direitos* in Recife in 1832,
Floresta's life was to be dominated by motherhood and her teaching career,
and it would be ten years before she published a work of her own. When
she did return to writing, her early publications continued to indicate an
overwhelming concern for, and at this time an exclusive focus on, female
education.[26] Between 1842 and 1847 Floresta published four short works,
three didactic texts (one of which is now lost), which it seems likely she
would have used as teaching aids in the Collegio Augusto, and the text of
a speech given to her pupils at the end of the academic year in 1847. The
three known texts are all written in a style suited to an adolescent audience,
with a simplistic moral positioning often bordering on the trite, as seen in
phrases such as 'o mau [...] não pode ser jamais feliz, embora o pareça, pois
a felicidade é sempre o resultado da virtude' (*Conselhos*, p. 46).

The first, and longest of these works, entitled *Conselhos a minha filha*, was
ostensibly written for Floresta's daughter Lívia on her twelfth birthday, although
it seems clear that she wrote it with publication in mind. In the course of ten
short chapters, Floresta outlines the behaviour appropriate to a young woman
and includes a warning against seducers whose false flattery brings ruin to many
women. The text was first published in 1842 and a second edition appeared
three years later with the addition of forty short verses reiterating the message
of the main text. It is from this extended second edition that all quotes are taken.
This was to be one of Floresta's most successful works, translated into Italian
and French and published in Florence in 1858 and 1859 respectively.

The year 1847 saw the publication of two short pieces of didactic fiction,
apparently written specifically for her pupils, but also published for public
sale. One of these texts, *Daciz, ou a jovem perfeita*, has sadly been lost,
although some notion of its content can be gleaned from an apparent reference to the text in the medical thesis of Floresta's brother-in-law Henrique
Medeiros, on the advantages of maternal breast-feeding. He quotes from 'a
interessante *Daciz*, quando dizia à sua digna preceptora: "Fugindo ao mundo

---

[26] It is not until 1849 that Floresta turns her attention to any other subject with the publication of *A Lágrima de um Caheté*.

para ocupar-me sómente de minha filha, eu esqueço junto d'ella o mundo e seus attractivos"'.[27] This reference suggests that Floresta may have used this piece of fiction to outline a woman's maternal duties. Further, the eponymous central character is likely to have been an example of saintly virtues similar to Fany, the heroine of the second of these two fictitious lessons. *Fany, ou o modelo das donzelas* recounts the life of an adolescent, the oldest of twelve children, living in Porto Alegre during the Farroupilha War, in which her father, who fights for the liberal republican rebels, is killed and the family is consequently ruined.[28] The text serves in part as a simple history lesson, including some historical detail regarding the capture of the provincial capital by the rebels and its subsequent recapture by Imperial troops (*Fany*, pp. 69 and 70). However, the political situation provides the palest of backgrounds to a narrative concerned with Fany's behaviour as the ideal daughter, and she is in fact specifically praised for remaining aloof from political concerns in the daily practice of virtue.

The last of these early educational publications, *Discurso que a suas educandas dirigio N. F. B. Augusta em 18 de Dezembro de 1847*, appears to have been published primarily as an advertisement for the Collegio Augusto: Floresta describes the 'assiduo trabalho a que [...] me dei sempre para conseguir ornar-vos com as flores, que no facil caminho da sciencia incansavel procurei colher para vós' (p. 3), and stresses the satisfaction of her pupils' parents. However, she also urges her students not to waste the education they have received and identifies the importance of that education for the fulfilment of their duties as women. Despite their different genres, all three surviving texts from this period are extremely similar in content and tone and firmly establish the relationship between education and virtue in Floresta's thinking at this time. The dominant focus in each is the virtue which education fosters and the happiness, security and social regard that women can only earn by showing themselves to be virtuous. Moreover, the Catholic basis of Floresta's vision of feminine virtue is clearly identified in her frequent reiteration of the value and power of faith for women, and in her specific concern for the threat of seduction, which reflects the need to control female sexuality that lay at the heart of Catholic, and patriarchal, constructions of virtuous womanhood.

It is particularly important to read these three pieces in the context of Floresta's teaching career, since their publication was undoubtedly influenced

---

27 José Henrique de Medeiros, *A Mamentação Materna é quasi sempre possivel*, medical thesis (Rio de Janeiro: Typ. Imparcial de Francisco de Paula Brito, 1848), p. 8.

28 The Farroupilha War, Rio Grande do Sul, 1835–45, was a liberal separatist revolt which saw regional interests turn against the central rule of the Imperial government and declare the province of Rio Grande do Sul a republic. This uprising, with its federalist ideology, posed the most serious and protracted threat to the Brazilian nation-state during the turbulent years of the regency. See Roderick J. Barman, *Brazil: The Forging of a Nation, 1798–1852* (Stanford, CA: Stanford University Press, 1988), pp. 182 and 187.

in large part by a concern for the success of the Collegio Augusto. At this time, the school was her most important project and, as far as is known, her primary source of income. In the stifling social conventions of the Rio *corte*, Floresta could not afford to attract polemic by putting her name to ideas which might have damaged her reputation and that of her school.

As the most explicitly instructive of the three texts, *Conselhos* offers the clearest example of the moral lesson Floresta hoped to impart to her students. After a short dedication to her daughter, the text begins with a lengthy preface in which Floresta states her motivation for writing, which she identifies as maternal devotion. She writes: 'Se há no mundo um título, que enobrece à mulher, é sem dúvida a de mãe; é ele que lhe dá uma verdadeira importância na sociedade' (p. 36). Most significantly, she suggests that it was this title 'que me deu o gosto pelo estudo na esperança de poder gozar um dia da ventura de dar-te as primeiras lições' (*Conselhos*, p. 36). The veracity of this statement is doubtful, as Floresta's 'taste for study' is likely to have begun at a much earlier age; however, her purpose in suggesting it is clear. Here we encounter the first allusion to the idea that education enables women to be better mothers, and that one of a mother's tasks is to educate her children. As we shall see, however, the value of motherhood plays a minor part in these texts, and Floresta does not engage fully with this maternal justification until 1853, after which it becomes central to her defence of female education.[29]

An interesting feature of *Conselhos* is that she states categorically that the education she seeks to impart to her daughter was laid out by her deceased husband. She writes: 'foi ele que traçou o plano de educação que, pelo meio mesmo de meus acerbos desgostos, e vicissitudes, tenho procurando [*sic*] ministrar-te; é a sua vontade que eu sigo ainda a teu respeito' (p. 40). Lívia was in fact only two years old when her father died, and it seems unlikely that he would have devised a specific curriculum for her at such an early age, although her parents may have discussed her future education in general terms. I would suggest that Floresta's inclusion of this 'factual' information for her readers reflects a desire to claim a rhetorical male authority to validate her position on female education. As her first original publication, written at a time when she was dependent on public opinion for her livelihood, not only in terms of the sale of her work but also in attracting parents to her school, it is not surprising that she was keen to stress this legitimising paternal support. Although, on many occasions through the course of her work, Floresta continues to make reference to her husband and the tragedy of his premature death, in subsequent texts his presence does not serve as a male affirmation of her opinions, reflecting Floresta's growing self-confidence and conviction as a writer.

---

[29] Although it must be remembered that Floresta's other piece of didactic fiction, *Daciz*, may have looked more specifically at a woman's role as mother.

Over the following eight chapters Floresta lists with examples the 'deveres e virtudes filiais [...] que servem de base a todas as outras [virtudes]' (p. 38). This long list includes simplicity, generosity, modesty, charity, resignation, docility, compassion, patience, and obedience and loyalty to one's parents. Floresta also stresses the importance of the Christian faith, without which 'a virtude mais austera naufragará' (p. 44). Certain vices are also identified, such as self-interest, ingratitude and vengeance. However, the vice which receives most attention in the text is vanity, which is described as 'esse terrível escolho da mocidade, em que tantas vezes tem naufragado a inocência mesmo' (p. 42). This identification of vanity over other vices is by no means unique to this text. In fact it can be found in much of Floresta's writing, including her prologue to *Direitos*, in which she expresses the hope that the text will not inspire vanity in its female readers (p. 21). Such a focus is inevitable, in the light of Floresta's appeal for better education for women, because those opposed to women's education could claim that it led to vanity (an idea also noted and dismissed by Sophia in *Woman Not Inferior*). Significantly, in *Conselhos* Floresta also reiterates Sophia's argument that only limited education leads to vanity, whilst a deeper knowledge has the opposite effect (*Direitos*, p. 49 [25]). Floresta writes, 'como não pretendo limitar-me a dar apenas a teu espírito uma leve notícia da ciencia, que, diz o vulgo, não ser necesario à mulher, eu não temo que a vaidade [...] infeccione tua alma' (*Conselhos*, p. 42), and later she states that 'a vaidade só é própria de uma alma baixa, de uma medíocre educação' (p. 47). In this way Floresta, like Sophia before her, seeks to pre-empt any accusations of vanity which might be levelled against her claims, turning a criticism into a further justification for improving women's education.

In *Conselhos* we find a constant reiteration of the idea that virtue is a woman's only route to both happiness and social regard. In fact, Floresta makes it clear that virtue is essential for a woman to defend herself against the many difficulties, threats and temptations life presents, describing kindness, patience and faith as a woman's 'armas poderosas' (p. 60). Floresta's emphasis on the importance of virtue is such that she suggests that without it 'nada pode brilhar em uma mulher' (p. 43), and even a woman's education is worthless: 'Instrução sem virtude na mulher, / [...] brilhar não pode' (p. 62). This is an explicitly gendered argument (Floresta makes no attempt to impose such standards on men), and as such, it is an extremely limiting discourse, which allows women's achievements only to be evaluated through the prism of feminine virtue. Here we find the first faint echo of the construction of women as moral boundary-markers of the nation, an idea embraced by Floresta in her later works, and discussed in the next chapter.

Together with virtue, Floresta also states the importance of reason over passion, suggesting that spiritual calm and contentment can be achieved by obeying one's conscience and 'dirigindo tuas ações conforme os ditames da sã razão' (p. 46). In fact the exercise of reason becomes a further virtue, and the failure to do so a vice, to be found, like vanity, only in 'as almas medíocres' (p. 57). In implying women's equal capacity for reason Floresta is perhaps also reflecting the influence of *Woman Not Inferior*, in which reason, and the empirical conclusions it enables, form the very basis of Sophia's claims. However, it must be noted that Floresta's definition of reason is very different from that found in *Woman Not Inferior*. Whilst the Cartesian reason of the English text provides a logical, dialectically argued route to knowledge and leads to the empirical conclusion that women are equal to men, Floresta's essentially gendered definition serves only to limit passion and so prevent unvirtuous and unfeminine behaviour.

A further echo of the text she translated that can be detected in *Conselhos*, particularly in the forty verses added to the second edition, is the identification of a deliberate policy on the part of men to keep women from education, and the ignoble personal motivations which inspire that policy, for example when she accuses men of selfishness in keeping women from knowledge (p. 59), and in the succinct and surprisingly uncompromising verse: 'Os homens leis fizeram parciais, / Que a mulher julgar deve naturais' (p. 60). Significantly here, a woman is not only expected to see the biased laws which govern her fate as fair, she must also consider them natural. Once again however, unlike Sophia, Floresta fails to develop or effectively muster this argument. It is perhaps no coincidence that the few more radical positionings expressed in *Conselhos* are all contained within the forty verses. Verse provided an ideal medium for Floresta to introduce an idea without allowing the space to develop an argument, as she might otherwise have been expected to do, and so avoid offending her largely conservative readership without completely excluding these more critical and confrontational positions. This is nowhere more evident than in verse 35, arguably the most challenging and tantalising moment of the text, in which Floresta warns her daughter not to aspire to success beyond the domestic sphere:

> Em um mundo, que justo ser não sabe,
> Não desejes brilhar, filha querida;
> Da mulher os talentos fazer devem
> Os encantos domésticos da vida. (p. 63)

What is so significant here, and subversive in the context of her work as a whole, is that Floresta implies that it is only in the unfair world in which her daughter, and all women, must operate that a woman's achievements are limited to domestic life. Thus she clearly implies that women should in fact be able to participate in the public sphere, and would be able to in a truly just society, although she appears to hold no hope for such a fundamental change. This short, sad verse is possibly the closest Floresta comes in her own work to reiterating the fundamental belief in women's equal rights and abilities in the public sphere expressed by Sophia in *Woman Not Inferior*, but in contrast to Sophia's aggressive tone, Floresta can only tell her daughter to accept this injustice. This pessimistic tone may hold some clue to why she never returned to the radical claims made by her English predecessor. However, Floresta's increasing belief in woman's role as wife and mother – as moral guardian and producer of virtuous citizens – which is charted in the next chapter, suggests that over time she moved away from this early concept of a fair society and public participation for women, perhaps due to its incompatibility with her Catholic beliefs and patriotic priorities.

Peggy Sharpe, reading these more challenging and confrontational moments in the text, concludes that *Conselhos* is 'radically subversive' and 'inspired by the author's *lack* of desire to corroborate the patriarchy'.[30] Yet this is a difficult position to maintain. Constância Lima Duarte quotes from a review of the 1858 Italian edition of the text in which the reviewer states that 'estes conselhos [...] não saem do círculo daquelas virtudes mais frequentes e menos rumorosas que são necessárias na reclusa vida de uma mulher',[31] clearly indicating that this individual saw *Conselhos* as corroborating, and indeed asserting, the patriarchy. It can only be assumed that the Bishop of Mondovi, who requested a re-edition,[32] and the text's many other readers in Brazil and Europe, viewed it the same way. In contrast to Sharpe, Duarte herself sees the text as conservative and limiting, and notes none of the moments of radicalism that emerge from between the prescriptive virtues and threats of ruin. The truth, perhaps, lies somewhere between the two positions, as Floresta struggles to reconcile a belief in women's essential equality with the profoundly differentiating discourse of Catholic patriarchalism.

The two short pieces that followed the publication of *Conselhos* are essentially a reiteration of the ideas expressed in that first text. The eponymous heroine of *Fany, ou o modelo das donzelas* is the living embodiment of the daughterly virtues outlined in *Conselhos* and Floresta urges all girls, particularly her own students, to imitate her. We are told that Fany believed obedience to her parents and 'o desempenho exato dos deveres de uma donzela' to be laws written by God (p. 67) and she is variously portrayed as modest, kind, charitable, compassionate, courageous and utterly devoted to her siblings. As in *Conselhos*, vanity receives special attention as the gravest feminine vice,

---

[30]   Peggy Sharpe, 'Reading Nísia Floresta: A Feminist Perspective', *Linea Plural*, 1: 2 (Spring 1998), 28–32 (p. 28).

[31]   Duarte, *Vida e Obra*, p. 223.

[32]   An event Floresta herself informs us of (see *Trois Ans 2*, p. 327).

and the reader is reassured that this great evil 'não havia infeccionado sua alma cândida com seu pestilento hálito' (p. 67).

As well as being a perfect example of feminine virtue, Fany is also a model student. Her dedication, Floresta suggests, is in sharp contrast to so many girls who, on leaving school, spend their time in complete idleness and never again pick up a book, fooling themselves that they have gained 'uma coisa que chamam liberdade' (p. 68). Curiously Floresta does not draw an explicit connection between education and virtue in *Fany* as she does in *Conselhos*, instead relying on the juxtaposed descriptions of her heroine's successful studies and her array of virtues to suggest the relation between the two. However, by condemning the degenerate daily routine of young women who turn their backs on their education and wrongly believe themselves to be free, she does appear to suggest that, as well as a more virtuous and purposeful existence, a degree of genuine 'liberdade' can be achieved through the continued pursuit of knowledge, although she does not indicate how.

Significantly, the implied criticism of women's restriction to the private sphere glimpsed in verse 35 of *Conselhos* (as discussed above) is no longer apparent in *Fany*. On the contrary, Fany is praised for knowing her place in the domestic sphere and not becoming involved in the political interests synonymous with public life (p. 70). Floresta emphasises the value of women's domestic role, telling the reader that Fany helps her mother with 'o peso dos trabalhos domésticos que, longe de desdenhar sabia, ao contrário, que é a prática deles que reunida a outras qualidades, pode conferir à mulher o mais nobre título de – boa mãe de família!' (p. 68). Here, together with the notion of social esteem through virtue, which was central to Floresta's defence of education in *Conselhos*, we also find the first clear expression of the notion that women can earn a higher position in society through the fulfilment of their domestic role, and quite specifically through maternal duties. Although the importance of motherhood is stated more emphatically here than in *Conselhos*, in *Fany* Floresta fails to establish a clear link between education and maternal duties, as she does, if only briefly, in the earlier text.

The short *Discurso* delivered by Floresta at the end of the school year in 1847 echoes the content of *Conselhos* even more closely than *Fany*, perhaps in part because both texts are non-fiction and therefore focus more precisely on Floresta's specific concerns regarding the teaching of girls. In fact *Discurso* offers a succinct expression of some of the writer's core ideas at that time. Interestingly, it also provides a striking indication of the extent to which Floresta's early thinking on women's education was influenced by the seventeenth-century French writer Fénelon, whom she had previously mentioned in *Conselhos*.[33] She includes a lengthy quote from his work regarding the need to introduce girls to study from an early age to protect

---

[33] June Hahner observes that François de Salignac de la Mothe Fénelon's 1685 text,

them from idleness and negative influences, and refers to the Frenchman as 'o sublime Fenelon' and 'este oraculo da educação' (*Discurso*, p. 5).

This influence takes on a curious irony when viewed alongside the considerable influence that Fénelon's contemporary Poulain de la Barre also had on Floresta, through Sophia's use of his work. Fénelon and Poulain adopted completely opposing views; in fact it seems likely that the former was specifically replying to Poulain's text when he wrote, in his famous and much quoted *De l'Education des Filles*, 'a woman's intellect is normally more feeble and her curiosity greater than those of a man; also it is not desirable to set her to studies which may turn her head. Women should not govern the state or make war or enter the sacred ministry.'[34] The juxtaposition of these two powerful and contradictory influences (unbeknownst to Floresta, who was not aware of the seventeenth-century French origins of the text she translated), offers a useful insight into some of the non sequiturs to be found in her writing, and is typical of the conflicting discourses that vie for position throughout her work.

The point at which a certain development can be seen between *Discurso* and the preceding texts is in the purpose Floresta begins to ascribe to women's virtue. Although the importance of motherhood remains undeveloped (in fact, maternity itself receives no mention in this text), for the first time we begin to see the emergence of a notion of woman as moral guardian. At this point the concept remains simplistic and undeveloped: she states only that a woman is 'destinada pelo Creador, para amenisar a existencia de seu semelhante', describing how 'a pratica exacta e constante das virtudes [...] a constituem sobre a terra um anjo de consolação, um anjo de paz!' (p. 4). Most importantly, Floresta makes it clear that education is indispensable in the fulfilment of this role (p. 4).

Considering these three texts together, the common message they share is that education, based on a sound moral and Catholic doctrine, is the only route to virtue, which in turn is the only means for a woman to properly fulfil her duties and achieve happiness, security and public esteem. We also see the beginnings of an idealisation of maternity and a realisation of the value that this exclusively female experience can afford, although Floresta does not yet make a clear connection between a mother's duties and her need for education. Neither does she establish a link between motherhood, or indeed women's wider condition, and the nation; and the absence of the forcefully patriotic rhetoric which dominates her subsequent writing suggests that Floresta had yet to realise the potential power that lay in constructing

---

De l'Education des Filles, was frequently quoted by those addressing the question of female education in Brazil through the nineteenth century (*Emancipating the Female Sex*, p. 48).

[34] Quoted in Clarke, pp. 19–20.

her defence of women's education in terms of the progress and status of the nation.

Opúsculo Humanitário (Rio, 1853) is the first text Floresta wrote and published after returning from her initial visit to Europe and it is undoubtedly her most ambitious Brazilian text. From it we gain an insight into Floresta's views on a wide range of subjects concerning contemporary Brazilian society, but it is immensely significant that, despite touching on many varied and controversial topics, including slavery, the condition of the native Indian and the corruption of the Brazilian clergy, the essential focus and purpose of the text is a discussion and defence of female education, and all other issues are approached from within the framework of this basic remit.

Opúsculo also offers clear evidence of the progression of Floresta's ideas since the publication of her early didactic texts, suggesting that she was greatly influenced by her experiences in Europe, where she had been between 1849 and 1852, and where she would have encountered new intellectual currents. In fact the tension between liberal and conservative discourses, already evident in her early works, is particularly apparent in *Opúsculo*. Peggy Sharpe considers the text to be an amalgam of Enlightenment, Romantic, Positivist and Utilitarian sources,[35] to which a powerful foundation of conservative Catholic doctrine must be added, as well as the last echoes of Sophia's Cartesian rationalism, which Sharpe was unaware of, writing before the exposure of *Direitos* as a translation of *Woman Not Inferior*. Furthermore, Floresta's time in Europe appears to have given her a new awareness of her own nation and national identity, which results in an overtly patriotic tone and justification of her ideas.

Alongside the by now familiar argument that a sound religious and moral education provides the best and only route to virtue and thus to social regard and happiness, we find the first clear expression of Floresta's support for education within the home and her belief that a properly educated and virtuous mother is the best educator of her own daughters. Most importantly, though, Floresta now goes to considerable lengths to show how an improvement in women's education is vital to Brazil's future well-being and progress. The opportunity to observe the nation from beyond its boundaries, and to encounter foreign perceptions and constructions of it, clearly alerted the writer to her country's position within an international hierarchy and she repeatedly employs the concept of the state of women's education as an index of civilisation. She also makes frequent comparisons with the situation in Europe and the USA, highlighting the national shame such comparisons provoke.

Opúsculo is structured as a comparative history of women's education,

---

[35] Sharpe, 'Brazilian Women and Social Reform in Nísia Floresta's *Opúsculo Humanitário*', *Brazil: A Journal of Brazilian Literature*, 1 (1988), 17–29 (p. 18).

beginning with the ancient civilisations and ending with a detailed consideration of the current state of the education system in Brazil. First to be considered are the ancient civilisations of Babylonia, Egypt, Persia, and India,
ancient Greece, and the Roman Empire (*Opúsculo*, pp. 2–9). It is implied
that the demise of all these civilisations came about because they did not
appreciate the importance of female education and women's contribution to
society. Floresta then moves on to look at the condition of women in Europe
from the Middle Ages onwards. She comments on 'o anticristão e nunca
assaz detestável regime feudal, que oprimia cruelmente as mulheres' (p. 15),
and observes that for much of this period 'a educação da mulher ficou esta-
cionária' (p. 16).

Floresta now arrives at a discussion of the current situation, and she states
her intention to look specifically at 'as três grandes nações da Europa moderna
e os Estados Unidos' (p. 17). She first turns her attention to Germany, praising
the sound education of the population (male and female) and the consequent
virtue of its women. Germans, she suggests, base their domestic happiness
'na moral esclarecida das mulheres (p. 18), who in turn enjoy certain privileges, whilst understanding the supreme importance of their role as mothers,
and educators of their children (pp. 17 and 20). Next to be considered is
England (or Great Britain, which is also used with no distinction), where
women are educated 'nos severos princípios de uma sã e esclarecida moral'
(p. 23). This education instils in English women a consciousness of their
own dignity and an understanding of 'a nobreza do sexo a que pertence e a
importância do cumprimento de seus deveres' (p. 23). Floresta then moves
on to France, stating that French women are able to cultivate their intelligence alongside men (p. 30), although she is less complimentary about the
women of France than about their northern cousins (pp. 35–7), a position she
maintains in her later works, despite making France her permanent home.[36]
Despite generally praising the condition of women in these three countries,
Floresta does not merely hold them up as an example to be emulated, instead
suggesting that 'muito tem ainda a sociedade que fazer para que cheguem ao
aperfeiçoamento da educação' (p. 37), indicating that her hope was not just
to see Brazil raised to 'civilised' European standards.

Last of all, the writer turns her attention to the United States, which offered
Floresta a particularly valuable comparison with Brazil because, sharing her
own nation's colonial heritage, it could be offered as an example of what
Brazil might also achieve with good government, and a sound education
system. Significantly, Floresta returns to this comparison in the final conclusion to *Opúsculo*, making clear her belief in Brazil's ability to match its
powerful Northern cousin when she writes:

---

[36] This increasingly critical posture is discussed in the final chapter.

A Providência, colocando-vos tão vantajosamente, pareceu chamar-vos a comandar um dia os destinos de toda a América do Sul, assim como aos filhos da União os de toda a América do Norte.

Eia! Se com mais rico solo do que o dos Estados Unidos, faltou-vos a mola principal – a educação – para a par deles marchardes. (pp. 159–60)

Here and throughout her comparative discussion of the condition of women through time and across continents, Floresta explicitly sets out her belief that education, and specifically female education, is essential to the moral foundation of society and thus to the spiritual and material prosperity of each nation. Her appeal for the improved education of girls in Brazil is therefore presented as patriotic in motivation and necessary for the new nation's development on an international stage.

In her description of the history of women's education in Brazil, Floresta adopts the common post-independence discourse of blaming the Portuguese, suggesting that disdain for female education was inherited from Portugal, where women were similarly neglected (p. 47). Moreover, she suggests that Portugal's own collapse as a European power is attributable to the poor condition of its women (pp. 51–2). She acknowledges the many benefits which the arrival of the Portuguese court in 1808 brought to Brazil, but, she points out, 'a educação da mulher permaneceu como nos férreos tempos coloniais' (pp. 66–7). Thus Floresta arrives at the moment of Brazilian independence, 'grandiosa época [...] de regeneração e de glória', but once again the opportunity to address the issue of female education was lost. She suggests that D. Pedro I, for whom she has high praise, could have done much to improve women's education, but 'uma triste fatalidade pesava sobre a sorte das nossas mulheres, e [...] outros fins, outro destino estavam reservados ao célebre fundador do Império Brasileiro' (p. 74). Floresta clearly presents Brazil's independence as a missed opportunity, not only for women, who have not reaped the benefits to be expected from the process, but also, by extension, for the progress and status of the nation as a whole.

Floresta begins her consideration of the current situation by making it clear that, despite blaming the Portuguese for the continuing disregard and disdain which characterises Brazilian attitudes to female education, she does not consider the nation's colonial past to be an adequate excuse for the reality of the 1850s, and that the government of the second reign must be held accountable. She writes: 'desde 1831 goza o Brasil de um governo inteiramente nacional [...] É, pois, sob este governo que devemos criticar os progressos de nossa educação física e moral, quer doméstica quer pública' (p. 76). This is an extremely important statement, with which Floresta establishes a clear point of departure from Brazil's colonial inheritance into an era of self-determination and responsibility, indicating not only that legal

and political changes can and must be made in the arena of female education, but also that the government is directly responsible for as yet failing to
address the issue.

In her discussion of the current state of education, Floresta identifies three
distinct agents: the government, the teachers and the parents, all of whom
receive criticism for their part in perpetuating its neglect. With regard to the
government's contribution, she observes that although they freely confess to
the poor state of public instruction (p. 85), in reality the nation's legislators
busy themselves with other issues, and not one voice is raised in defence of
reform, which, she asserts, 'merece incontestavelmente a mais circumspecta
atenção dos homens pensadores' (p. 81). However, she maintains a constant
hope that one day the government will take action, painting a picture of
herself rushing to the newspaper each morning for news of any discussion
of educational reform in the Chamber, always in vain: 'dobramos a folha
desconsolados e aguardamos o dia seguinte, que se escoa na mesma expec-
tativa, no mesmo desengano' (p. 81). This passage offers an effective, even
melodramatic image of personal and profound disillusion with the government, but it has another more interesting significance. The daily report of the
Chamber's sessions would have been considered appropriate reading for men.
This vignette of the writer's private actions, occurring within the domestic
sphere of her own home, serves as a subtle advertisement for women's right
and duty to take an interest in and thus, within the limited means available,
interact with the political landscape that shaped their lives.[37]

On more specific aspects of legislation, Floresta criticises the limited
curriculum taught to most girls, outlining the banalities which most Brazilians considered to be a good education (p. 110), and condemns the lack of
secondary education available to them, which was offered by very few private
schools (the Collegio Augusto being one such rare example) and not provided
at all within the public system (p. 86). She is also extremely critical of the
lack of regulation of private schools, which she suggests are set up by anyone
who can read (p. 80), and is particularly emphatic in her condemnation of the
number of Europeans who arrive and open schools without any capacity for,
or experience of, teaching. By allowing individuals to run schools without
ensuring that they are fit to do so, Floresta accuses the government of actively
jeopardising national well-being: 'seria difícil explicar vantajosamente a
negligência com que um governo ilustrado deixa practicar assim abusos que
tanto se opõem a nossa futura prosperidade' (p. 80).

---

[37] Floresta gives a number of other examples of the active interest she takes in the political
and legislative discourse surrounding education, as when she quotes from the recent report to
the General Assembly on education in the Northern provinces, which the poet Gonçalves Dias
was commissioned to write and in which he too called for major reform (*Opúsculo*, pp. 83–4),
and when quoting statistics from official surveys.

Floresta is equally critical of her fellow teachers, for although she blames the government for allowing inadequate teachers to work, she also questions the motivations and morals of those directly involved in education, observing that public primary schools for girls have become so discredited that they are frequented only by the daughters of those who cannot afford private education (p. 78). That said, she also points out that many private teachers are no better than those to be found in the public system (p. 71). In particular she notes this problem with regard to foreign teachers, commenting from personal observation that qualified teachers in Europe have no need to look for employment outside their own countries, where education is valued so much more highly, meaning that the kind of people who come to Brazil to teach are quite unable to fulfil their pedagogic duties (pp. 78–9). The specific issue of European women setting up schools without regulation would have been a source of personal chagrin to Floresta, who would have found herself competing against these women in recruiting pupils for her own school, and this comment could even be seen as a deliberate ploy to discredit such establishments.

In the end, despite passing harsh judgements on both public and private education, Floresta settles in favour of private schooling, believing that, because those who operate private schools must develop and maintain a reputation for themselves in order to remain solvent, they are obliged to make at least some small effort in the administration of their duties (p. 71). However, this preference clearly establishes women's education as an elite prerogative and she makes no suggestion as to how the poor might afford the private education she favours; in fact she addresses the issue only in terms of the quality of education provided. Her failure to defend, or even discuss, the right to free education is clear evidence of her overwhelming concern for and identification with the privileged, elite social classes, which will also be observed in subsequent chapters.

Floresta acknowledges the existence of a few dedicated women who genuinely set out to provide a broad and solid education to their pupils, amongst whom she clearly includes herself, and comments on the difficulties they encounter in the face of negative social attitudes. It is likely that she is speaking from personal experience when she describes the pressure to conform with parental expectations in order to fill the classroom (p. 111). Floresta observes that a good teacher cannot produce 'indivíduos morigerados, conspícuos e modestos' if parents do not encourage the lesson with their own example. Likewise good parents cannot bring their children up as such if their teachers are not adequately qualified to teach. In fact it is 'da comunhão das boas práticas de uns e de outros que somente poderão sair homens e mulheres capazes de firmar o renome da Nação Brasileira' (p. 111). Thus the writer establishes the patriotic duty of both teacher and parent, as well as the government, in the process of improving Brazil's education system.

In fact, although only the men in power can bring about material, legislative changes, she hopes that parents can provide 'um remédio mais pronto e porventura mais profícuo ao nosso melhoramento moral' (p. 88).[38] Floresta stresses parents' responsibility to find good schools 'cujas diretoras sejam reconhecidas por seu zelo e dedicação ao ensino' (p. 92), but parental support within the formal education system is not her primary concern. Instead she is interested in the education, in the widest sense, which parents themselves offer their children. She is vehement in her condemnation of those parents who expect teachers to do their job for them, neglecting the most basic moral lessons of infancy (p. 77). She highlights the importance of the earliest years of a child's development, stating that 'a educação, para ser perfeita, deve começar no berço' (p. 94), and quoting Fénelon on the ease with which children learn in infancy and the influence of example at this time. It is therefore essential that parents set a good example to their children at all times, and it is mothers, who have most contact with their children, particularly daughters, who have the most important role to play. Nothing, Floresta asserts, is worse for a girl's education than a bad mother: 'uma mãe é [...] o modelo que devem primeiro copiar: se esse modelo não é perfeito, como poderá a menina apresentar uma cópia perfeita?' (p. 103).

Interestingly, it is not this belief in the importance of a mother's example which leads Floresta to advocate the education of girls by their own mothers. Her ostensible motivation for adopting this argument, as expressed in *Opúsculo*, is her belief in the benefits of small class size, extended to a logical conclusion in favour of individual over collective tuition (pp. 89–90). Moreover, she believes that a well-educated and knowledgeable mother will always obtain better results than a teacher, most importantly in inspiring 'o sentimento da própria dignidade, que qualquer diretora não conseguiria obter de suas educandas' (p. 91). However, she suggests that at present many mothers are performing their duties badly, observing that, having inherited men's indifference and disdain for female education, they pride themselves on a duty they have failed to fulfil (p. 112).[39] She condemns what she sees as the widespread social disregard for childhood innocence (pp. 77 and 97), describing the use of bad language and inappropriate topics of conversation in front of children as revolting and unchristian behaviour which degrades

---

38   It is important to bear in mind that the Portuguese 'pais' can mean 'parents' or 'fathers'. Although there are instances in which Floresta might be specifically addressing fathers, the fact that she goes on to ascribe such fundamental importance to the role of mothers in education leads me to translate 'pais' as 'parents'.

39   Curiously, elsewhere in the text Floresta praises Brazilian women as devoted mothers. These contradictory positions indicate a tension within *Opúsculo* between a desire to highlight, and thus improve, the many faults she perceived in her society, including in the behaviour of its women, whilst simultaneously seeking to emphasise women's value in the eyes of their male compatriots.

humanity (p. 98), and observing how young girls are dressed up in all the restrictive finery of women. In fact this criticism of the treatment of children appears alongside a wider condemnation of the frivolities and corruption of modern 'civilised' life, which Floresta sees as interfering with education (e.g. p. 114). Moreover, she observes how the bright lights of Rio's social scene lead many to suggest that education has progressed, commenting that this is the belief only of those who confuse 'a instrução com a educação, a licença com a civilização'(p. 84). Such foolish blindness is contrasted with the writer's own position, which once again reveals her vision of education and progress to be synonymous: 'nós [...] não costumamos julgar da educação e dos progressos de qualquer povo pelas numerosas instituições de bailes, nem pelo desprezo da mocidade pelas coisas mais respeitáveis' (pp. 84–5).

The educational issue which perhaps receives the harshest criticism, however, is the teaching of religious doctrine, which Floresta believed to be so essential to a woman's education and her future happiness (p. 134). She writes: 'Podemos dizer, sem receio de que nos tenham por exagerados, que em nenhuma paróquia do Brasil a nossa religião é devidamente ensinado à mocidade' (p. 135). This state of affairs she blames entirely on the Brazilian clergy, who not only fail to teach the catechism, but also, through their own corruption, set a bad example to their flock (pp. 133–43). She continues to state, perhaps even more clearly than in earlier texts, that 'a religião deve ser a base da educação da mulher' (p. 25). Guacira Lopes Louro notes how references to the Christian faith in nineteenth-century Brazil invariably implied Catholicism, and it is certainly true that Floresta's own Catholic faith is evident throughout her work, and is clearly what she taught and held to be true. However, it is interesting to note that she does not preclude Protestantism from her notion of a sound moral education. In fact she observes English women's superiority over their French counterparts, in terms of morality and duty, and attributes this difference to the better religious education they receive (p. 24).

Woven through the many tacks of this dense and complex text, we find a constant reiteration of the essential arguments with which Floresta defends her claims for improved female education. The core argument identified in her early texts, that education leads to virtue, happiness and social regard for women, is still very much present in *Opúsculo*. In fact it continues to form the foundation of Floresta's positioning and is at times developed further. An example of this development is Floresta's emphatic statement that, if it were proved that educated women were less virtuous than uneducated women, 'certo que não hesitaríamos em ser do número dos apologistas da ignorância da mulher' (p. 68). One of the most important additions to Floresta's vision of virtue through education, however, is that in *Opúsculo* she offers an indication of how it might bring about a tangible positive change in women's own lives and provide some of the 'liberdade' which she so unsatisfactorily hinted at in her earlier work (*Fany*, p. 68, see discussion above). She repeatedly stresses that with a sound moral and religious education women will be able to maintain a sense of their own dignity (e.g. p. 34) and, most importantly, she describes how firm moral values enable a woman to govern herself, and thus escape the 'humilhação de uma vigilância que degrada a mulher, porque faz pensar ser-lhe necessário um guarda para que ela permaneça pura' (p. 24). This kind of moral autonomy, which she suggests English women already enjoy, would make a very real difference to the shuttered and chaperoned existence of most Brazilian women.

Yet although this association with virtue remains at the root of Floresta's discussion of female education, it no longer constitutes her primary defence. Instead it serves as a starting point for a more tangible and targeted appeal which identifies the real, practical benefits of women's education for men, society and the nation. By specifically pointing out the advantages that men can gain from better educating women, Floresta makes a calculated play for the self-interest of her male readers, in whose hands any hope of change inevitably lay. She does not only suggest that no Brazilian woman wants the kind of existence encouraged by superficial instruction, she also challenges Brazilian men, asking: 'qual é aí o homem razoável e honesto, que se contente de uma esposa [...] entregue às futilidades de uma vida de dissipação e indolência, antes que no empenho constante [...] de ilustrar-se pela prática das virtudes' (p. 61). She also describes the domestic unhappiness which can afflict men whose wives are not properly educated, comparing the harmonious and contented family life to be found in Germany, where women enjoy a sound moral education, with the subterfuge, caprice and dissolution suffered by French men, who foolishly criticise the instruction and freedom offered to women by their northern neighbours (pp. 18–19).

Yet Floresta's interest does not really lie in these small-scale effects of female education on individual lives. She is concerned instead with the progress of the nation and, perhaps most importantly, with Brazil's reputation and standing within the supposed civilised world. This concern with international judgements of her country is the obvious and inevitable result of her two-year visit to Europe where she would have gained her first real insight into the abundance of prejudices and perceptions, accurate or otherwise, regarding the New World. Her encounter with these opinions is made very clear in the text by the large number of comparisons she draws between European and Brazilian practices, the many quotes she takes from published accounts of European travellers to Brazil and the several occasions on which she describes the personal shame felt when hearing Brazil's education and the condition of its women criticised or ridiculed (e.g. pp. 101 and 136).

Central to this concern for her nation's status is Floresta's employment of the notion of women's education as an index of civilisation. She states this idea clearly and categorically on the opening page of *Opúsculo* (p. 2) and continues to remind her reader of it throughout the text. In fact it becomes clear that it is the question of Brazilian standing in the world which is of greatest importance to Floresta. In an extremely important passage within the text, in which Floresta states her purpose in writing *Opúsculo* and clearly establishes her patriotic motivations, she writes 'o desejo ardente que nos cala n'alma, de ver o nosso país colocado a par das nações progressistas, nos impõe a obrigação de franca e imparcialmente analisar a educação da mulher no Brasil, esperando excitar [...] penas mais hábeis que a nossa a escreverem sobre [o] assunto' (p. 45).

I would suggest that this passage represents a deliberate attempt by Floresta, which can also be identified elsewhere in the text, to protect herself against accusations of radicalism and inappropriate engagement in public, political debate. By emphasising her own patriotism she effectively silences those who might suggest her claim for women's education is subversive and prejudicial to society, and draws authority from dominant male discourses of national independence and maturity. Moreover, the limited hope which she claims to have for the effect of her work might be seen as an apology or justification for what is in fact a deeply political text which is highly critical of the Brazilian establishment.

Floresta's other core defence of women's education is, of course, the importance of women's role as mothers and specifically the advantages of mothers educating their own daughters. In *Opúsculo* Floresta makes it clear that this is one of her primary motivations for educating women: 'desejaríamos proporcionar a todas conhecimentos, aptidão e gosto a fim de preencherem elas mesmas, como deviam, a honrosa e sublime missão de preceptoras de suas filhas' (p. 91). This vision of the mother-educator can be interpreted as indicating the influence of Positivism, which Floresta first encountered during her initial visit to France. However, it also echoes growing mater-nalist discourses and can be found in other Brazilian writing at the time.[40] Moreover, to attribute Floresta's position to her contact with Comte's philos-ophy at this time is problematic. In his utopian Positive society every woman educated her own children during their formative years, and in later European publications Floresta can be seen to suggest something similar. For example, in her consideration of women's role in society in 'A Mulher' (1859), she writes 'quando a sociedade for bem ordenada, a mãe será o único diretor e o único mestre dos próprios filhos, até a idade em que a razão deles mostra-se formada' (p. 143).

In *Opúsculo*, however, she specifically advocates the idea of mothers educating their daughters; with regard to sons she describes only the

---

[40] Including Zaira Americana's lengthy 1853 text and the articles written and published by Joana Paula Manso de Noronha in her *Jornal das Senhoras*, both referred to earlier in this chapter.

responsibility of both parents to set a good example to their children. It is extremely surprising that Floresta overlooked the idea of women educating their sons, when we consider what a powerful argument this offered in terms of women's contribution to the nation through the production of good citizens. This massive omission suggests that at the time of writing *Opúsculo*, Floresta was indeed concerned primarily with the education of girls, and not with establishing a specific claim for female value in society, the focus of subsequent European texts. It must also cast doubt on the extent of Comte's influence on her thinking at this time.

It is also curious that it is only in the conclusion to *Opúsculo* that Floresta fully identifies women's specific influence over men and starts to outline the role of moral guardian, a notion that we saw beginning to emerge in *Discurso* (1847) and which in later writings comes to play such an important part in her definition of a woman's duty. She comments on the often pernicious influence that wives or mistresses can have over men, an influence which can affect judicial, military, or even royal decisions and so have a considerable effect on the nation (p. 157). She concludes: 'quem mais precisa de uma boa educação [...] de sorte a não abusar do império que exerce sobre o homem e dirigir este à sua própria ventura e ao bem da humanidade?' (p. 158). This is an extremely powerful argument in favour of women's moral education and it is certainly surprising that Floresta does not make more of it through the text. A partial explanation for this apparent reticence can perhaps be found in Floresta's obvious allusion to Domitila de Castro, the mistress of Pedro I who had risen to Pompadour status in the royal court during the 1820s.[41] Although providing an excellent example of the point she wished to make, this situation was probably still perceived as a black mark on the Imperial family's reputation and Floresta may well have wished to avoid dwelling on such a sensitive issue.

Although Floresta's concern with women's domestic virtue, and her employment of patriotic, national-building discourse, dominate her defence of education in *Opúsculo*, certain ideas can still be glimpsed regarding women's essential right to education, ideas which remind the reader of the humanist arguments employed by Sophia in *Woman Not Inferior*. This right is implied in *Opúsculo* through the parallel signifiers of religion and nature. Very early in the text Floresta appears to suggest that God destined women to be properly educated and hold a position of importance in society, and that men's failure to allow this is a gross hypocrisy and neglect of God's will (pp. 3 and 14). She also makes use of the argument, found in *Woman Not Inferior*, that men and women alike are 'uma alma servindo-se de corpo' (p.

---

[41] See Roderick Cavaliero, *The Independence of Brazil* (London: British Academic Press, 1993), p. 171.

62), suggesting that it is a profanation to neglect any soul, in favour of the adornment of the body.

However, it is not only women's souls which are equal to men's; Floresta also asserts that God created Adam and Eve with 'o mesmo sentir, a mesma inteligência, as mesmas prerrogativas' (p. 6). Like Sophia, Floresta also holds that 'a inteligência [...] não tem sexo' (p. 63) and, since it is not physical force but intelligence that makes one individual superior to another, it is implied that women can well be superior to men (p. 63). Moreover Floresta observes the frequent excuse that physical weakness precludes women from study and dismisses such an idea, suggesting, in fact, that women's very fragility makes the exercise of her intellectual faculties more important if she is to properly fulfil her domestic duties (pp. 61 and 64). Despite acknowledging women's spiritual and intellectual equality with men, however, on only one occasion in the text does Floresta categorically state their right to education 'a fim de que elas possam vencer as trevas que lhes obscurecem a inteligência, e conhecer as doçuras infinitas da vida intellectual, a que tem direito as mulheres de uma nação livre e civilizada' (p. 44).

Interestingly, here Floresta inverts the usual relationship that sees women's education as a signifier of civilisation, instead suggesting that civilisation brings with it the right to education. This passage is clearly aimed at her readers' sense of national identity. The implicit message is that, whilst it may have been acceptable for women to remain in ignorance before independence, when men and women alike suffered the yoke of colonial repression, now that Brazil has gained the status of free nation in which it takes such pride, its women are also entitled to claim some of the privileges which its men are already enjoying. That said, it is by no means implicit that the education to which women have a right is equal to men's education, and Floresta stops far short of extending this right beyond the classroom and into the public sphere of the street and workplace.

It is not only in these fleeting claims to women's intellectual, if not social equality with men that we feel the last resonances of *Woman Not Inferior* in Floresta's work. In fact, where they can be felt most clearly is in the writer's continuing identification of men's deliberate desire to repress and control women. Whilst this accusation is by no means expressed with the frequency, or the audacious tone with which it is found in Sophia's work, it remains a consistent, underlying presence. Just like her English inspiration, Floresta declares that from the earliest times men took gross advantage of their physical pre-eminence, maintaining women in ignorance 'para que mais facilmente desempenhasse a humilhante missão a que a destinava' (p. 6). Floresta notes how this notion continues to shape most men's attitude to women's education, and, like Sophia, she also observes how through this policy men have shot themselves in the foot. More importantly though, it is also presented as being fatal to the prosperity of the nation (p. 60) and so their actions are cast not only as foolish, as Sophia suggests in *Woman Not Inferior*, but also as unpatriotic. This subtle but significant shift reveals how the specific context of Brazilian independence, and the nation-building discourse it engenders, leads to a fundamental redirection of the ideas Floresta takes from the text she translated.

Opúsculo is Floresta's only text to include a discussion of Brazil's 'classes pobres' and, as I will discuss in more detail in subsequent chapters, it is a subject she struggles to engage with in a meaningful way. Her thoughts on the education of poor women are particularly brief and simplistic. Despite indicating her support for their access to gainful employment, discussed in the next chapter, Floresta does not advocate a practical education teaching useful skills through which these women might contribute to the family income. Instead her concern remains clearly in the realm of feminine virtue and she suggests that, because money and title can protect and hide a rich woman's fall into vice, poor women have an even greater need for education. It is 'a voz da humanidade, primeiro, e, depois, a da honra do nosso país' (p. 131) which therefore impels her to appeal for the education of lower-class women. It is telling that in Floresta's eyes it is of greater value to the nation to ensure a virtuous female population than to equip women to contribute to the practical alleviation of poverty. This position is particularly striking when we consider that Floresta supported herself and her family for many years through her teaching.

It is clear from a reading of *Opúsculo* that a fundamental shift in approach has occurred since the didactic texts of the 1840s. *Opúsculo* is founded almost exclusively on a nation-building discourse which allows Floresta to hide her challenge to the more conservative and reactionary attitudes still prevalent in Brazilian society behind a façade of patriotic devotion. This overt nationalist construction is precisely what is absent from her earlier writing and this difference certainly reveals the influence of Floresta's stay in Europe on her perception of Brazil as a nation-state whose prosperity and reputation lie in the collective actions and beliefs of its people. More importantly, she is acutely aware of the power this patriotic rhetoric can afford when harnessed to her appeal for improved education.

Floresta's time abroad can be seen to have given her a greater confidence as a writer, expressed, for example, in her use of the authorial 'we' and her direct criticisms of the government and its legislation, yet the education she endorses is no broader than that suggested by her early texts. The focus remains absolutely on morality and Catholic virtue. In fact, the role for women, which education is now required to facilitate, is even more clearly demarcated within the confines of the family and home since her continuing assertion of women's intellectual equality is no longer accompanied by the wistful implication, glimpsed in *Conselhos*, that women's entrapment in the private sphere is unfair and unnatural. This move away from the humanism of *Woman Not Inferior* towards a social construction of woman, and the increasingly rigid boundaries that imposes, is even more marked in her later writing, published in France and Italy from 1857 onwards. In this final phase of Floresta's writing, which I shall now go on to consider, her demands for women's education are sidelined in favour of more expansive claims regarding the value of women in society. Yet education remains a starting block for the supreme role of regenerator she comes to identify. Within this context, Floresta's definition of women's education becomes even more rigidly and narrowly defined by the specific functions of women's domestic imprisonment and sanctification.

Writing in Europe

Opúsculo is the last of Floresta's works to devote such attention to the subject of female education, and her move away from this focus reflects her definitive move to Paris in 1856 and the end of her teaching career, something she appears never to have pursued in Europe. Although she continues to refer to education in almost all her works, and her writing maintains its familiar didactic tone, women's education ceases to be her primary focus. As she moves on to consider women's role as regenerator of society, their education becomes a means to an end, and not an end in itself, and her interest lies increasingly with the education of society as a whole.

Floresta is now emphatic in her identification of the role of mother-educator, favouring maternal education for all children, male and female, during their formative years. Not only does she state the importance of this role, in 'A Mulher' Floresta offers lengthy and detailed advice to mothers on how to educate their children. She notes the importance of setting a good example from the earliest age (p. 117), and forcefully condemns parents who do not respect the innocence of youth, as she does previously in *Opúsculo*, describing it as an unforgiveable sin (p. 119). She advises mothers to avoid lectures, threats and cajoling, which only diminish a child's respect for his/her mother, in favour of simple examples of virtue through action (pp. 143–5). By this method, mothers must teach the difference between truth and falsehood, merit and status, the useful and the superfluous (pp. 145–7). Children should be brought up to know the nobility of work and to love humanity (pp. 147–9). Floresta urges mothers to 'privai-vos sempre [...] de uma excursão de prazer [...] para ir com [os filhos] sob o esquálido teto do pobre que implora vossa caridade' (p. 147). Yet it is, of course, only the middle class (and above) that is in a position to sacrifice leisure time to acts of charity. This recommendation, with its undertones of bourgeois condescension, provides further evidence of Floresta's inability to engage with the domestic realities of the lower classes, and their consequent exclusion from her vision of womanhood.

It also becomes clear that Floresta now considers it the responsibility of mothers, as much as, if not more than, men, to break the cycle of female repression. She stresses the importance of teaching boys to respect and appreciate women from an early age, observing that 'o ensinamento da igualdade que deve reinar entre homem e mulher, começa neles em relação às proprias irmãs em seus jogos infantis' (p. 149), although this 'igualdade' does not stand up to examination, even assuming the public and private spheres allocated to each sex to be of equal value, since Floresta advocates obedience and submission on the part of wives (see Chapter 3). Floresta even suggests that women are in part to blame for their own abuse, through the poor upbringing of their sons, astutely observing that 'aquele orgulho excessivo e aquela pretensão do rapazola que tanto vos diverte, [...] nada mais é, ó mulheres, senão o germe deste presunçoso egoísmo que vos oprime por toda a vida ...' (p. 149). On the one hand this notion excuses men of some of the blame for their ignoble treatment of women, and typifies the burden of responsibility for male morality, which, as moral guardians, women are now expected to carry. On the other hand, this is the only instance in which women's self-sacrificing role as mother-educator offers an explicit opportunity for them to bring about a real improvement in their own quality of life. However, it must be noted that this passage (quoted immediately above) concludes '... com prejuízo da própria felicidade deles'. Once again, despite addressing women directly, Floresta's concern for social well-being leads her to a primarily androcentric vision of the benefits to be obtained from a more respectful relationship between the sexes.

It is evident from the advice given to mothers that Floresta's concern now lies exclusively with moral education and she repeatedly stresses this fact and emphasises its importance for society and the nation. In 'A Mulher' she identifies a lack of faith as the cause of the horrors and misery of 'civilisation', which she in turn blames on a lack of moral education (p. 111). In Três Anos she notes 'a influência incontestável da educação moral da mulher sobre a felicidade das nações' (p. 168), and later asserts that the moral education of the people (i.e. men and women alike) is the only solution to the degeneration of contemporary society (p. 302). In fact, in Floresta's overwhelming concern for morality, scholarly education apparently ceases to be of interest to her. She suggests that it does not matter how many schools are opened (or scientific discoveries made or laws passed), 'não se chegará nunca a curar as chagas gangrenadas da sociedade, se se continuar a desleixar a educação moral dos povos' ('A Mulher', pp. 111–13).

This focus on an exclusively moral education has a particularly profound effect on the education appropriate to women in order to prepare them for their role as mother-educator. Floresta begins by suggesting that, in order to foster the virtue with which nature has blessed women, 'é preciso dirigi-[la] bem com uma educação culta e fortificada na prática do dever e na razão' ('A

Mulher', p. 115). However, one of the most significant passages to be found in all Floresta's European writing on education clearly confirms her definitive abandonment of the broad and equal education advocated by Sophia in *Woman Not Inferior*, and which, to an inevitably lesser extent, Floresta herself offered in the Collegio Augusto. She states that women do not need intellectual instruction to fulfil their duty as mother-educator, which requires them only to be loving, fair, honest and modest:

> Para serdes assim, percebereis muito bem que não é preciso ter estudado os grandes mestres; se tendes coração, achareis aberto o maior, o mais eloqüente e útil dos livros, onde toda página oferecer-vos-á uma lição muito mais proveitosa [...] do que quantas possam se encontrar nos melhores livros, ou na palavra dos mais hábeis preceptores. ('A Mulher', p. 145)

Having embraced the full extent of women's role as moral regenerator of man, and the supreme patriotic value ascribable to this domestic definition of womanhood, it would seem that Floresta no longer saw the need for the foreign and ancient languages, history and much more besides which she had worked so hard, and faced criticism and ridicule, to teach her own pupils in Rio.

It is therefore interesting to note that on several occasions in her European publications Floresta reminds her readers of her previous teaching career in Brazil, even informing them of the extent of her curriculum when she re-encounters the man who, as papal nuncio, had witnessed the examination of pupils in the Collegio Augusto (*Três Anos*, pp. 97–8) (as discussed at the beginning of this chapter). However, Floresta's endeavours as a teacher are clearly and emphatically represented as a noble, patriotic vocation, and even a sacrifice, but never as an occupation pursued for personal fulfilment, nor as a financial necessity (e.g. *Itinerário*, p. 162; *Três Anos*, p. 97; 'Luxemburgo', p. 195). In the same passage from *Três Anos* in which she recounts the prelate's visit to her school, the radical potential of her far-reaching curriculum is denied when Floresta states her motivation as 'a esperança de formar para a pátria mulheres dignas de ilustrarem-na pelas virtudes do coração e pelos atrativos do espírito consagrados à felicidade da família' (p. 97). As well as being part of Floresta's wider construction of herself as a patriot, seen in *Opúsculo* and throughout her European writing, this specific emphasis on the patriotic motives behind her teaching appears to be an attempt to reconcile her own public life with the exclusively private sphere of operation which she now assigned to her fellow women.

Inevitably, it is this fundamental contradiction between Floresta's writing and her personal reality that makes an analysis of her position on education so challenging, but it simultaneously offers insights into the forces affecting her work. Floresta's own intellectual formation, her life spent in elevated intellectual circles, the curriculum she taught, her decision to translate *Woman*

Not Inferior and her continued use of that text's arguments regarding the equality of the soul and mind, all combine to suggest that the writer was herself convinced of women's equal intelligence, and therefore also of their ability to receive an education equal to that of men.

However, a gulf divides this fundamental belief, and the practice of it in her own life and her school, from the definition of education to be found in her writing. Whilst Floresta's published works all stress the importance of moral education and the teaching of womanly virtues, the broad curriculum she taught suggests that this was not the primary focus in the reality of her classroom. Similarly, in her writing she continually emphasises the purpose of education as a preparation for motherhood, yet in the Collegio Augusto she taught her pupils subjects that furnished them with knowledge far beyond that required to be good and virtuous mothers, even when allocating them the role of educator. It is unlikely that the many advocates of female education, who made this same connection with motherhood through the second half of the century, envisaged mothers across the land teaching their daughters Latin or ancient history.

At no point in her work does Floresta suggest that education can be a source of personal fulfilment for a woman, although this was undoubtedly the primary motivation behind her own lifetime of learning and erudition. Neither, in her writing, does she discuss female education in terms of employment and women's possible need for financial independence, despite the fact that she herself depended (at least in part) on her teaching to maintain her family for many years. It cannot be doubted that Floresta reaped considerable rewards, both financial and intellectual, from her own unusually broad knowledge and it seems that she sought to share these advantages with her pupils, even though she was unwilling or unable to include them in the rhetoric of patriotic duty by which she constructed herself and her fellow women in her writing.

The writer's continued reference to women's equal intelligence and ability to reason challenges one of the founding principles of patriarchy, entrenched in Western philosophy. But the potential radicalism of this position is defeated by Floresta's inability to shake off a Catholic valuation of feminine virtue which limited women's sphere of influence to the realm of sentiment, a construction which finds its own reflection in Positivist gynolatry. Furthermore, by appealing to concerns regarding national progress and status in order to gain power for her arguments, Floresta makes female education a male issue, and a means by which to protect men's interests.

In her essay on *Opúsculo*, Peggy Sharpe suggests that Floresta addresses 'the question of education as a solution to the problem of gender as a cultural construct'.[42] Floresta's own intellect undoubtedly challenges expectations

---

[42] Sharpe, 'Brazilian Women', p. 24.

and grants her an autonomy that defies an easy defininition; and she equips
her own students to follow suit. But in her writing, whilst she may challenge the image of woman as an idle, foolish play-thing, education is not a
liberating or degendering tool. Rather, by embracing Catholic and nation-
building discourses, and later Positivism, to shore up her defence, she can
only offer an alternative construction of woman, still predicated exclusively
on gendered natural and spiritual differences. Essentially, Floresta is trapped
in the inevitable paradox of early liberal feminism, in which even the smallest
step forward for women could only be achieved by addressing any appeal
in terms of men's interests. In doing so, of course, and as we shall see even
more clearly in the next chapter, the notion of women's rights is lost from
view.

3

The Feminist

Within Brazil, Floresta has long been and continues to be considered the forerunner of women's emancipation, and her early works to be founding texts of Brazilian feminism.[1] Whilst her position in Brazil's feminist canon owes much to her supposed adaptation of the ideas of Mary Wollstonecraft, it is also based on her own lifetime of writing on women. Since *Direitos* can no longer be considered her own work, we must turn to the many discussions of women's condition, behaviour and role in society to be found in her own subsequent writing in order to assess her feminist positioning and the space that she comes finally to advocate for her fellow women. In looking at Floresta's writings on women, I will outline the main themes that emerge from her increasing adherence to the discourse of separate spheres, and consider the intellectual, cultural and social influences which may have helped to shape her work. I shall also continue to note those instances in which the influence of Floresta's early translation can still be perceived in her own writing, despite its fundamentally different approach and conclusions.

It is possible to identify two basic roles at the heart of Floresta's vision of womanhood: the duties of motherhood, in particular the notion of the mother-educator, and the role of moral guardian and regenerator of men. Both are portrayed as a means by which women can secure a position of greater value in society, since these roles are expressed in terms of their benefit to society and the nation. In fact the two are essentially aspects of the same gendered nation-building discourse, in which woman is cast as producer and influencer of citizens. This definition of woman, central to the construction of patriarchal liberal democracy, ensures her entrapment within the private sphere. To women falls the responsibility of producing good citizens, yet they themselves are denied that right to citizenship, a denial which is encapsulated in Rousseau's *Émile* when he asks: 'Is it not the good son, the good husband, the good father, who makes the good citizen?'[2]

---

[1] For example, Seidl, p. 9; Câmara, *Historia*, p. 57; J. J. Barreto, 'Precursora da emancipação feminina no Brasil: Nísia Floresta – (1885–1985)', *O Poti*, Natal, 26 May 1985; Duarte, *Vida e Obra*, p. 167.

[2] Jean-Jacques Rousseau, *Émile*, trans. Barbara Foxley (London: J. M. Dent & Sons, 1911), p. 326.

All Floresta's writing on women reveals this core concept of the potential value of their position at the heart of the family, and I will therefore look at her various publications together, identifying the sub-themes which emerge across them. However, during the course of my discussion, I will also observe certain discrepancies between her Brazilian writing (namely *Opúsculo*) and her subsequent works written and published in Europe. Some of these differences can be seen as the result of Floresta's acute awareness of the needs and restrictions imposed by different national contexts and audiences. In fact such instances are examples of a concerted tactic, driven by her own patriotic motivations, which Floresta employs through her work after her first visit to Europe between 1849 and 1852. With regard to a range of issues, Floresta attempts to awaken a sense of national shame in her compatriot readers by constantly emphasising Europe's social and cultural superiority, whilst she presents Brazil in a positive light and identifies European failings when writing with a European reader in mind.[3] However, certain discrepancies between *Opúsculo* and later texts also reflect the influence of different intellectual currents on her work, in particular the increasing influence of Positivism after her return to France in 1856 and her ensuing friendship with Auguste Comte.

Comte proclaimed the vision of a Positive social utopia, to which all societies must eventually, inevitably, progress. Under his Humanitarian System, beyond the temporal order of financial and social hierarchies, human existence would be modified, reformed, and indeed defined by a superior spiritual order of moral worth.[4] Gender therefore played a crucial part in his social theory because Comte believed that women naturally possessed a moral superiority over men, meaning that much of this reforming spiritual power fell to women. In fact, particularly after meeting Clotilde de Vaux, with whom he had a passionate but entirely celibate relationship, he elevates women to a quasi-divine status.[5] Wernick comments that such elevated rhetoric regarding women's virtue is hardly original, noting that it owes much to the Romantic discourse of the *culte de la Femme*.[6] However, he suggests that such excessive gynolatry is one of the details of the Positivist System which has exposed Comte to ridicule.[7]

---

[3]   Such conflicts and contradictions between her Brazilian and European writing will be highlighted through the course of the chapter. This phenomenon is discussed in detail in Chapter 6 with regard to Floresta's engagement in discourses of political and national identity.

[4]   See Raymond Aron, *Main Currents in Sociological Thought*, vol. 1, trans. Richard Howard and Helen Weaver (Harmondsworth: Penguin, 1965), pp. 63 and 76–9.

[5]   Andrew Wernick, *Auguste Comte and the Religion of Humanity: The Post-Theistic Program of French Social Theory* (Cambridge: Cambridge University Press, 2001), p. 4.

[6]   Wernick, p. 147.

[7]   Wernick, p. 23. In fact, it is not uncommon for scholars to write off the 'dottily punctilious prescriptions' of his later works as 'the ramblings of a ruined mind' (pp. 23–4).

Behind this overpowering veneration of womanhood, however, lay a fundamentally androcentric and patriarchal concept of the family and a rigid sexual division of labour in which women's unequivocal restriction to the private sphere of the home was constructed as a biological given, as well as a social necessity. Despite Comte's claims, Positivism could not offer a genuinely emancipatory discourse for women because it allowed no place for the concept of gender equality.[8]

It is important to remember, though, that Comte was by no means alone in espousing the notion of female value through social regeneration from within the family. Although Floresta's connection with the founder of Positivism is one of the most famous aspects of her biography, and Brazilian positivists were the first to recover and reproduce her work, claiming her as one of their own,[9] it certainly cannot be assumed that his ideas came to have exclusive influence on her work.[10] When writing in Europe, Floresta was in fact contributing to a well-established Enlightenment feminist discourse that Karen Offen terms 'relational feminism', which sought to elevate women's social status by emphasising their natural role as mother-educator and 'their responsibilities to a broader collectivity'.[11]

Whilst the vision, embraced by Floresta, of womankind regenerating society and guiding man on the path to true progress is undeniably Comtian, a closer consideration of her work reveals that Floresta's engagement with Positivism is not straightforward. I will therefore attempt to identify the aspects of her writing which most clearly reveal this influence, as well as those points of divergence, and the continuing evidence of other influences, which challenge her reputation as a positivist.

As discussed in the previous chapter, the primary focus of *Opúsculo* remains the question of female education, but it is also the first of Floresta's texts to include, amongst various other social issues, a discussion of women's wider condition and behaviour in Brazil and Europe, and a consideration of

8 Wernick, pp. 126–7 and 148, note 71.

9 Duarte, *Vida e Obra*, pp. 197–8.

10 Evaluating Floresta's adherence to Positivism as a whole (not just with regard to women), Duarte observes the parallel influence of other intellectual currents and concludes 'uma adesão bem limitada' (*Vida e Obra*, pp. 184–5). There is a note of relief in this conclusion (p. 198) which perhaps reflects the ridicule that has come to accompany Comte's final philosophy. However, whilst I do not agree with all of Duarte's conclusions regarding Floresta's positioning vis-à-vis Positivist theories (see, for example, Chapter 5, p. 155), I would support her suggestion that Floresta selects only those elements that suit her own discursive purposes, and that much of what might be interpreted as the influence of Comte can be equally identified in other Enlightenment and contemporary discourses.

11 Karen Offen, 'Contextualizing the Theory and Practice of Feminism in Nineteenth-Century Europe (1789–1914)', in *Becoming Visible: Women in European History*, ed. Renate Bridenthal, Susan Stuard and Merry Wiesner, 3rd edn (Boston and New York: Houghton Mifflin, 1998), pp. 327–55 (p. 331).

the rights and responsibilities attached to her sex. In fact, Floresta appears to use her explicitly identified educational focus as a cover under which to introduce a more comprehensive social commentary. This impression is confirmed by her assertion, in the opening words of the text, that, whilst the rest of the world clamours for women's emancipation, she is concerned only with education (p. 2). Furthermore, in a blatant attempt to distance herself from more radical European thought and reassure her conservative Brazilian readers, Floresta writes that she leaves the defence of women's rights to 'Wollstonecraft, Condorcet, Sièyés, Legouvé, etc.', stating instead that 'a nossa tarefa é outra, e cremos que mais conveniente sera às sociedades modernas: a educação da mulher' (p. 29).[12]

This statement clearly implies that the education of women is of benefit to society whilst 'women's rights' are of benefit only to women. Significantly, by including Wollstonecraft amongst the defenders of women's rights and separating Opúsculo from this issue, it appears that Floresta may even be publicly distancing herself from the more radical tone of her own first publication, bearing in mind that Direitos was published and received as a translation of Mary Wollstonecraft. A reading of Opúsculo soon reveals that Floresta by no means abides by this self-imposed distinction, as will become clear from the discussion below. As Duarte observes, it is in fact impossible to talk of women's education as something distinct from emancipation,[13] and I would suggest that Floresta does not genuinely believe that they are discrete issues, suggesting as much only to make her publication more palatable and less overtly challenging. However, it must be acknowledged that for much of her writing on women Floresta does not address the question of women's rights; instead her focus moves increasingly in the direction of women's many responsibilities, to their family, society and the nation.

It is in Opúsculo that we first encounter the writer's focus on women's domestic role as wife and, most importantly, as mother, and the notion that the proper fulfilment of this role and an improvement in women's behaviour, facilitated by education, is of great interest and benefit to society. In fact, Floresta stresses throughout the text that her concern for her nation's well-being is her primary and sole motivation for writing. These interconnected discourses of maternalism and patriotism/nation-building, largely absent from her early educational writing, come to dominate her work. Therefore, for the purposes of this chapter, I shall take Opúsculo as the starting point of Floresta's own full and conscious engagement in the debate over women's

---

[12]   It is interesting to note that women writing about education at the turn of the century, a decade after the end of the Empire, still felt obliged to issue equivalent disclaimers in their work in order to 'reassure readers that women wanted reform, not revolution' (Costa, 'Patriarchalism', p. 263).

[13]   Duarte, 'Posfácio', p. 122.

part and participation in society. Her later writings about women, written and published in Europe, complete the shift away from an educational focus. It is amongst her European writing that we find the essay 'A Mulher', which Duarte describes as the most interesting and best constructed of her works on women.[14] This essay undoubtedly offers the most complete expression of the writer's vision of regenerated and regenerating womankind.

Although 'A Mulher' is the only piece of writing published in Europe which offers a comprehensive discussion of women's condition, and only two other short essays, 'Abismo' and 'Luxemburgo', can be considered to specifically address issues relating to women, Floresta's interest and concern for the detail of women's lives remains a consistent theme in almost all her writing. This is most clear in her lengthy travel journals, in which the writer is constantly 'woman-watching', commenting on the behaviour of women of different nationalities, recalling their historical deeds whenever a location prompts it and creating a privileged space for women as actors in the events she experiences and recounts. She is keenly aware of women's oppression, both in her native country and in Europe, drawing frequent comparisons between the two and between different European nations. Floresta's shifting approach, determined by her own patriotic motivations, is particularly visible in these comparisons. In *Opúsculo* she is generally positive about the condition of women in Germany, England, France and the USA, suggesting that the Brazilian woman 'nada é ainda pelo espírito e nenhuma liberdade goza das que honram as mulheres do Norte' (p. 112). When publishing in Europe, however, she describes the repression of all women, writing that 'a companheira do homem [...] acha-se ainda oprimida como nos tempos do paganismo!' ('Abismo', p. 79), and observing the severe laws under which women live, 'mais ou menos humilhada em sua própria dignidade' ('A Mulher', p. 127).

What is most notable about Floresta's depiction of women's oppression is that she frequently reiterates the accusation, made by Sophia in *Woman Not Inferior*, that men have deliberately held women back by denying them an education and encouraging the very faults of which they are so critical. She notes how weak men 'bradam e gritam contra os defeitos que eles mesmos enxertaram naquele sexo por demais ingênuo a fim de que se embelezasse das qualidades a eles agradáveis em seus próprios passatempos' ('A Mulher', p. 125). In fact, in her later, European essays, when she is no longer constrained by the need to appeal to and appease her conservative male compatriots, the biting sarcasm with which she condemns men's behaviour is almost as powerful, though certainly not as constant, as that found in Sophia's text. When Floresta writes: 'mas deixemos de lado todas essas aberrações do intelecto viril, que dariam material para grandes volumes a quem quizesse delas se ocupar' ('A Mulher', p. 127), it is easy to imagine that we are once

---

14 'Posfácio', p. 241.

again reading her translation of Sophia, in which the same idea and tone can be found in comments such as 'além disso, para obrigar os homens a provar com razão, seria reduzi-los ao silêncio' (*Direitos*, p. 58 [31]).

The influence of *Woman Not Inferior* can also be noted in *Opúsculo* when Floresta observes the difficulties involved in challenging 'prejuízos inveterados' and the belief that things are 'em muito bom estado só porque tal era a opinião de seus antepassados' (pp. 44–5). It is precisely prejudice and custom that Sophia identifies, from the opening paragraph onwards, as the root causes of men's assumed superiority (e.g. *Direitos*, pp. 23 and 28 [1 and 6]). Sophia sets out to defeat these forces with the Cartesian weapons of reason and truth, whilst Floresta declares that her patriotic hopes for the nation oblige her to face the challenge with a 'frank and impartial' analysis (*Opúsculo*, p. 45). A second clear example of Floresta borrowing ideas from *Woman Not Inferior* can be found on page 9 of *Opúsculo* when, in order to demonstrate the selfishness of Roman men, Floresta quotes the same passage from Cato that appears in Sophia's work (borrowed, like so much of her text, from Poulain de la Barre).[15] It is important to note, however, that Floresta appropriates this quote for a somewhat different purpose in her own work. Whilst Sophia mocks Cato's argument as evidence of men's lack of reason, Floresta pities the philosopher for the misery such attitudes brought to his door, suggesting that his own unhappy demise might have been avoided 'se uma mãe religiosa e esclarecida lhe tivesse dirigido os primeiros passos na vida' (*Opúsculo*, p. 10). It is illustrative of the fundamental difference between Floresta's translation and her own work that arguments for women's equality founded on reason in Sophia's work are now harnessed in support of a very specific demarcation of female behaviour through the dual discourses of maternity and patriotism.

The claims Sophia makes regarding women's equality to men can still be glimpsed in *Opúsculo*, as when Floresta states that God created man and woman with equal intelligence and the same souls but 'o homem, ainda semi-selvagem, arrogou a si a preeminência da força física' (pp. 5–6). However, because Sophia's claims for women are all based on the fundamental notion of equality between the sexes, she goes to considerable lengths to rationally 'prove' that the two sexes are the same in every aspect except reproduction (*Direitos*, pp. 47–9 [23–4]). Floresta, on the other hand, makes no attempt to back up her suggestion of women's spiritual and intellectual equality, a notion which appears as little more than a few passing comments. When considered in the wider context of the work, it can only be concluded that her lack of interest in emphasising such a fundamental and radical idea lies in the fact that equality was not a prerequisite for the domestic role she envisages for women. In fact an emphasis on sameness, as found in *Woman Not Inferior*, could be seen as contradictory to a system which draws such clear

---

15   The quotation appears in *Direitos* on p. 58 [31].

delineations based precisely on women's biology. Floresta's move away from a notion of equality is confirmed in her later essays, in which it is replaced by an explicit discourse of female moral superiority, which I will discuss below. In embracing this stance, it seems likely that Floresta is revealing the influence of Positivism, which elevated woman to the status of near-domestic deity whilst denying her any sphere of operation outside the confines of her own home.[16] Thus moral superiority goes hand in hand with political, social and financial inferiority, indeed infancy: Comte believed that women's biology held them in 'une sorte d'état d'enfance continue'.[17]

Throughout her discussion of women's repression, it is the Enlightenment image of woman as adornment and play-thing, incapable of rational thought (most famously espoused by Rousseau in *Émile*), which Floresta challenges most forcefully (e.g. *Opúsculo*, pp. 62, 64–5, 122, 158; 'A Mulher', pp. 117, 119). In *Opúsculo* she has harsh criticism for Voltaire, Montesquieu and Rousseau for their attitude to women (pp. 27–8), although she is careful to acknowledge the importance of the wider work of these three philosophers, hinting at the powerful influence of the Enlightenment on her own, and her compatriots', intellectual formation. In a later chapter she spells out the effect of such widely adopted ideas: 'todos esses princípios subversivos, espalhados com tanta profusão por penas mais ou menos hábeis [...], só têm feito com que se aumente o número de escravas, procurando iludir despóticos ou fanáticos senhores' (p. 62), and in 'A Mulher' she notes that all women's faults and weaknesses 'têm origem no desejo doentio de agradar seus amáveis dominadores, que se empenham para nelas incuti-lo' (p. 129).

This last quote also begins to illustrate a subtle shift that can be observed once Floresta is publishing in Europe. Although it is still understood that men are ultimately to blame for women's condition, the women she addresses are no longer cast as entirely helpless pawns in men's domination; rather they are portrayed as weakly and foolishly pandering to the whims of a male-ordered society. In *Opúsculo*, Floresta highlights inappropriate female behaviour and informs her readers of a woman's proper duties, but she shows a distinct solidarity with her Brazilian sisters, pointing out their successes, rather than disparaging their failures: 'muitas de nossas brasileiras, apesar da atmosfera de subversivos príncipios em que respiram, são, todavía, o modelo do sexo e a honra da humanidade' (p. 104). This conciliatory tone, which it must be noted is not entirely consistent through the text, reflects Floresta's desire to elevate, rather than lower, her countrywomen in the esteem of her male readers. Moreover, since she must include herself in the ranks of 'brasileiras', it is in her own interests to demonstrate women's ability to rise above the stifling cultural milieu of their up-bringing.

16 Wernick, pp. 4–5 and 127.
17 Quoted in Wernick, p. 127, note 31.

By the time she is writing in Europe, however, her vision of women's duty has become clearer, and her expectations of their behaviour are proportionately higher. Positioning herself as objective, removed observer, she now offers an uncompromising condemnation of their faults. She describes the sight of women gambling in Germany as 'um espetáculo tão revoltante' (*Itinerário*, p. 183), and notes the 'índole ciumenta, [...] insipidez e menosprezo' common to married women ('A Mulher', p. 143). But her harshest words are reserved for those who neglect their maternal duties: 'faltam-lhes coração, mas não o orgulho e a vaidade' ('A Mulher', p. 107).

Such criticisms hint at the extent to which virtue remains central to the position Floresta envisaged for women in society, something which lay at the heart of her early work on education. However, the part feminine virtue plays in her vision of womanhood has shifted considerably. In her early didactic writing virtue is itself the goal, through which women can achieve social value and esteem. Moreover, it must be nurtured through education; in fact, in her early texts the attainment of virtue forms the basis of Floresta's defence of improved female education, as discussed in Chapter 2. In her later work, Floresta takes women's virtues as a starting point for a more active role in society. Although she continues to see education as a necessary means of developing virtue (e.g. 'Abismo', p. 79), not least to counteract the 'subversive principles' described above, which she clearly saw as fostering weak and immoral behaviour in women ('A Mulher', p. 133), it is significant that Floresta now begins to emphasise women's innate tendency to virtue, as opposed to their need to learn it; that is to say, their natural moral superiority as identified by Comte.

Thus Floresta notes 'os nobres sentimentos, de que não por acaso dotou [à mulher] tão largamente a previdente natureza' ('Abismo', p. 79). She particularly identifies charity and tenderness as women's natural domain (*Opúsculo*, p. 35; 'A Mulher', p. 113), but the noblest virtue possessed by women is self-denial ('A Mulher', pp. 115 and 133). It is through the practice of these virtues that Floresta now suggests that women can set an example to those around them and exert a positive moral influence on men's lives and actions. This concept of woman as moral guardian is present in *Opúsculo*, but the argument is not yet fully developed. Only once do we find a clear reference to this role, when Floresta describes 'esses anjos de paz que tão salutar poder exerceriam sobre os destinos dos homems, se os homems soubessem compreender bem sua grande missão na sociedade!' (p. 9).

It is only on her return to Europe, and her closer involvement with Comte's system, in which Man is saved by Woman,[18] that Floresta categorically assigns to women 'o sublime ofício de regeneradora do homem' ('Abismo', p. 79). And it is not just the men around them who will be regenerated; through

---

18   Wernick, p. 149.

their virtuous example women can exert 'a mais poderosa influência sobre o desenvolvimento da humanidade' (*Três Anos*, p. 79), and by influencing men's destiny, she states, women will have a real influence over the destiny of nations ('A Mulher', p. 117). Thus women's role is clearly constructed within a nation-building discourse: it is every woman's patriotic duty to embrace this responsibility.

This regenerative role for women is undoubtedly what most attracted Floresta to Comte's philosophy. In fact she makes this clear in 'Luxemburgo', the only work in which she explicitly states her support for Positivism, when she writes:

> o sistema Humanitário, de que és fundador e digno representante, estabelece para a mulher um grau particularmente distinto, que a habilita a poder utilizar com segura vantagem as faculdades da própria inteligência e as do coração no exercício das virtudes, que farão dela um dos primeiros ornamentos e a base mais sólida dos progressos da civilização. (p. 193)

It is interesting to note, however, that Floresta is selective in the aspects of Positivism which she adopts or gives voice to. It is probable that Comte would not have been in complete agreement with this passage and its emphasis on women's intelligence, since the founder of Positivism was convinced of women's inferior intelligence and inability for abstract or scientific thought.[19]

However, it is evident that Floresta saw in this concept of social regeneration a powerful discourse for women, and she words her appeal to women carefully to emphasise this point. The emancipatory rhetoric is loud and clear when she writes:

> É tempo, enfim de se enxugarem as lágrimas inúteis causadas pelas opressões sofridas ou por um arrependimento estéril, e de assumir uma heróica resolução de fazer o máximo para erguer-se da sua prostração [...]. Não há para a mulher condição tão aflitiva da qual não possa sair-se dignamente, quando sentir no peito uma firme crença e uma verdadeira bondade de coração. ('A Mulher', p. 131)

Yet by urging women to 'trabalhar para tornar-se útil à família e a toda a humanidade' ('A Mulher', p. 129), it is far from clear what real benefits Floresta saw for women. The significance of self-denial becomes clear as Floresta outlines women's duty as regenerators of humanity: 'é sobretudo a grande obra do porvir que deveis ter em vista, sacrificando a ela o vosso próprio bem' ('A Mulher', p. 143). In truth Floresta gives voice to a fundamentally androcentric discourse which severely reduces women's sphere of

---

19 Wernick, p. 127, note 31.

operation and potential for autonomy, offering in its place nothing more than a hollow veneration, which in fact differs little from Rousseau's notion of woman as adornment and play-thing, which she condemned so forcefully. Woman is still an 'ornamento' (in the passage from 'Luxemburgo' quoted above), only now it is her spiritual, rather than her physical beauty which is to be worshipped. Moreover, within this discourse of self-sacrifice, women are denied any practical means of improving their own situation; on the contrary they remain entirely dependent on men's perception and reception of their behaviour. Added to which, women are burdened with the responsibility for men's own moral failings.

At no point in Floresta's exposition of women's regenerative influence is there a suggestion that it is to be exerted anywhere but within the confines of the family. She clearly states that the family is the foundation stone of society and the starting point for social reform, from which virtue and prosperity must flow (*Três Anos*, p. 243). In this belief she is, of course, not only repeating Comte, who took family bonds as a paradigm for social unity,[20] but also the prevailing notions of her day as well as Enlightenment constructions of society.[21] The image of the unified patriarchal family was central to Enlightenment concepts of citizenship and civil society, in which it was seen as the basis of society and a 'miniature fatherland' where devotion to the state is learned through devotion to one's family members. Floresta states this same idea in her own work: 'o santo amor à família [...] constitui a base principal do grande e nobre amor à Pátria' (*Três Anos*, p. 104).

Long before Comte elevated women's domestic virtues to the status of cult, Enlightenment thought held that by becoming better mothers, and with it better wives, women could bring about a transformation of family life, making men better husbands and fathers, strengthening marital ties and affections and exercising greater moral influence over their husbands.[22] Diana Coole observes that 'the potential radicalism of seventeenth-century individualism was thus surrendered to a vision of the sentimental family, which would offer a new rationalization for women's private and subordinate role and which would thrive from the eighteenth century on'.[23] In Floresta's work,

[20]   Wernick, pp. 128 and 132.

[21]   In *The Social Contract*, Rousseau writes that 'the family may be regarded as the first model of political society' (Jean-Jacques Rousseau, *Discourse on Political Economy and The Social Contract*, trans. Christopher Betts (Oxford and New York: Oxford University Press, 1994), p. 46). It is hugely significant that within this model, in which 'the leader corresponds to the father, the people to the children' (p. 46), the wife/mother is conspicuously absent.

[22]   This belief is clearly shared by Floresta a century later: in 'A Mulher' (p. 143), she states that the surest way for a woman to secure her husband's respect and affection is to be a good mother to his children.

[23]   Diana H. Coole, *Women in Political Theory: From Ancient Misogyny to Contemporary Feminism* (Brighton: Wheatsheaf, 1988), p. 103.

women's exclusion from the fruits of their own labour is unspoken, but very apparent: 'Constituindo boas famílias, formareis gente laboriosa, morigerada, justa e feliz. E as famílias, os povos, as nações, de que o gênero humano se compõe, abençoar-vos-ão em seu verdadeiro progresso, em sua prosperidade' ('A Mulher', p. 151). In this quote, women are implicitly excluded from the families, peoples and nations that thank them, whilst the progress and prosperity women foster is not theirs to enjoy.

Floresta's increasing conviction in the value to be accrued from the role of moral guardian and regenerator appears to prevent her from questioning the massive restrictions which such a discourse imposes on women's operations. Her positioning is now starkly opposed to the idea of female participation in the public sphere, which she translated from *Woman Not Inferior* twenty-five years earlier. Sophia, for example, argued for women's equal ability to govern, offering Elizabeth I as an obvious example (*Direitos*, pp. 65–6 [38]). Even when writing *Opúsculo*, Floresta is not immune to the allure of such a remarkable female figure, noting the military and cultural developments that occurred under her reign and suggesting that through her, all the women of England have the right to the esteem of their male compatriots (p. 23). Only a few years later, however, a considerable shift in attitude can be observed. Whilst travelling in Italy, Floresta has the chance to observe the deposed queen of Spain and the writer asks herself 'como era possível que uma mulher, cercada de um esposo e filhos que a amam, pudesse desejar outra felicidade na terra e ambicionar outra glória, além da que consiste em recomendar seu nome através de virtudes dignas desses dons que Deus lhe concede' (*Três Anos*, p. 70). This passage contains a clear denouncement of any woman's desire to wield power beyond the passive 'power' of moral influence within her own family.

Floresta was by no means unusual as a woman embracing the patriarchalism of the public/private divide. Carol Pateman observes that 'almost everyone' in the nineteenth century, even the early feminists, accepted the doctrine of public and private spheres, holding them to be separate but of equal importance and value to society and the nation. But beneath the rhetoric of the social value of motherhood and a stable family, this division was maintained by 'the belief that women's natures are such that they are properly subject to men and their proper place is in the private domestic sphere'.[24]

It is therefore family relations which come to dominate Floresta's very definition of women, and so emerges the most distinct and dominant motif in her discussion of women: the 'holy trinity' of daughter, wife and mother (to which a fourth, sister, is sometimes added, for example, 'Abismo', p. 79 and 'A Mulher', p. 117). The concept of this moral triumvirate appears

---

[24] Carol Pateman, *The Disorder of Women* (Cambridge: Polity Press, 1995), pp. 120 and 127.

repeatedly in all her writings on women, so much so that Floresta herself writes: 'filha, esposa e mãe (repeti-lo-ei ainda uma vez)' ('Luxemburgo', p. 191). In support of her Brazilian compatriots, in *Opúsculo* she states how well most Brazilian women fulfil the duties of these three roles (p. 104); but in her European texts, influenced by Comte's dream of a future Positivist utopia and the powerful discourse of female-led social regeneration, women's threefold domestic identity is portrayed as a role yet to be appreciated by men or women and 'A Mulher' is a fundamentally instructive text, in which Floresta sets out the behaviour appropriate to each role. Floresta ascribes to these three-roles-in-one such profound value that they become an earthly equivalent of the Christian Holy Trinity, apparently reflecting Floresta's own Catholicism, mingled with the cult of womanhood in the Positivist Religion: 'Esta sublime tríade sois vós, ó mulheres, que a representais sobre a terra. Santificai-a com o honrar de cada um destes belos títulos, mediante o exer-cício daquela excelsa virtude que nos faz sempre volver em prol dos outros o bem que fazemos' ('A Mulher', p. 133).

   Although Floresta always includes the role of daughter in her definition of woman's identity, she in fact has little to say regarding the duties pertaining to that position. In *Opúsculo* she notes only that good Brazilian daughters 'respeitam seus pais, lamentando no silêncio d'alma suas faltas, seus crimes, se os cometem, sem que a mais ligeira censura lhes escape dos labios' (p. 104). The advice offered in 'A Mulher' is even briefer: the simple instruc-tion to love and respect one's parents is reinforced with the reminder that they can never be truly repaid for everything they do (pp. 133–5). These passing references to the role of daughter are at odds with her early didactic texts which, aimed at adolescent readers, are almost exclusively concerned with the behaviour and virtues appropriate to daughters, as discussed in the previous chapter. A clue to Floresta's diminishing interest in this role can be found in its corresponding duty, as set out in the above quotes. Due to a daughter's eternal indebtedness, coupled, no doubt, with the imbalance of status imposed by the generational divide, the role of daughter is a passive, unquestioning one, in which all power and influence lie with the parent. It is significant that in the first passage quoted above, the possibility of offering moral guidance is expressly denied. Once Floresta has fully recognised the power and value to be secured for women through the discourse of male/ social regeneration, the passivity inherent to 'daughter' is no longer of interest to her. So it is to 'wife' and 'mother', as shaper of man in his adulthood and infancy respectively, that she devotes her attention.

   A wife, Floresta instructs, should be a prudent and devoted friend, an inseparable and necessary companion to her husband, and she should ensure that happiness, harmony, cleanliness and economy rule in her household ('A Mulher', p. 135). Floresta advocates an active role for women within marriage, and this includes taking some responsibility for the success or failure of the relationship. She urges women to 'expulsai a sedutora frase *Lua de mel*' and suggests that if a marriage does only have a honeymoon period, it is often the woman who is to blame, for neglecting the practices which ensure her husband's respect and behaving like 'uma caprichosa menina, que acaba por aborrecer, não obstante seus agrados' ('A Mulher', pp. 135–7). Although critical, Floresta would have seen this as a positive discourse for women, since it allows them a degree of control over their relationship, and therefore their destiny. Floresta extends this argument further by claiming that 'a mulher é omnipotente sobre o homem, quando sabe prendê-lo' (p. 143); however, it is a fundamentally hollow power that she affords to wives, since it can only ever be properly used to improve man at the expense of women's own interests and autonomy.

In fact, it soon becomes clear that women's particular capacity for self-sacrifice, highlighted above, plays a significant part in Floresta's vision of the ideal wife. In *Opúsculo* she notes that good wives are happy to 'sacrificar a seus esposos toda a ventura de sua vida, antepondo à sua inconstância ou à sua dureza a incessante prática das virtudes domésticas' (p. 104). This clearly unequal relationship is still very much in evidence in 'A Mulher', although Floresta tries to cast it within an empowering rhetoric, writing: 'a vós compete saber identificar a hora e o lugar de manter a dignidade na submissão, e a autoridade na obediência' (p. 137). Once again she appears to reveal the influence of Comte in adopting this naïve and idealised notion of power in weakness. The founder of Positivism advocated 'a complex relationship of authority–obedience between man and wife' in which the husband's obvious authority was cast as inferior to women's morally superior submission.[25]

Floresta not only addresses the issue of women's behaviour within marriage, she also has much to say on the state of the institution, 'tão caluniada, tão profanada, e tantas vezes fracassada' ('A Mulher', p. 137), and is extremely critical of contemporary attitudes towards matrimony. She notes that most men marry with money in mind, or as a means of producing legitimate heirs, whilst women see in it only status, or 'uma mal interpretada liberdade que a libere de certos preconceitos' ('A Mulher', p. 137). She criticises the cynicism which sees gestures of affection between husband and wife ridiculed and, observing the popular notion that marriage destroys love, she comments that since wealth and status do not ensure domestic happiness, 'não se deve [...] acusar o casamento como causa de esfriamento do amor, mas antes ao homem ou à mulher que se ligam levianamente e sem amor' (*Três Anos*, pp. 319–22). Without love as a foundation, families fall apart, and the only route is unhappiness, dishonour and misery ('A Mulher', p. 121), but when based on mutual love and understanding, marriage 'seria enfim o non plus ultra da humana felicidade' (p. 137).

[25] Aron, p. 97.

Although Floresta's condemnation of loveless marriages is equally vehement in all her discussions of the subject, a subtle shift can be observed in her attitude towards marriage between *Opúsculo* and her subsequent European works. In the former, although it is never clearly stated, the text appears to offer the occasional hint that Floresta favoured, or at least did not condemn, divorce. She praises the equality in marriage enshrined in German law, and refutes Mme. de Staël's accusation that the availability of divorce there has led to 'uma sorte de anarquia' (pp. 17–18). Instead, she implies, the absence of divorce in France, which renders matrimony 'um jugo imposto pela lei' (p. 18), causes greater social problems and unhappiness. Later in the text, Floresta recalls the example of a loyal wife who is abandoned by her husband, and warns that a woman cannot merely base her happiness on 'laços julgados indissolúveis e santos por aqueles que facilmente os profanam quando as paixões os agitam' (p. 126). However, since Floresta recommends instead that women must work constantly to maintain the affection of their husbands, it is unclear whether she is genuinely advocating divorce as a solution here, or simply highlighting the hypocrisy and immorality of men.

Regardless of how much one chooses to read into these passing allusions to divorce, what is certain is that they are entirely absent from her European works. It seems likely that the more liberal, critical approach to the indissolubility of marriage which we see in *Opúsculo*, no doubt developed under the influence of more liberal ideas encountered during her first visit to Europe, was subsequently countered by the increasing influence of Positivism on her thinking. Marriage was so fundamental to Comte's Positive system, that it was not only unbreakable, but also compulsory for everyone.[26]

Although Floresta clearly attributes a considerable significance to women's duties as wives, it is motherhood to which she ascribes the greatest value and devotes the most space in her work. Motherhood is 'a [...] mais doce, mais nobre, mais relevante obra a cumprir' ('A Mulher', p. 139), but it is also 'a mais negligenciada coisa que há do princípio do mundo até nossos dias!' (p. 109), an 'excelso título' which too many women treat with thoughtlessness and disdain (p. 139). The concept of motherhood in Floresta's work inevitably extends far beyond the mere act of producing children, in fact she states her definition clearly: 'ser mãe, no sentido moral, não consiste em se ter filhos, mas em saber bem educá-los' ('A Mulher', p. 139). This notion is very much in line with 'the Victorian ideal of the enlightened mother, devoted exclusively to the domestic sphere', which Ania Loomba identifies.[27] However, it was not only patriarchal male discourse that emphasised women's natural role in the private sphere: for nineteenth-century feminists 'maternity had

---

[26] Wernick, p. 146.
[27] Ania Loomba, *Colonialism/Postcolonialism* (London: Routledge, 1998), p. 219.

become not only the strategic common ground for women's solidarity, but also the vehicle for their liberty'.[28]

The notion of mothers as the first and best educators of their children is already firmly established in *Opúsculo* (e.g. pp. 92 and 104), but it is interesting to note that whilst *Opúsculo* is primarily concerned with women educating their daughters, in 'A Mulher', their responsibility now clearly lies with sons and daughters alike. Once again it is possible to attribute this important shift to the growing influence of Positivism, since Comte saw the early education of sons as one of women's most valuable contributions to his ideal Positive society. However, since the education of sons inevitably held a greater value than the education of daughters, it can also be seen as part of the natural development of Floresta's ideas as she moves away from a specific concern for female education, still dominant in *Opúsculo*, towards the question of woman's value to society as moral guardian and regenerator of man.

The fundamental concept behind this vision of mother-educator, particularly once mothers are educating their sons, is the concept of woman as the producer of citizens. Floresta is careful to emphasise this point, and the supreme value which women can therefore claim in society: 'a posteridade abençoar-vos-á nas obras de vossas crianças, as quais permanecerão marcadas com aquelas boas máximas de que embeberam em vossa escola' ('A Mulher', p. 141). Motherhood is 'a gloriosa obra que deveis cumprir para dar à sociedade homens e mulheres que sejam dignos e capazes de melhorá-la' ('A Mulher', p. 151). It is interesting to note that Floresta here implies the production of citizens of both sexes, and their equal value. However, it is clear that these worthy men and women will 'improve society' in very different ways. Enclosed in their triple relational definition, the daughters must go on to become wives and mothers themselves, and once again influence society only indirectly through their moral influence over men. That is to say, they can only ever be 'citizen-mothers'.[29]

One specific aspect of a mother's duty finds a particular focus in Floresta's writing on women, and offers an interesting insight into some of the social and intellectual factors at play in her work. That is the subject of maternal breast-feeding and an accompanying condemnation of the use of wet nurses. In addressing this specific issue Floresta was contributing to a distinct and lively debate in both Brazil and France, which was fuelled predominantly by the medical profession and concerned with the still-widespread belief that both physical and moral attributes were passed on to a child in the breast milk. As a woman participating in a traditionally male, medical discourse, Floresta creates a discursive space for herself as subject rather than object. Two of Floresta's texts address this issue, *Opúsculo* and 'A Mulher'.

---

28 Offen, p. 351.
29 Offen, p. 337.

The definition of women's 'natural' domestic role is particularly evident in the breast-feeding debate. To breast-feed was widely described by doctors, philosophers and essayists as a woman's 'natural' duty or ordained by nature, and those mothers who neglect this duty are frequently portrayed as denatured.[30] The concept of the repellent unnaturalness of a mother who neglects this sacred responsibility can be found in both Floresta's texts. In *Opúsculo* we find an expression of instinctive repulsion: 'Nada nos parece tão revoltante como ver uma mãe, sem causa justificada pela natureza, consentir que seu filho se alimente em seio estranho' (p. 93). In 'A Mulher', this idea has crystallised into a direct accusation: 'Ó mães sem coração, que abandonais os mais sagrados deveres da natureza. [...] ante vossos olhos quero eu delinear o deplorável quadro que [...] verbalizará o processo de vossa desnaturação face às gerações porvindouras!' (p. 87).

A noticeably different approach can be observed in Floresta's engagement with the subject of breast-feeding in the two texts. Whilst *Opúsculo* touches only briefly on the issue, 'A Mulher' includes a lengthy and detailed discussion of the circumstances of wet-nursing in France, a discussion which constitutes the first quarter of the essay and serves as an introduction to, and perhaps a disguise for, a wider discussion of women's role in society. In fact, it seems valid to suggest that Floresta made use of the burgeoning anti-wet-nursing sentiment in France to attract a greater readership and provide a vehicle for the expression of her views on women's education and position.

Wet-nursing had become a source of increasing concern in France as the century progressed. George Sussman identifies the 1860s as the most significant time in the anti-wet-nursing movement, with the establishment of a 'Société protectrice de l'enfance' authorised by the government and the appearance of a large number of texts, mostly medical, condemning the practice and detailing the abuses that children suffered under it.[31] With a publication date of 1859 (although the essay is itself dated 1857), this puts Floresta's essay 'A Mulher' at the very forefront of this trend. A similar concern can be observed in Brazil during the mid-nineteenth century, with the appearance of a number of medical texts. However, criticism of wet-nursing was by no means a new phenomenon. Enlightenment philosophers and medical doctors had condemned the practice, most famously Rousseau in *Émile* (1762).

Opúsculo Humanitário and 'A Mulher' both portray breast-feeding, like women's wider domestic responsibilities, as every mother's patriotic duty

---

[30] E.g. Jose Lino Coutinho, *Cartas sobre a educação de Cora, seguidas de um cathecismo moral, politico e religioso* (Bahia: Typ. de Carlos Poggetti, 1849), p. 145; Emilio Joaquim da Silva Maia, *Ensaio sobre os perigos à que estão sujeitos os meninos, quando não são amamentados por suas proprias mãis* (Rio de Janeiro: Typ. de R. Ogier, 1834), p. viii.

[31] George D. Sussman, *Selling Mother's Milk: The Wet-nursing Business in France, 1715–1914* (Urbana, Chicago and London: University of Illinois Press, 1982), pp. 121–2.

to the nation. This was a common theme in anti-wet-nursing discourse in Brazil and France. The primary concern of most writers was to reduce infant mortality rates at a time when industrial capitalist societies required an ever greater workforce to develop and compete;[32] however, most observers looked beyond simple demographics. A mother's duty was to raise sons that were both physically and morally robust, that they might be properly equipped to become good citizens and defenders of the nation. Hence the considerable concern that a wet nurse's milk might not only contaminate the child with disease but also with her vices. This dual interest can be seen, for example, in a medical essay published in Rio in 1834:

> Assim mãis Brasileiras, se verdadeiramente amais nosso bello paiz, pondes em pratica a aleitação materna, que desta maneira muito concorrereis para a reforma de nossos costumes de que tanto precisamos, e para o augmento de nossa população, da qual o Brasil tanta necessidade tem para o desen-volvimento de suas immensas riquezas naturaes, e para a sua futura pros-peridade.[33]

Once again, though, the ideas expressed in this passage are certainly not new. In fact it closely echoes Rousseau's observation in *Émile* that 'when mothers deign to nurse their own children, there will be a reform in morals'.[34]

The practice of using a wet nurse was common in Brazil and France during the nineteenth century, but the circumstances under which it occurred were extremely different. In Brazil the nurse was almost invariably a black slave woman, sold or hired out, usually without her own child, and who lived and worked within the suckled child's household. The mother who employed her was white, bourgeois or upper class, part of the urban elite or from a plan-tation-owning family.[35] In France the wet nurse was usually a poor woman living in a rural area who nursed the child in her own home alongside or after her own child, unless that child had died. The mother who employed her was most commonly an urban, working woman, employed in a factory or family business.[36] This effectively means that, although in both cases breast-feeding is essentially a question of female behaviour, and is approached as such by Floresta, race comes to the fore in Brazil, inextricably tied in with attitudes towards slavery and the captive black population, whilst in France, class is the underlying factor which shapes the discourse in terms of the social status of both nurse and mother.

---

[32] Sussman, p. 7.
[33] Maia, p. 10.
[34] Rousseau, *Émile*, p. 13.
[35] Sonia M. Giacomini, 'Ser escrava no Brasil', *Estudos Afro-Asiáticos*, 15 (1988), 145–69.
[36] See Sussman.

   Although Floresta clearly found the Brazilian and French systems equally abhorrent, condemning the neglect of mothers on both sides of the Atlantic with equal vehemence (*Opúsculo*, p. 93; 'A Mulher', p. 87), she never draws parallels between the two, despite close similarities in the debates provoked by each. In fact, in each case the writer uses the other nation as a positive contrast to the evils of the country whose system she is considering. When describing the situation in Brazil in 1853 she writes:

> Se Rousseau, com o seu *Emílio*, fez corar as mães francesas pelo esqueci-
> mento em que estavam desse primeiro dever da maternidade, em França,
> onde as amas têm mais ou menos alguma educação e se distinguem pelo
> asseio, o que sentiriam as mães brasileiras que bem comprendessem aquele
> livro, à vista de seus filhos pendentes do seio de míseras africanas, que
> passam, muita vez, do açoite [...] ao berço do inocente para ofrecer-lhe
> seu leite? (*Opúsculo*, p. 93)

However, just four years later, when she writes about the circumstances characteristic of the system in France, she describes French nurslings as:

> Essa inocente porção do gênero humano, abandonada pelo aparente
> progresso da civilização em meio às misérias que minha boa mãe deplo-
> raria tanto quanto eu, se coubesse também a ela ser-lhes espectadora! Mas
> ela nunca saiu de seu país, onde tais enormidades são desconhecidas até
> agora. ('A Mulher', p. 95)

The reason for this seeming economy with the truth is not difficult to determine. When writing for a Brazilian readership she is appealing to the popular conception in Brazil of Europe, and in particular of France, as a model of all things enlightened and progressive and an example to be followed, suggesting that at least some French women have seen the error of their ways, and that the situation is ameliorated by education and hygiene. On the other hand, when writing for a European audience Floresta remains patrioti-cally silent on the equivalent situation in Brazil, in fact implying that there is no such equivalent. Conscious of the role patriarchal ideology ascribed to women as figurative representatives of the nation, Floresta omits this nega-tive femininity on the part of her Brazilian compatriots, reconstructing Brazil through its women's sanitised behaviour. Anne McClintock identifies this construction of women emphatically: 'excluded from direct action as national citizens, women are subsumed symbolically into the national body-politic as its boundary and metaphoric limit'.[37] Floresta's desire to distance the neglect of maternal duties from Brazil's national identity can also be observed in

---

[37] Anne McClintock, *Imperial Leather: Race, Gender and Sexuality in the Colonial Contest* (London: Routledge, 1995), p. 354.

Opúsculo when she states, rather vaguely, that the practice was introduced from abroad, 'porque não é [...] de origem brasileira' (p. 93).

A comparison of the two texts, of Floresta's portrayal of wet-nursing practices, and of the nurses and mothers in the very different contexts of Brazil and France, indicates that the writer was able to engage with the class issues of the French system more comfortably than with the racial issues which were so essential to a consideration of wet-nursing in Brazil. The very fact that she makes little more than a passing reference to the system in her own country whilst entering fully into the debate in France would seem to support this analysis.

In contrast to the lack of concrete detail and the figurative imagery found in Floresta's very brief consideration of infant feeding in *Opúsculo*, she describes the French system in painstaking, almost journalistic detail, painting a vivid picture of the dirty and impoverished surroundings in which the nurses live and informing the reader of neglect on the part of both wet nurses and more particularly parents who fail to send payments. More significantly, Floresta portrays the nurses she meets as humble, polite women and pities their poverty and the sacrifices they must make to support their families ('A Mulher', pp. 85–105). She reserves her condemnation for the neglectful mothers.

Wet-nursing was still a 'significant commercial enterprise' in France throughout the nineteenth century, contributing massively to the rural economy of some areas.[38] However, demand had fallen since the eighteenth century when the practice was at its most widespread. One of the reasons for this decline was a move towards maternal feeding amongst the educated upper and middle classes. In fact it was amongst the expanding urban petit-bourgeoisie – the shopkeepers and craftsmen, as well as single mothers, that the employment of rural wet nurses remained common practice.[39]

Although she is sympathetic to the nurses' hardship, Floresta fails to consider, or even to acknowledge the strong economic impetus behind the wet-nursing business for the child's urban working mother. Dispensing with the task of feeding and caring for young children allowed urban women to continue contributing to the household income uninterrupted, often as factory workers, where children were not allowed, or participating in the family business where an infant was no less at risk or inconvenient. In fact Floresta's own reading of the situation is that most parents of nurslings were from the urban bourgeoisie, and their motivation for sending their children away was laziness and the allure of the social scene. Yet documentation shows that in the mid-1800s this was certainly not the case. It may be that Floresta found it easier to condemn a mother on those terms than when the mother was acting

38 Sussman, pp. 123–5.
39 Sussman, p. 101.

out of economic necessity, although it seems more likely that she was aware that her readership would be from the higher classes and so chose to address her appeal to them. Moreover, her discussion of class issues elsewhere reveals her predominant interest in middle- and upper-class concerns. In truth, by condemning wet-nursing in France, where the motivation was financial for both mother and nurse, Floresta effectively contributed to a discourse that sought to deprive women of the opportunity to enter and participate in the public sphere as wage-earners. This was typical of the bourgeois feminism that was to be condemned by socialist feminists by the end of the century.[40]

The detailed and sympathetic description of the French rural wet nurse is the complete antithesis of Floresta's portrayal of the black nurse in Brazil. She is able to acknowledge the white French nurse as the victim of a corrupt system, despite the importance of wet-nursing to the rural economy in France, whilst casting the black slave much less favourably as corruptor and infector. She also portrays the French nurses as individuals in their own right, something which is entirely lacking from her references to slave nurses, whom she considers en masse purely in terms of their effect on the white children they suckle. Most significantly, though, she is able to recognise the French nurses as fellow mothers, making frequent reference to the nurses' own children whom they must endeavour to nourish as best they can alongside the nurslings ('A Mulher', p. 97). In contrast, when describing the black slave nurses she makes no acknowledgement of their own maternity, although a wet nurse was by definition also a mother. Slave mothers are firmly excluded from her vision of universal motherhood. By extension they, and their offspring, are also excluded from the Brazilian nation which patriotic motherhood produces, whilst their French counterparts, who are depicted as struggling to support their families, are cast as better citizens than the French urban mothers who neglect their children, although it is implied that these nurses too could fulfil their own maternal duties more effectively if they were not also responsible for nurslings.

In the French text, it is implied that a return to maternal breast-feeding would enable women of all social classes to claim a position of value as 'citizen-mothers'. In the Brazilian context the black slave woman is not given the chance to be natural or patriotic for she is not recognised as a fellow mother. Thus when writing in Brazil, and concerned primarily with the importance of breast-feeding in representations of female patriotism, Floresta's own patriotism, coupled with the inherent racism of the time, which she shares, disable her feminist concerns, precluding a universal vision of womanhood.[41]

---

[40] Offen, p. 332.

[41] For a more complete analysis of Floresta's participation in the debate on maternal feeding and its gender and class implications, see Charlotte Liddell, 'Nature, Nurture and Nation: Nísia Floresta's Engagement in the Breast-feeding Debate in Brazil and France', *Feminist Review*, 79 (2005), 69–82.

Floresta's exclusion of slave women from her construction of the Brazilian nation, and her engagement with gender issues within her general discussion of slavery, are considered in more detail in Chapter 5.

Floresta may be able to embrace the poor French wet nurse as a mother, on an equal footing with her bourgeois client and counterpart, but her approach to class divisions and the question of women's employment in her wider work is neither clear nor consistent. As the case study of the rural wet nurses suggests, Floresta's overriding concern lies with the middle and upper classes, and she struggles to find a discursive space from which to address the problems of the working class. A clear example of this natural bourgeois focus can be found in *Itinerário*. Whilst travelling, Floresta sees a group of lace makers in Brussels and notes the damage such intricate work does to the eyesight of these 'pobres mulheres'. However, she immediately goes on to observe that their handiwork 'serve apenas para excitar a galanteria, para aumentar o luxo frívolo das mulheres da sociedade' (p. 58); in other words, her sympathy for the labouring poor is soon pushed aside by her concern for the moral degeneracy of the higher classes. Moreover, her thoughts on this situation and its larger social implications are prematurely curtailed: she is 'distracted' by a memory of her own mother making lace, an image which effectively recasts the process as a bourgeois leisure activity, and so undermines the implication of poor working conditions and social imbalance which lie behind the scene.

It is significant that Floresta's only consideration and advocation of female employment appears in *Opúsculo*, when the full extent of women's domestic duty to the nation has still not been realised. Even then it is not always clear what exactly she has in mind for her fellow women. For example, she condemns the general idleness of Brazilian women who 'desprez[am] o trabalho e pass[am] todo o seu tempo ocupadas em frivolidades' (p. 120), but it soon becomes apparent that it is not remunerative work they disdain. In the following sentence, Floresta notes with pity the many girls who languish in complete inactivity, despite possessing the necessary elements to become excellent 'mães de família' and women of note. It is clear, then, that the work Floresta is advocating here is that which is involved in the fulfilment of domestic duties.

However, when she turns her attention specifically to Brazil's 'classes pobres' (p. 124), she does clearly advocate gainful employment for women (although, as noted in the previous chapter, she fails to advocate the sort of practical education that might have facilitated this). She holds up French and English mothers, rearing children, managing the home and contributing to their husbands' business, as a model to be emulated, and praises them also for fostering a good work ethic in their children (pp. 124–5). Floresta goes on to issue a direct appeal for the establishment of 'uma classe pública de operárias' (p. 132), observing that this would offer 'uma parte das famílias desvalidas [...] um meio seguro de as livrar da miséria' (p. 132).[42] The subject of working women, and of a working class in general (the distinction becomes blurred here), is once again couched within a patriotic, nation-building discourse: 'essa classe tiraria e faria ao mesmo tempo com que a pátria tirasse proveito dos grandes recursos que encerra o nosso riquíssimo solo' (p. 132).

Although Floresta appreciates the need for lower-class women to contribute to the family economy, and identifies this need clearly, it is telling that the issue of female employment occupies only a few brief paragraphs in a text that runs to 160 pages. Moreover, Floresta's discomfort in addressing class issues can be detected in the fact that, despite declaring her intention to discuss Brazil's poor, she is twice distracted, almost immediately, by other issues: in the first instance, marriage (where the example she cites is of an elite, educated couple, p. 125), and on the second occasion, the natural wealth of the nation and the end of slavery (p. 132). Perhaps not surprisingly, a distinct note of bourgeois condescension can also be detected when she compares the simple and modest dress (and, reading between the lines, aspirations) of the French working classes with those in Brazil who 'não se resignando com o estado em que Deus as colocou, querem mostrar-se aos olhos do mundo trajadas acima da sua condição' (p. 126).

In her subsequent European texts it is clear that the powerful combined discourse of moral guardian and mother-educator have left no room for a consideration of women's employment. Although she continues to show sympathy, and even a degree of admiration, for women of the lower classes who have no choice but to find work as well as caring for the home and family ('A Mulher', p. 121), we no longer find any suggestion that these women should be encouraged to do so, and certainly not that it might be in the interests of the nation. On the contrary, the only space now endorsed for women of all classes is the home: 'esquecei de vós mesmas, dignas mães de todas as nações, e de todas as classes [...] no cumprimento de vossa sublime tarefa' ('A Mulher', p. 153).

Floresta's reluctance to engage fully with the issues of poor or working-class women may partly be the inevitable response of a writer addressing a subject beyond her own experience and which she cannot fully comprehend. However, it is also plain to see that female employment conflicts irreconcilably with women's regenerative role, as constructed by Floresta, enacted through the family and home. She is unable to deny that the opportunity to earn is essential for many women, and therefore cannot condemn those who

---

42 Floresta's differentiation between the 'poor classes' in Brazil and the 'working classes' in Europe (and, in the future, Brazil) suggests that she understood the distorting effect of slavery on Brazil's labour economy, although this does not prevent her from criticising 'idle' lower-class parents for failing to encourage a taste for work in their children in *Opúsculo* (pp. 126–7).

work, although she implies that they could fulfil their 'sacred' domestic duties better if they did not. Unlike Comte, Floresta's project does not extend to a wholesale restructuring of society; therefore she must accept the economic realities of her day and allow women to continue working, although this prevents them from realising their true mission as women. What this irresolvable tension means, of course, is that Floresta's vision of female value through social regeneration, and the opportunity for patriotic participation which it purports to offer, eventually becomes an exclusive discourse for the social elite, which devalues lower-class women's direct contribution to the public economy and reinforces class division.

A reading of Floresta's own writings on women's condition, behaviour and role in society reveals how the humanism of Sophia's defence of absolute equality, which initially finds an echo in Floresta's work through her assertions of women's intellectual equality, gradually and inexorably loses ground in the face of her growing adherence to a profoundly differentiating construction of woman founded on moral superiority. This shift in part reflects the influence of Positivism on her thinking, and Comte's influence might also be observed in Floresta's increasing focus on the roles of wife and mother. However, her position was also, and I would suggest rather more, profoundly shaped by her own increasingly patriotic focus, operating in tandem with deeply entrenched Enlightenment constructions of the family as a practice-ground for the nation, and the nineteenth-century relational feminist revalorisation of womanhood through the prism of biological difference, which projected women within the private sphere of family and home, thus continuing to cast them as the producers of citizens.

What is certain is that Sophia's revolutionary Cartesian reasoning can never be claimed for Floresta, as faithful translator of *Woman not Inferior*. Rather, I would suggest, she earns the title of feminist through her lifelong desire to see women occupying a position of greater dignity and regard in society. This desire is manifest in her pedagogical practices and her impressive body of work, spanning a period of more than four decades and almost always privileging women's concerns and experiences. If her search for an effective means to achieve this goal eventually led her down the blind alley of domestic sanctification, she was by no means alone, although the weight of the patriotic mission she sets herself certainly made a retreat more difficult.

Floresta's specific engagement with the subject of infant feeding, a debate which hinged on discourses of nation-building, reveals the extent to which patriotism directed her vision and discussion of women's role and status in society. It also offers a valuable insight into the intersections between gender, class and race in Floresta's writing, revealing the difficulties she encountered in attempting to reconcile her vision of womanhood with her own white, elite identity, and more importantly, with the image of a white, middle-class, 'civilised' Brazil which she sought to encourage in her Brazilian readers and project to her European audience. The strategies Floresta employs to resolve and/or evade this fundamental incompatibility will become increasingly clear over the course of the following chapters, in which I will repeatedly highlight the patriotic premise behind her social and political positionings.

4

The Indianist

In the first three chapters I have shown how Floresta constructed an image of idealised womanhood, and how that image was fundamentally tied to a concept of national identity and standing. I shall now turn to the writer's engagement with a more traditional symbol and representative of Brazilian national identity: the indigenous population. The primary focus of this chapter will be *A Lágrima de um Caheté*, published in Rio in 1849. This poem is arguably Floresta's most unusual and surprising work, her only concerted use of poetry as a medium, and her only overtly political, anti-establishment publication. The poem laments the defeat of a Pernambucan *nativist* uprising, of the same year, but its central figure and 'hero' is a Caeté Indian. For this reason the poem is generally referred to as an example of, and Floresta's only contribution to, Indianist writing.

This definition is problematic, however, because the text differs from the norms of the Indianist movement in a number of fundamental ways. I will therefore analyse this work closely to consider how Floresta borrows from and manipulates this popular and influential genre to suit her very specific literary and political purpose and to assess the validity of the text's Indianist label. To do this, I shall first look at the development of the wider Brazilian literary and social movement known as 'Indianism', and the ideologies behind it, before looking at the political motivation of Floresta's poem and how it shapes the text and sets it apart. I will then discuss the poem through the portrayal of its various 'characters' – Indian, Portuguese and allegorical, comparing Floresta's approach with that of her male Indianist contemporaries.

However, *Lágrima* is not Floresta's only work to address the subject of the Brazilian Indian, and I will conclude the chapter by looking at her subsequent writings, which include a discussion of the Indian in the context of both social commentary in *Opúsculo* and *ufanismo* in her European essays 'O Brasil' and 'Viagem Magnética'.[1] Since these texts attempt to address the real circumstances of the nineteenth-century Indian, they provide a valuable contrasting insight into Floresta's attitude towards the indigenous population

---

[1] *Ufanismo* is the name given to a particular, long-established style of nativist discourse in Brazil which emphasises the natural wealth and beauty of the Brazilian land.

as a social reality rather than a literary mechanism. I will show how her engagement with issues of material, historical Indian identity and citizenship offers both contrasts and parallels with her representation of the symbolic Caeté, highlighting his figurative purpose whilst simultaneously revealing the continuing influence of Indianist stereotypes and idealisations on Floresta's thinking.

Indianism was the most important element of the Brazilian Romantic movement, spanning most of the nineteenth century, from the 1830s onwards; evident in literature, poetry, drama and the visual arts. It arose as a direct response to independence and the need for a new Brazilian national identity, enjoying the patronage of the Emperor Pedro II and mirroring a renewed interest in and public debate over indigenist politics. In fact the movement became 'a central element in the Empire's project of state- and nation-building'.[2]

David Brookshaw identifies the mid-1850s to the mid-1860s as 'the most intense period of Indianism in literature',[3] which positions *Lágrima* amongst the early examples of the trend and ahead of its fashionable peak. However, the earliest examples of romantic Indianism date from the 1830s and the movement started to take off in the 1840s. Poetry was the preferred medium of these early Indianists, with the novel, itself a very new literary form, only finding favour in the 1850s.[4] This fact may well have influenced Floresta, possibly explaining her decision to use poetry in this instance, despite her clear preference for prose.

David Treece distinguishes between two distinct phases around mid-century. The first phase of the movement, which he suggests extends into the mid-1850s, is characterised by a pessimistic, often tragic and critical tone; a focus born, at least in part, out of the social and political tensions and frequent violent uprisings of the 1840s.[5] Texts from this period lament the demise of the Indian, and condemn the colonial process and internecine fighting which brought about their downfall, and they are founded on the construction of 'the mythology of a heroic indigenous ancestry and of a shared tradition of anti-colonial military resistance, through which the Brazilian national and the Indian could be identified as partners in a natural alliance'.[6] The second phase was dominated by the presence of José de Alencar and characterised by apologists of both the colonial project and the Imperial establishment of the day. Although very different in tone, both phases were fundamentally concerned with, and celebrated, inde-

---

[2]   See David Treece, *Exiles, Allies, Rebels: Brazil's Indianist Movement, Indigenist Politics, and the Imperial Nation-State* (London: Greenwood Press, 2000), pp. 91–2.

[3]   David Brookshaw, *Paradise Betrayed: Brazilian Literature of the Indian* (Amsterdam: CEDLA, 1988), p. 34.

[4]   Macedo's *A Moreninha* (1844) is usually identified as the first Brazilian novel.

[5]   Treece, pp. 98–100

[6]   Treece, p. 96.

pendent national unity. Chronologically and in terms of the tone of the text, *Lágrima* was influenced by, and must be considered as belonging to, the first phase of the movement, although, as will become clear through the course of the chapter, Floresta's poem presents a real challenge to such definitions.

Treece names two leading proponents of the first phase of the movement: the renowned Gonçalves Dias, whose First and Second *Cantos* were published in 1846 and 1848 respectively, and his more obscure contemporary Antônio Gonçalves Teixeira e Sousa, whose first and best known work, *Os Três Dias de um Noivado*, was published in 1844.[7] We can be quite certain that Floresta was familiar with the work of both these writers. Dias's *Cantos* received immediate critical acclaim, and whilst his contemporary never enjoyed the same recognition, a quick glance at the first edition of Teixeira e Sousa's work reveals that Floresta was among the list of the poem's subscribers. These and other contributors to the emergent Indianist movement would undoubtedly have influenced Floresta in her writing of *Lágrima*.

It is important to note, however, that *Lágrima* is not mentioned in studies of Brazil's Indianist movement, although the poem's existence is not a recent discovery; it was re-edited in the *Revista das Academias de Letras* in 1938. As a woman writer, Floresta is not alone in suffering this fate. At least one other Indianist text written by a woman, a little-known novel by Ana Luísa de Azevedo Castro entitled *D. Narcisa de Villar* (1859), has also been entirely overlooked by studies of the movement.[8]

One of the most significant factors in the development of the literary Indianist movement was the Instituto Histórico e Geográfico Brasileiro, founded in 1838. The institute, whose president and patron was the Emperor himself, was influential in fostering and maintaining the movement through financial support and intellectual endorsement and encouragement. However, Imperial patronage came at a price. It is known that Gonçalves Dias struggled with a personal conflict between principle and patronage, on the one hand seeking to criticise the second reign whilst simultaneously depending on the Emperor for financial backing.[9] Floresta, writing and publishing independently, was subject to no such constraints (although censorship was still a problem, as I will discuss futher below), which may be a contributory factor in explaining the more explicit nature of her criticisms.

Although *Lágrima* certainly shares many characteristics of early Indianist texts, it also differs markedly in a number of ways from the norms and themes generally identified in early Indianist writing. These divergences provide a crucial insight into Floresta's motivations for writing *Lágrima* and clearly

---

[7] Treece, p. 100.

[8] Ana Luísa de Azevedo Castro, *D. Narcisa de Villar*, 3rd edn (Florianópolis: Editora Mulheres, 1997).

[9] Treece, p. 93.

reveal the author's capacity for adapting a prevailing discourse to voice her particular concerns. Through the course of my analysis of the poem I will therefore draw attention to these fundamental differences, as well as to the many typically Indianist features, in order to consider what social, political and literary factors shaped the text and its Indian.

The Indian as a literary device

The poem begins with a lone figure on the banks of the Beberibe river, identifying the location as Pernambuco. A description of the figure soon reveals him to be an Indian. There follows a lengthy consideration of the idyllic life he has lost at the hands of the colonisers and of his moral virtues, at all times contrasted with the vices of the Portuguese. The young Caeté Indian is thirsting for vengeance when, in the distance, he hears the sound of gunfire. The fighting he can hear is a nativist uprising known as the Praieira Revolt, which rocked the province of Pernambuco during the final months of 1848 and early 1849. It soon becomes clear that this event is an important focus of the poem, and the author's chief motivation for writing it. From this point on, the Indian not only mourns the loss of his land and the destruction of his family and culture, but also laments the defeat of the rebellion and in particular the execution of one of its leaders, Nunes Machado, who is glorified as hero and martyr.

The final third of the poem takes on a more mystical element as a series of allegorical figures appear to the Indian. Firstly he is comforted by the 'Genio do Brasil', a spirit representation of the nation, who reassures him that Nunes Machado has earned a place in history. Thus inspired, the Indian sets out to avenge Machado's death but is stopped in his tracks by an ugly old woman who reveals herself to be Reality. Reality advises the Indian to turn back, saying that no one cares for him, but at that moment a beautiful virgin appears in the clouds, and hot on her heels a monster, with the Furies behind it. The Caeté instinctively wishes to defend the virgin, but is unable to reach her. Reality then identifies the virgin as Liberty and the monster as Despotism, and whilst she reassures the Caeté that Liberty can never be dethroned, and that Despotism will be conquered and cast out from Brazil, she indicates that the Indian's own future is not so bright, advising him to return to the forests.

As this brief synopsis makes clear, *Lágrima* is a complex text in which a number of often-conflicting literary and socio-political factors are at play. Whilst some aspects of the poem reveal characteristics common to classically Indianist texts, others distance the poem from the norms of the movement, making its definition more problematic. Most importantly, each aspect requires equal consideration because the political, Indianist and allegorical aspects are inextricably linked and the poem cannot be seen from one angle alone. I will therefore consider each of these three factors in turn, and draw conclusions about Floresta's intentions from the interactions and symbiosis between them.

Whilst the political and social context of post-independence Brazil led Indianist writers to return to a pre-Columbian idyll or the early days of conquest in their quest for an uncontaminated Brazilian identity, the political realities of the day were to have a much more direct influence and presence in *Lágrima*, for Floresta does not locate her Indian in Brazil's colonial past, but in the absolute present. In fact this contemporary setting is one of the most significant features that distinguish *Lágrima* from previous and indeed subsequent Indianist texts. The reason for such a departure from convention is, of course, the fact that Floresta's true interest and motivation for writing was the extremely contemporary events of the Praieira Revolt, and her primary aim was to defend and express her support for the uprising, its federalist cause and its defeated hero Machado.

The province of Pernambuco had always been a hotbed of nativist sentiment and the scene of regular uprisings since before independence. The Praieira Revolt was to be the last of these uprisings, for Pernambuco and for Brazil as a whole. The revolt came about as a result of political events in Rio. In September 1848 the Liberal, nativist cabinet had introduced an unpopular bill relating to the slave trade. The bill failed, and the cabinet resigned in protest. Rather than replacing the ministers with another Liberal cabinet, the Emperor formed a government from the Conservative opposition. The new cabinet then set about removing Liberals from all positions of national and local control. Most factions put up no resistance, but in Pernambuco the Praieira faction, which had enjoyed total control for a number of years, was confident of public support and the uprising began on 7 November 1848. On 2 February 1849 the rebels launched an attack on Recife, the last stronghold of the government troops. The attack was successfully repelled and in the face of defeat the revolt lost momentum and, after the capture of the remaining leaders in March, collapsed, although guerrilla fighting was reported in the southern forests until 1850.[10]

Floresta presents the aims of the uprising in a romantic light: the first allusion to Machado in the text, before he is named, establishes his altruistic motivations: 'Desde lá do berço aprendeo a amar / O triste opprimido; d'ell' é defendente' (p. 22). This heroic image is obviously a very romantic and simplified version of the complex political motivations behind the uprising. However, the Praia manifesto did include such liberal ideals as the redistribution of land amongst the population, and the degree of popular support the faction enjoyed in the province would suggest that Pernambucans believed that they were indeed defending their interests.[11]

Whatever Floresta's opinion of the Praieira Revolt and its objectives, her

[10]   Barman, pp. 231–2.
[11]   Amaro Quintas, *O Sentido social da Revolução Praieira*, 6th edn (Recife: Editora Massangana, 1982), p. 142.

interest within the context of *Lágrima* seems to have been in Nunes Machado as an individual, for he was by no means the only figure behind the revolt but is the only one to be mentioned in the poem. This is in large part explained by the fact that the author had a personal connection with Machado, although the extent of their acquaintance/friendship is not documented. Floresta's second husband Manuel Augusto de Faria Rocha and the rebel leader were both born in Goiana in Pernambuco and graduated together from the Olinda law faculty in 1832. Duarte states that the two men were childhood friends, and Adauto da Câmara refers to 'estreitas ligações de amizade' between Floresta herself and Machado.[12] We can at least be fairly certain that the young Floresta had met Machado in person, and the homage she pays him in *Lágrima* suggests that he left a considerable impression. Beyond this personal association, Machado was the obvious choice as a figurehead for the revolt and the ideals it represents in the poem. He was to be its martyr and Floresta remembers him alongside the martyrs of previous Pernambucan uprisings such as Domingos José Martins, executed leader of the 1817 rebellion; and Frei Caneca, one of the driving ideological forces behind the 1824 *Confederação do Equador* Revolt, who was also captured and executed (p. 23). Floresta is not alone in ascribing such significance to Machado's death; the Pernambucan historian Amaro Quintas describes him as 'o mais gigantesco de seus vultos (do partido praieira), o grande mártir da Democracia no Brasil'.[13]

Ultimately, *Lágrima* serves more as an expression of support for the nativist and federalist cause, and an elegy to Nunes Machado, than as a lament for the condition of the native Indian and a condemnation of the processes which created and maintained that situation. In this, Floresta's poem does not differ greatly from most classic Indianist texts. The Indian is always a device: a romantic construction; a symbolic figure, be it the noble savage or the 'degenerate cannibal'; an allegory for the Brazilian people. The actual way of life, rights and welfare of the Indians themselves were not the motivation for Indianist literature, as the political and social reality of their treatment makes clear. Any difference lies in the fact that Floresta's employment of the Indian as a vehicle for political expression is more explicit than that of her contemporaries.

The timing of the poem also confirms where her true concern lay. *Lágrima* was originally completed for publication in the February of 1849 – immediately following Machado's death and even before the revolt had been fully defeated, but its publication was delayed. Floresta states this fact in a short foreword to the poem, in which the delay is explained by what can only be understood as an allusion to censorship: 'é sómente agora que lhe permittirão apparecer, e isto depois de o terem feito passar aqui por mil torturas inquisi-

---

12   Duarte, *Vida e Obra*, p. 111; and Câmara, *História*, p. 89.
13   Quintas, p. 142.

toriaes!' (p. 5). The immediacy of the political content no doubt contributed to this censorship and the resulting delay of several months in the poem's publication. In fact, considering the overtly pro-Praieira and pro-federalist stance of the poem, which even called for Machado's death to be avenged, and the less than subtle parallels drawn between the current political regime under Pedro II and the much-hated and vilified Portuguese colonisers, it is surprising that the poem was published at all, particularly so soon after the rebellion had been put down. The author herself goes some way to explaining how the poem came to be published when she implies, again in the prologue, that it was due to the efforts of someone with influence (someone who remains tantalisingly anonymous), that *Lágrima* made it to publication. She writes: 'Graças à bemfazeja mão, que o fez renascer, qual Phenix, das cinzas a que o havião ou querião reduzir!' (p. 5).

The inflammatory political message of the poem no doubt also explains the author's decision not to use her usual, and by then well-known, pseudonym. Instead she chose the entirely obscure, but significant pseudonym Tellesilla.[14] This is the name of a figure from ancient Greece, a woman who, in the absence of the men who were away at war, armed her fellow women and slaves to successfully defend their city from attack by the king of Sparta. Floresta apparently casts herself in the role of defender of her region, and by extension her nation, from what she perceived to be the despotism of Imperial rule.

In light of the poem's overtly political context and focus, it is not surprising that a consideration of the history of the Caeté reveals a likely political motivation behind Floresta's choice of Indian 'hero'. Moreover, it is a choice that sets *Lágrima* apart from the norms of Indianist literature. Most writers, both prior to and after 1849, preferred to draw their heroes from peaceable tribes such as the Guarani of southern Brazil, or those who had formed allegiances with the Portuguese colonisers such as the Tobajara and Potiguar Indians of Rio Grande do Norte and Ceará immortalised in Alencar's *Iracema*. David Brookshaw states that 'no Brazilian Indianist exalted those Indians who had actually resisted the Portuguese'.[15] The Caeté (from northern Bahia and southern Pernambuco), on the other hand, had maintained a persistently anti-Portuguese stance during the first century of colonisation. If their preference for forming alliances with the French log-wood traders were not enough, the Caeté had sealed their fate as 'bad Indians' when, in 1556, they captured the shipwrecked first Bishop of Bahia and ate him.[16] This reputation had

---

14 For whatever reason, this new pseudonym appears to have been ineffective in securing anonymity, since Floresta's first appearance in a bibliographical dictionary, in 1862, includes *Lágrima* in the list of her works (Silva, *Diccionario*, p. 295).

15 Brookshaw, p. 35.

16 John Hemming, 'Indians and the Frontier', in *Colonial Brazil*, ed. Leslie Bethell

even earned the Caeté a place in the literary canon, where they featured as
enemies of Diogo Álvarez and Paraguaçu in Santa Rita Durão's influential
epic *Caramuru* (1781).

Although it is clear that Floresta's choice of the Caeté Indian was partly
geographic, they were not the only Indian tribe whose territories included
parts of Pernambuco. Both the Potiguar and the Tobajara encroached from
the north.[17] What is more likely to have attracted the author to the Caeté in
her quest for a Pernambucan hero was the combined fact of their historical
refusal to ally themselves with or accept the colonising force, and their particularly harsh treatment in consequence. In 1562 the Governor of Brazil, Mem
de Sá, had declared a 'just war' on the Caeté nation. Although the reason
given was retribution for their unfortunate taste for bishops, H. B. Johnson
suggests that the move was more likely made to satisfy the restless colonists'
need for slave labour as supply was dwindling with the expansion of the
Jesuit *aldeias*.[18] Whatever the reason, the colonists took full advantage of
the situation, enslaving Indians from their own settlements and also illegally
seizing them from within the *aldeias*. Further ruthless Portuguese campaigns
between 1575 and 1590 decimated those few who had survived the Caeté war
and the waves of disease that struck the area in 1562 and 1563.[19]

In the Caeté, a people who suffered greatly at the hands of their oppressors and who went down fighting, the author had found a figure to represent
Pernambuco, fiercely independent and *nativist* in sentiment and the scene
of regular violent uprisings that had produced a number of martyrs to the
federalist cause, of whom Nunes Machado was just the latest. This symbolic
purpose of the Caeté, as metaphor of the Pernambucan people, lies at the
heart of the poem's political and Indianist duality, and absolutely determines
the construction of Floresta's Indian, his character, his desires and his beliefs.
It is the identification of the Caeté as the original Pernambucan that provides
the foundation for Floresta's political expression and her defence of the
Praieira Revolt, its ideals and its hero. Furthermore, not only is the Caeté
Pernambucan, by a logical extension the true Pernambucan is also a Caeté.

In fact, Floresta is adamant in her identification of the Pernambucan people,
and Nunes Machado in particular, as descendants of the Caeté people. Describing Machado she says 'Dos bravos Cahetés se diz descendente, / Sua triste
raça jurou de vingar ...' (p. 22) and on the following page: 'Cahio o chefe
immortal / Dos bravos Pernambucanos!' (p. 23), as if the Pernambucans were

(Cambridge: Cambridge University Press, 1991), pp. 145–89 (p. 159).

[17] Hemming, pp. 165–6.

[18] H. B. Johnson, 'Portuguese Settlement, 1500–1580', in *Colonial Brazil*, ed. Leslie
Bethell (Cambridge: Cambridge University Press, 1991), pp. 1–38,(p. 25).

[19] See Johnson and Hemming for an overview of the history of the Caeté and other Indians
under colonial rule.

themselves an indigenous people fighting in self-defence against a foreign coloniser. This association is so central to the text, and the message that Floresta sought to communicate through it, because it is only by establishing Pernambuco's Indian ancestry that everything which is claimed for the Caeté, his natural and God-given ownership of the land, his noble character and his right to vengeance (all of which I will discuss below), can also be claimed for Machado, the Praieira Revolt and the wider federalist cause. This claim is explicit in the verse which first introduces the uprising:

> De peitos Brasileiros sahe o brado,
> ...
> – Eia! àvante! guerreiros libertemos
> A terra dos Cahetés, a terra nossa! (p. 22)

It is here, in Floresta's use of the Caeté as a symbol of a *nativist*, regional sense of identity, and as the source of legitimacy for federalist, separatist ideals, that *Lágrima* poses its most fundamental challenge to the ideology of the literary Indianist movement. The writer subverts a discourse founded on the need to establish national identity and unity, employing it instead to attack the very political system it is meant to endorse, and defend the forces that opposed the Imperial hegemony. This subversion from national to regional, unifying to dividing discourse is not only a radical and daring literary move on Floresta's part. I would suggest that it is also a profoundly insightful act of discursive appropriation: it could well be argued that the reality of the 'Brazilian Indian' – a patchwork of diverse peoples with differing customs and traditions – serves as a much better model for a federal system, recognising the social and economic interests and identity of each regional 'pátria', than for the unified and uniform Imperial Brazil which the Indianist movement was marshalled to construct.

This fundamental political difference between Floresta's text and those of other Indianist writers is the one overwhelming factor which shapes her portrayal of her Caeté 'hero', and indeed of the other human forces that appear in the poem. That said, Floresta's depiction of the Caeté simultaneously echoes many of the common motifs of Indianist texts. From the first moment that Floresta introduces the Caeté, which occurs towards the end of the first stanza, he is alone and sad: 'Vagava solitario um vulto de homem' (p. 7). This shadowy presence reflects the status of the Indian in Brazilian society: all but absent from view except in a symbolic role. Later in the poem Floresta goes on to acknowledge the limited number of surviving Indian communities when the Indian appeals to his 'Patria' saying: 'Recolhe o pranto meu, quando dispersos / Pelas vastas florestas tristes vagão / Os poucos filhos teus à morte escapos' (p. 11).

In describing the sad state of the surviving Indian population and their

severely reduced numbers, Floresta echoes her most famous contemporaries
Gonçalves Dias and Teixeira e Sousa. In Dias's 'O Canto do Piaga' the
unhappy fate of the Indians under colonial rule is predicted:

> Fugireis procurando um asilo,
> Triste asilo por ínvio sertão;
> Anhangá de prazer há de rir-se,
> Vendo os vossos quão poucos serão.[20]

In *Os Três Dias de um Noivado*, on the other hand, Teixeira e Sousa's Indian
hero recounts what has already befallen them:

> As que escaparam [...] se esconderam
> Lá pelas virgens matas do Amazonas!
> Destroçadas familias só ficaram
> [...] estes tristes, derradeiros restos.[21]

Both writers suggest that the only freedom and happiness the Indian community can hope to achieve is by isolating itself in the forests and backlands, an
idea which Floresta in turn expresses through the uncompromising figure of
Reality (p. 38). This suggestion flies in the face of the process of assimilation
favoured politically at the time, and throughout much of Brazilian history,
and a process that Floresta clearly advocates in her later writing, as I will
discuss in the final part of this chapter.

The opening pages of *Lágrima* are spent describing the Caeté both physically and morally. He is painted in typical aboriginal dress with bow and
arrows and feather adornments. At this early point in the poem Floresta has
referred to him only as a man, but the physical description she gives leaves
the reader in no doubt as to his Indian identity. He is strong and healthy, but
more importantly he is virtuous and from the beginning the writer establishes
a sharp contrast with the vices of the Portuguese coloniser, and in fact with
modern society as a whole, be it Portuguese or Brazilian, as the following
verse indicates:

> Em seu rosto expansivo não se vião
> Os gestos, as momices, que contráe
> A composta infiel physionomia
> Desses seres do mundo social. (p. 8)

The Caeté is also courageous, in juxtaposition to the cowardly Portuguese.

[20] Gonçalves Dias, *Poesia Indianista* (São Paulo: Martins Fontes, 2002), p. 12.
[21] Antonio Gonçalves Teixeira e Sousa, *Os Três Dias de um Noivado* (Rio de Janeiro: Typ.
de Paula Brito, 1844), pp. 71–2.

Floresta not only states this bravery explicitly, as when she describes him as 'O bravo, o destemido, o grão selvagem' (p. 9); the contrast between Indian and coloniser is also implicit in a consideration of the weapons they use: the Caeté carries a bow and arrows, but not a gun. That, we are told, is the weapon of tyrants and cowards, 'sob as quaes / Succumbe o rijo peito, vence o inerte! (p. 7). The Caeté has no riches of the sort valued by society; his soul is enriched by virtues 'que valem muito mais qu'esses thesouros' (p. 9), and he finds all his worldly wealth in nature.

The physical description Floresta gives of the Caeté is all but indistinguishable from the descriptions to be found in the eighteenth-century epics of Basílio da Gama and Santa Rita Durão, in which adornment with feathers and the carrying of non-firearm weapons, in particular a bow and arrows, are predominant motifs. In da Gama's *O Uraguay*, for example, the Indians describe themselves thus: 'E o arco e as settas e as vistosas pennas / São as nossas fantasticas riquezas.'[22] Where Floresta differs from these colonial forerunners, and in particular from Durão, who was vociferously pro-Portuguese and showed none of da Gama's sympathy for the indigenous way of life,[23] is in the value she ascribes to those motifs. For Floresta the Indian's feathers create an image of man in a state of natural innocence, which displays his health and strength.

Durão, on the other hand, condemns the Indians' nakedness, describing them as 'gente tão nojosa'.[24] Further, in *Lágrima*, the Caeté's bow and arrow are symbols of his bravery, guns being the weapon of cowards, a significance absent from the eighteenth-century texts. In fact, in *Caramuru*, it is precisely the firing of his gun that saves Diogo Alvarez from certain death at the hands of his Indian captives and earns him status and influence amongst them. For Durão the gun is a blatant symbol of the power and superiority of the 'civilised' Portuguese over the ignorant barbarity of the Indian.

These motifs of physical appearance are less apparent in the works of Floresta's early Indianist contemporaries, and those she is likely to have drawn most influence from. However, in *Os Três Dias de um Noivado* the absence of traditional Indian dress is equally significant. Teixeira e Sousa's hero Corimbaba is an educated, urbanised Indian and the author stresses that he never learnt how to shoot a bow and arrow, but he handles a rifle well (p. 92), whilst other Indians in the village still use traditional weapons. The poem is in part a consideration of the problematic identity of the assimilated Indian and the mestizo, accepted by neither the white nor Indian communities. As

---

[22] Basílio da Gama, 'O Uraguay', in *Epicos Brasileiros*, ed. F. A. de Varnhagen (Lisbon: [n. pub.], 1845), p. 23.

[23] See Treece, p. 59.

[24] José de Santa Rita Durão, 'Caramuru', in *Epicos Brasileiros*, ed. F. A. de Varnhagen (Lisbon: [n. pub.], 1845), p. 133.

such, Corimbaba's lack of bow and arrows, which differentiates him from his fellow Indians, is as significant as the Caeté's proudly displayed weapons. As a symbolic, 'original' Indian, whose purpose is to provide a contrast to the Portuguese, the Caeté's feathers, bow and arrows are indispensable.

Floresta's description of the Caeté's moral virtues echoes her contemporaries more closely, in particular Teixeira e Sousa. Whilst Gonçalves Dias primarily emphasises the Indians' bravery in battle,[25] *Os Três Dias de um Noivado* attributes to the Indians many of the same virtues as *Lágrima*. There is a mention of '... os seus talentos, / Seus feitos, seu valor, suas virtudes!' (p. 107), and we are told that 'Os crimes d'ambição desconheciam, / As fraudes, as intrigas, as versucias' (p. 16). The latter is echoed by Floresta's Caeté: 'Por nossos costumes singelos e simples / Em troco nos derão a fraude, a mentira' (*Lágrima*, p. 11).

Having completed her description of the Indian, Floresta goes on to describe the idyllic way of life that he has lost. In fact, shifting to the first person, she allows the Caeté to idealise his own life:

> Quanta vez, oh, lembrança doce-amarga!
> Depois de longa pesca fatigado,
> Ou voltando das selvas, onde eu ia
> As feras perseguir, alegres vinhão
> A meu encontro aqui, a esposa, os filhos
> Offerecer-me felises seus cuidados! ...
> Venturoso em triunfo me levavão
> Ao tosco asilo nosso, onde maior
> Que um pagé me julgava, onde Tupan
> Nosso puro prazer abençoava. (p. 16)

It is at this point in the poem that it becomes clear that Floresta's Caeté is not a nineteenth-century Indian long-since deprived of his land and culture; he is the timeless embodiment of the Caeté people, mourning the loss of a pre-Columbian paradise which lives on in the collective 'memory' of the Brazilian nation. His wife is given a name, Porangaba, which means 'beauty' in the Tupi language,[26] when the Caeté asks: 'Onde estão [...] / estes bens qu'erão nossos? / Porangaba perdi, perdi os filhos' (p. 17). The symbolism is clear: as figurative representative of his people, the Caeté has lost more than wife and children; he has lost the natural beauty of his way of life and more importantly, he has lost his future.

Gonçalves Dias and Teixeira e Sousa both make reference to the idyllic natural life which the Indians have lost, but neither go into detail, nor do they invoke the sense of nostalgia to be found in Floresta's writing. This

---

[25] See, for example, Dias, pp. 3, 4, 17, 19 and 42.
[26] According to Gonçalves Dias in his *Dicionário da Língua Tupi*, in Dias, pp. 193–360.

nostalgia serves to heighten the melancholy tone that pervades the poem, reaffirming its true purpose as a lament for the failed revolution and the death of Machado. The positive portrayal of pre-Columbian life was in fact a vital aspect of the Indianist movement as it contested the colonial concept of a barbarous, immoral existence from which the Indian had been saved by European civilisation and Christianity. In fact, it is in these romantic, idealised descriptions of the indigenous way of life before colonisation that *Lágrima* can most clearly be considered an Indianist text.

Following on from the loss of this idyllic existence is the popular Indianist motif that the Native Indian would choose death in preference to a life of slavery, and this can be found in the works of both Dias (pp. 22, 23 and 30) and Teixeira e Sousa (p. 54). In *Lágrima* this concept of preferring death is in fact transferred onto Machado (an honourary Caeté). It is the Gênio do Brasil that anounces this: 'De quarenta e nove o Heróe preclaro, / Que jamais com outro s'ha de confundir, / A morte a opprobrio soube preferir' (p. 29). By borrowing this stereotype of Indian bravery and nobility for her real hero, Floresta not only affords him the attributes of the noble savage, but also implies that the centralised, hegemonic rule of Empire, which the defeat of the revolt secured, is itself a form of slavery.

Throughout Floresta's poem a strong link is made between the Caeté and nature, establishing his simultaneous origins in and claim to the land. In the opening lines of the work he is located in a rural setting, and nature shapes him: 'Era da natureza o filho altivo, / Tão simples como ella' (p. 9). The Indian is both son and lord of the natural elements which surround him; he is referred to as the 'filho das bosques' (p. 35), but his ownership is also frequently stressed (e.g. pp. 9 and 17).

The Indian's claim to the land is in fact established in three ways: through his close relation with nature itself; as his birth-right, inherited from his fore-fathers: 'Ó terra de meus pais, ó Patria minha!' (p. 11); and finally as a God-given right: 'Era um Caheté, que vagava / Na terra, que Deos lhe dêo (p. 9). This Indian ownership is vital to the underlying purpose of the poem, because it is through the symbolic ancestral Caeté that the Pernambucan people – that is to say the supporters of the Praieira Revolt and defenders of 'liberty' – are also constructed as rightful owners of the land, and the Portuguese coloniser is automatically cast as thief and usurper: 'os tyrannos / Que a nossa terra tomarão!' (p. 18).

The need to establish the Indian's link to and ownership of the land was in fact central to the ideology behind the Indianist movement, since the Indian, as symbolic representative of true Brazilian identity, also establishes the Brazilian people's right to the land; that is to say, to independence. It is therefore not surprising that Floresta can again be seen to echo common Indianist motifs, particularly in the close association of the Indian with nature. One of these motifs is the use of epithets such as 'filho da natureza'. These are particularly common in Teixeira e Sousa's text and Dias uses 'filho das selvas' in the poem 'I-Juca-Pirama'.[27] Like Floresta, Dias also states the Indians' ownership of the land as an indisputable fact, writing: 'E a terra em que pisam, e os campos e os rios / Que assaltam, são nossos.'[28]

What is so significant in Floresta's construction of the Caeté's right to the land is that the god who bequeathed him the land is not the deity of an aboriginal belief system; it is the Christian God brought by the colonisers that Floresta uses to legitimise the Indian's cause. In fact the God of Christianity is an underlying presence throughout the poem. Ironically, whilst this allows her to give religious legitimacy to her hero Nunes Machado and the federalist cause of the Praieira Revolt, she is unable to denounce the process of catechesis which went hand in hand with colonialism and played a significant part in the destruction of the indigenous way of life which the poem laments, as that would mean denying Catholicism as the true and legitimate religion of the new Brazil she hoped for.

The question of religion and the process of conversion is a problematic presence in many Indianist texts and is dealt with in varying ways. For example, in his famous early poem 'O Canto do Índio', Gonçalves Dias describes how a young Indian chief falls passionately in love with a beautiful white virgin whom he sees bathing in a river. He declares that although he hates her kind, he is willing to be the white man's slave just to be able to possess her.[29] David Treece interprets this poem as an allegory of the process of subjection through the catechesis,[30] and it is hard to imagine that the poet could have intended it to be read literally, although many have done so, when elsewhere his warriors are brave, bloodthirsty and defiant, willing to choose death over slavery. Adopting Treece's reading, 'O Canto do Índio' is a harsh condemnation of the catechesis, in which the church is held directly responsible for the Indians' loss of freedom, status and identity.

Teixeira e Sousa, on the other hand, does not take his criticisms so far. In fact, in the prologue to *Os Três Dias de um Noivado*, he highlights the importance of Christian faith, writing that he wanted the idea of 'uma religião benefica', 'uma moral santa' and 'uma virtude inhabalavel' (p. xxi) to be at the heart of the poem. The Guarani Indians of the text are devout Catholics and, as the poem begins, the central couple are returning 'Da igreja de São Pedro, onde prestaram / O nupcial, solemne, eterno voto'. What Teixeira e Sousa condemns are the 'vãos pretextos religiosos' used to justify the persecution and extermination of the indigenous peoples. He returns to the theme

27   Dias, p. 48.
28   Dias, p. 17.
29   Dias, p. 15.
30   Treece, pp. 120–23.

later in the poem, stating: 'Tornou-se a religião vil interesse, / Monopolio, e pretexto de conquistas!'[31]

It is exactly this position that Floresta also adopts in *Lágrima*, describing the colonisers as, 'tyrannos oppressores, / Qu'em nome do piedoso céo viérão / Tirar-nos estes bens qu'o céo nos dera!' (p. 11). Constância Lima Duarte suggests that this passage is a condemnation of the catechism.[32] However, whilst it is clear that Floresta denounces the abuses inflicted in the name of conversion, like Teixeira e Sousa, what she is actually condemning is the wider condition of Portugal's colonial project, which massacred and enslaved under the banner of Catholicism. She is unable to denounce the conversion of the Indian because the Christian faith lies at the heart of her hopes for the future of the nation; therefore only a Christian Indian can represent the nation's people.

The Caeté's own religious beliefs, though not stated explicitly, are certainly evident in the text. Although he mentions Tupan and Anhangá (pp. 16 and 17), good and bad indigenous deities which had long-since been constructed by Christian observers as God and Satan, they appear as part of a nostalgic description of an idyllic past, and serve more as a device to evoke a romantic, exotic world rather than as a reflection of the Caeté's true beliefs. His Christian faith is revealed when, on discovering the body of Machado, the distraught Indian 'Os joelhos dobra! Do céo inda espera / Prodigio estupendo! que poz Las'ro em pé!' (p. 24) and Floresta makes it clear that she considers Christianity to be the best path for the Caeté (e.g. p. 36).

The only aspect of the Caeté's representation which might be considered 'unchristian' is the vengeance he seeks for Machado's death, but Floresta justifies this by portraying such an attack as divine retribution (p. 14). So not only does Floresta establish the cause of the Indian, as legitimate owner of the land, to be right in the eyes of God, she implies that the action he takes to avenge his loss is also sanctioned; in fact it becomes a virtue: 'Vingança de selvagem tão tremenda, / Tão nobre como elle!' (p. 17). Every unhappiness to befall the Portuguese nation is represented as punishment for the crimes committed against the indigenous peoples of Brazil, and both God and the massacred Indians achieve vengeance through this misfortune, which includes such events as the Inquisition and the Spanish occupation of Portugal from 1580 to 1640 (p. 14). The Caeté sets out to complete the task by avenging the death of Nunes Machado, saying: 'De uma inteira, infeliz, extincta raça ... / Vingando-te eu a vingo' (p. 32).

Duarte takes this thirst for vengeance as evidence that the Caeté is not a noble savage, observing that 'o selvagem não é tão bom assim', and therefore concluding that Floresta challenges the European philosophical origins of

---

31 Sousa, pp. 24, 71 and 108 respectively.
32 Duarte, *Vida e Obra*, p. 116.

the idealisation of the Indian, instead portraying him in a more real, human light.[33] Yet Floresta makes a clear distinction between the violence of the 'Portuguese' and the desire for violence in the Caeté. In fact she states quite categorically that it is a mark of nobility and sanctioned by God. What must be taken into account is that the Caeté's vengeful desire, and its religious and moral legitimisation, are essential to the purpose of the poem since it in turn justifies the violence of the Praieira Revolt and its hero Machado, and indeed of any future struggles for the political cause of 'liberty'.

One of the most striking contrasts between Floresta's portrayal of the Brazilian Indian and that of her Indianist contemporaries is her harsh criticism of those tribes that formed allegiances with the colonising power. It is curious that the historical figures she refers to are the very same characters who would be made famous by the two most important exponents of the Indianist movement, Gonçalves Dias and José de Alencar, although her interpretation of their actions differs considerably.

The first of these figures is Tabira (whom she refers to as Tapeirá), the subject of the poem of the same name by Gonçalves Dias, published in 1848. Tabira, fearless leader of the Tobajara, made a treaty with the Portuguese colonisers, who then renegued on that alliance, enslaving members of the tribe after they had defeated the Potiguares. Gonçalves Dias portrays Tabira as foolish and reckless: 'Chefe stólido, insano, imprudente' (p. 22), but also as extremely brave and loyal – the naive pawn in the oppressor's power struggle and therefore deserving of pity. Floresta, however, makes no excuse for his actions, unequivocally condemning the Indian chief for betraying his own people and going to war against fellow Indians of other tribes in the interests of the Portuguese:

> Maldito, ó maldito sejas
> Renegado Tapeirá!
> Teu nome em nossas florestas
> Em horror sempre será!
> Tabayares miserandos! raça escrava!
> Que a voz incautos desse chefe ouviste
> Mandando exterminar os irmãos teus,
> Para um povo estrangeiro auxiliar! (p. 12)

The second historical figure Floresta refers to is Antonio Filipe Camarão – the Portuguese name given to Poti, brother of the chief of the Pitiguara tribe immortalised by José de Alencar more than ten years later as the devoted friend of Martim Soares in *Iracema*. In this instance the contrast between the two writers' approaches is much more extreme, reflecting the more funda-

---

[33] Duarte, *Vida e Obra*, p. 128.

mental difference between Floresta's position and the pro-establishment, apologist position adopted by Alencar. In Alencar's novel Camarão, or Poti as he is primarily called, is a hero, a true and loyal friend to Soares and a brave, patriotic Brazilian because he had fought alongside the Portuguese against the French and Dutch.[34] Floresta, on the other hand, condemns him with the same vehemence as she does Tabira, saying: 'Desse Camarão, também renegado, / Que bravo guerreiro a Fama apregoa, / O titulo de nobre lá jaz despresado!' (p. 13).

If the author is scathing about those Indians whom she perceives to be traitors, she saves her real venom for the Portuguese. She accuses them of a vast array of vices, describing them as tyrants and usurpers, consumed by wild passions and steeped in vice (p. 8), ferocious, deceitful and barbarous (p. 11), miserable cowards (p. 17) and hypocrites (p. 19). She uses phrases such as 'Fero Luso ambicioso' (p. 17) and derides Portugal, suggesting the nation is in its final hour, 'em decadencia jasendo / Se debate, geme e chora! ... (p. 20). She describes the treatment of the Indians under colonial rule as a 'terrivel crime nefando' (p. 20). The colonisers' vices are held up in direct contrast to the Caeté's virtues, and Floresta points up the irony of the barbarous actions of the Portuguese next to the nobility of the Indian. The Caeté himself voices this idea, saying: 'De barb'ros nos dando o nome, que delles / na antiga e moderna Historia se tira' (p. 11).

Vilification of the Portuguese colonisers is typical of the early phase of Indianist literature, which vehemently condemned the abuses of colonisation. Where Floresta's approach differs so significantly from her contemporaries is that it is clearly not just the Portuguese that she is criticising in *Lágrima*, although that is what she seeks to imply. Within the contemporary setting of a *nativist* uprising, the enemy against whom she takes up her pen is essentially the conservative, centralised political elite under the Emperor Pedro II. When those responsible for Machado's death are described as 'Os anti-Brasileiros … Patricidas! ...' (p. 28), and when describing the barbaric displaying of the severed heads and hands of rebels, it is clearly the government forces of the day that Floresta is criticising.[35] Almost thirty years after independence, being 'Portuguese' in Floresta's poem is clearly determined by a person's political persuasions rather than place of birth. Therefore any criticism of the Portuguese also contains an implicit condemnation of the current political elite.

In fact, on occasion her criticism is considerably less than implicit. On the opening page of the poem, Floresta launches a brief but audaciously overt

---

[34]   See the 'Notas do Autor' in José de Alencar, *Iracema* (São Paulo: Editora Moderna, 1984), p. 47.

[35]   This is harsh criticism indeed: as 'patricidas', they have not only killed Nunes Machado, the father of the revolt and the ideals it represents (in the poem), by thwarting federalism they have also killed the nation.

attack on the very principle of monarchy when her first words to describe the wandering figure (not yet identified as the Caeté) are: 'Não lhe cingia a fronte um diadema, / Insignia de oppressor da humanidade' (p. 7). It is perhaps surprising that such a confrontational remark should have escaped the censorship which the poem apparently suffered, but it is the only explicit condemnation of Imperial rule to appear in the text. From then on, in order to facilitate the identification of hero and villain, Floresta attempts to establish a vastly over-simplistic dichotomy in which anyone who is not Indian is Portuguese, and vice versa. This fallacy she attempts to resolve with the equally improbable suggestion that all true Pernambucans are descended from the Caeté, as discussed above.

It is Floresta's attempt to reconcile the colonial setting of the Indianist genre with the contemporary context of her own political interests that leads her to rely on such problematic and unsustainable human definitions. Such difficulties may in part explain her decision to introduce allegorical figures into the poem, representations which can supersede the historical and geographical connotations and constraints of both Indian and Portuguese.

The first allegorical figure to appear is the 'Genio do Brasil', an ambiguous, faceless entity who appears to serve as both defender and personification of the nation. Earlier in the poem the Caeté had called upon this spirit for assistance: 'Ó Genio do Brasil, às plagas tuas / Volta ... oh! Volta a vingar os filhos teus!' (p. 21), but when the Genio does appear it is not to fight, but to comfort and reassure the Caeté. The spirit makes a lengthy speech praising Nunes Machado and confirming his place in history (pp. 28–30). This speech leaves the Caeté inspired to avenge Machado's death and with that purpose in mind he sets out for Recife. The 'Genio do Brasil' was already a familiar figure in Indianist literature, appearing in Ladislau dos Santos Titara's epic poem *Paraguassú* (1835). However, whilst Floresta's spirit appears as a disembodied voice to whom no physical characteristics are ascribed, Titara's figure, who defends the principles of 'Liberty, Courage, Unity and Glory', takes the form of an Indian warrior complete with feather headdress and animal skins.[36]

The 'Genio do Brasil' then disappears from the narrative, but is quickly replaced by Reality, in the form of an ugly old woman who stops the Caeté before he can reach the provincial capital and realise his plans for vengeance. Reality is the voice of cynicism in the poem, warning the Caeté that no political party is concerned for his welfare, and that all are driven by self-interest alone. She advises him to return to the depths of the forests, the only place where he has any chance of peace and contentment. However, while

---

[36] Treece, p. 95. Although not identified as such, the literary function of the Genio also appears to be fulfilled in Teixeira e Sousa's *Os Três Dias de um Noivado* by the figure of the old man whom Corimbaba encounters in the Forest.

she is speaking, another figure, a beautiful virgin, appears. This virgin, whom the old woman subsequently identifies as Liberty, is the complete antithesis of the figure of Reality. Whilst Reality's earthly origins are stressed, Liberty descends from above on golden clouds and remains suspended out of reach at all times. Reality stands beside the Caeté and talks to him at length, but Liberty does not speak or interact with him at any time and Reality's ugliness contrasts with the beauty of the virgin, her throne of roses and the sweet music that accompanies her arrival.

It is for the figure of Liberty, more than any other, that Floresta draws on a well-established and immediately recognisable representation. Maurice Agulhon states that 'Liberty, together with its image and attributes, came from Roman antiquity, and the whole allegorical apparatus was codified for artists in the seventeenth century.'[37] However, it was during the French Revolution and the subsequent Republics that the familiar figure of the young woman Liberty, or Marianne, as she came to be known, was firmly established in numerous poems, paintings and sculptures as the embodiment of the Republic itself. Floresta's representation of Liberty shows striking similarities to this nineteenth-century French image. Agulhon notes how she could be portrayed in poetry equally as virgin, goddess, lover and mother,[38] and there are aspects of all these in *Lágrima*: she is clearly identified as a virgin, but she also appears from heaven with a 'rosto divino' (p. 34), and the Caeté is immediately besotted by her: 'a sua alma começa a sentir / Vehemente amor, paixão primorosa' (p. 34). Meanwhile, those who fight to defend Liberty (i.e. the federalist rebels) are said to be her sons (p. 36).

Both Agulhon and Marina Warner comment on the significance of Delacroix's painting *Liberty Guiding the People* (1831), which was to become the most famous and influential visual representation of Liberty, and more particularly Revolution, in France and beyond.[39] As Warner observes, there is nothing vulnerable about the beauty of this woman – she surges forward with strong legs and muscly arms, gripping the flag and gun in big fists.[40] Likewise, Floresta's Liberty in no way needs the Caeté's protection, although he longs to offer it. The image presented is again one of commanding power and strength:

> Feiçoes tem risonhas, olhar cintillante,
> Um ar varonil, porte majestoso;
> Lê-se em sua fronte o fogo vibrante,
> Que o peito lhe abrasa, forte, grandioso! [...]

---

[37] Maurice Agulhon, *Marianne into Battle: Republican Imagery and Symbolism in France, 1789–1890*, trans. Janet Lloyd (Cambridge: Cambridge University Press, 1981), p. 11.

[38] Agulhon, pp. 40–1.

[39] Agulhon, p. 38, and Marina Warner, *Monuments and Maidens: The Allegory of the Female Form* (London: Butler & Tanner, 1985), pp. 270–2.

[40] Warner, p. 270.

> Da Liberdade um sorriso
> De desprezo esmagador
> Responde só aos uivos
> Do Despotismo eversor ... (pp. 34 and 37)

Where Floresta's portrayal differs from the traditional Liberty of the French
Republic is in her religious association. Although the French image tended
to 'borrow from the Catholic cult of the Virgin Mary its rhetoric of worship
and representation', it was in fact 'a secular allegory quite distinct from –
indeed opposed to – Christianity'.[41] Floresta, on the other hand, makes it
quite clear that Liberty and Christianity are indistinguishable: 'Tu dobras o
joelho! ... oh! sim adora; / Adora o, que na vida mais tu prezas; / A Liberdade adora e nella Deos' (p. 36). Floresta is clearly distancing herself from
the anti-Catholic discourse associated with the French Republic, indicating
that in her vision, Christianity is not just possible but an essential part of the
republic which, in *Lágrima* at least, she hoped and believed Brazil would
one day become.

However, this is the only point on which the two representations diverge
significantly. In fact, for the most part Floresta appears keen to emphasise
the origins of her divine virgin. The quotation from Victor Hugo with which
she introduces the poem (and which significantly also maintains the Christian
connection) is a clear declaration of Liberty's French inspiration: '... fille
sainte de Dieu, / Liberté! Pur flambeau de la gloire orageuse, / Non, je ne
t'ai point dit adieu!' (p. 1).[42] Floresta's employment of this self-consciously
French allegory would have created a clear iconographical link with the
French Revolution. Thus Floresta's use of this allegorical, female Liberty
takes on a double significance: not only does she represent freedom, both
political and social; she is quite specifically the symbolic representation of
the Republic, reiterating the justification of the Praieira faction's cause. If
Liberty is on the side of the rebels, Despotism must, by definition, walk with
the monarchy and ruling oligarchy against whom they fought.

However, the figure of Liberty also serves a third, somewhat different purpose
within the specifically Brazilian context of Indianist discourse. Floresta's depiction of the Caeté falling passionately in love with Liberty is in fact an interesting variation on a common motif in Indianist literature – that of the brave,
proud Indian falling in love with the white virgin and becoming her slave.
The most obvious examples of this are Gonçalves Dias's poem 'O Canto do

---

[41] Agulhon, pp. 8 and 57.

[42] By quoting Hugo, Floresta also establishes the poem's Romantic credentials: Hugo was
one of the early French Romantics whose work had a considerable influence on the development of Romanticism in Brazil. Gonçalves Dias also introduced the Indianist poem 'O Gigante
de Pedra', which appeared in his *Ultimos Cantos* (1851), with a quotation from Hugo.

Índio' (discussed above), which pre-dates *Lágrima*, appearing in his *Primeiros Cantos* in 1846, and the character of Peri in Alencar's 1857 novel *O Guarani*. These two examples adopt very different positions, with Dias offering an implicit indictment of the insidious suppression and enslavement of the Indian through conversion to Catholicism whilst Alencar praises and naturalises his submissive Indian's devotion. Despite this essential difference, both instances represent the repression and loss of identity of the Indian in the face of the colonising culture. By altering the symbolic significance of the virgin, Floresta turns a negative connotation into a positive one: the Caeté is rediscovering his love of freedom and is inspired to fight to defend her. He is strengthened by the encounter, not weakened, as is clearly the case elsewhere.

Constância Lima Duarte also draws attention to this relationship. However, she suggests that its significance lies in the fact that, unlike other Indian characters who fall at the feet of the 'virgem-branca-pura', as a religious or purely female image, the Caeté is able to 'resistir ao apelo da Virgem e ouvir a voz da razão que lhe diz: "Busca as matas, lá somente / Gozarás da Liberdade"'.[43] Such an interpretation denies the overwhelmingly positive value Floresta ascribes to the figure of Liberty, implying instead that, like the other white virgins of Indianist literature, she represents a dangerous threat to the Indian's cultural identity, from which the Caeté alone successfully escapes. Yet in truth it is Reality herself who reassures the Caeté of Liberty's indestructibility and even instructs him to adore her (*Lágrima*, pp. 36–7, quoted above). I would suggest that the ambiguous note regarding the Caeté's future freedom serves a different purpose: reading further, Reality goes on to say that he might indeed have enjoyed liberty 'aqui' (i.e. within society rather than hidden away in the forests), if others were more like Nunes Machado. In other words, Reality's pessimistic predictions function as a lament of Machado's death and the failure of the Praieira Revolt and not, as Duarte suggests, as a denunciation of what Liberty has to offer the Caeté.

Despotism, the last of the allegorical figures to be revealed, is a vision from hell, and thus completes the triumvirate with earthly Reality and heavenly Liberty. Interestingly, Floresta no longer employs the female form, or indeed the human form at all, to represent Despotism, choosing instead the image of the snake with its Satanic associations of corruption and trickery: 'um monstro enroscado, / Feroz simulando enorme serpente!' (p. 34). In this, Floresta is maintaining a long-standing tradition in Indianist literature in which the snake appears frequently, often as a symbol of the evils of colonial corruption, or as an omen of any unidentified danger. It is a snake, symbolising the corrupt control of the Jesuits, that kills the tragic Indian heroine of Basílio da Gama's *O Uraguai*,[44] and in Teixeira e Sousa's *Três Dias de um*

---

43 Duarte, *Vida e Obra*, p. 128.
44 See Treece, p. 58.

Noivado, an incident in which an Indian boy attempts to save a dove that is being killed by a snake, and accidentally kills them both, serves as an omen of the poem's tragic denouement.

Observing the depiction of the Caeté's miserable condition, Constância Lima Duarte concludes her analysis of *Lágrima* with a powerful claim for the text. She suggests that Floresta's focus on the Indian's defeat and destruction 'posibilita[m] considerar este poema como um protesto pela estereotipia que se fazia do indígena', and that 'mais que um poema "indianista" temos talvez uma das primeiras abordagens de cunho indigenista de nossa literatura'.[45] However, I would suggest that this claim misinterprets Floresta's motivation for writing the poem and considerably underestimates the idealisation and allegorisation of the Caeté.

One passage, which particularly fuels Duarte's interpretation, contains what at first appears to be a rare moment of brutal honesty and insight for the time. Through the voice of Reality, Floresta describes the social and political isolation facing her Caeté hero:

> Em campo eil-o agora co'as armas na mão!
> Mas seja um partido, ou outro que vença
> A tua ventura não creias farão!
> São outros seus planos, outra a sua crença ... (p. 33)

Yet, whilst this may be an accurate representation of the situation of the nineteenth-century Indian in Imperial Brazilian society, it is also essential to the political purpose of *Lágrima*. The poem is a lament of the defeat of the Praieira revolt and the death of Nunes Machado. As such, its symbolic Indian hero must be a defeated, tragic figure, just as the real hero Machado is. Considering that this is where Floresta's real interest lay, as I have already demonstrated, it seems that the primary motivation behind her portrayal of the defeated Indian is as a romantic image to enhance the mournful tone of the text. Such suspicions are confirmed by the contrasting, grossly unrealistic suggestion that things could have been different for the Indian:

> Busca as matas, lá somente
> Gosarás da Liberdade,

---

[45]   Duarte, *Vida e Obra*, p. 126. This claim is also supported and reiterated by Christina Ramalho in her discussion of *Lágrima* ('Um Indianismo transgressor: Nísia Floresta', in *Elas escrevem o épico* (Florianópolis: Editora Mulheres; EDUNISC, 2005), pp. 55–67. The distinction Duarte draws between Indianism and 'indigenism' is based on definitions established by Maria José de Queiroz in her unpublished manuscript entitled 'Do Indianismo ao Indigenismo – Nas letras hispano-americanas', in which the latter is defined as a discourse '[que] foge às considerações estéticas, ao exoticismo, ao espetáculo. Indaga pelo homem', which, in other words, represents the Indian 'como ele é'. Quoted in Duarte, *Vida e Obra*, p. 124.

Que aqui terias
Talvez gosado,
Se todos fossem
NUNES MACHADO! (p. 38)

It is evident that Floresta's comment on her symbolic hero's disenfranchise-
ment is in fact a reflection of her disappointment with the defeat of pure
political ideals in the face of corrupt political interests rather than a comment
on the very real, fundamental exclusion of the Indian from contemporary
Brazilian society. Besides which, the suggestion that Floresta expresses a
genuine concern for the condition of the Caeté Indians overlooks the very
core of the text: that the Caeté is here serving as a representation of the
Pernambucan people. It is therefore the political abandonment of the people
as a whole that Floresta is describing here, and in turn implying that only
federalism, embodied by Machado, can politically liberate the disenfran-
chised population.

Duarte is correct when she describes the Caeté as 'um índio vencido.
Desde o início, vencido. [...] de protagonista da história Brasileira ele passa
neste poema a mero espectador, uma vez que se encontra à margem do
processo histórico', and when she notes how this representation contrasts
with Alencar's submissive Peri and the idealised bravery of Dias's warriors.[46]
What she does not acknowledge is that this divergence stems from *Lágrima*'s
radically different political and ideological basis compared with other Indianist texts. Whether critic of or apologist for the colonial project, Indianist
writers celebrated the nation and the gaining of a genuine, united Brazilian
identity. Floresta, on the other hand, has nothing to celebrate.

In truth, I would suggest, Floresta's Indian is utterly and undeniably idealised: he operates outside of any specific time frame and all his characteristics,
including his desire for vengeance, are sanctified. He cannot be considered to
be a depiction of the nineteenth-century Indian after more than three centuries of contact, abuse, discrimination and miscegenation; he must be read
as a purely artificial device, a deliberate, abstract anachronism. It is for this
reason, over and above Floresta's use of the classically Indianist motifs I
have identified, that I would contest Duarte's interpretation of the poem and
suggest that *Lágrima* must be considered as an Indianist text, rather than an
indigenist one. However, the text very clearly does not fit the traditional Indianist mould either, and it might even be suggested that it has a part to play
in reshaping that mould. The Indianist movement in Brazil was at all times
ideologically and economically endorsed and appropriated by the Imperial
court in Rio, and Floresta subverts this nationalist discourse, turning it on
its head to defend federal republicanism and uncompromisingly condemn

---

46 Duarte, *Vida e Obra*, pp. 119–20 and 124.

the monarchy and pseudo-colonial power of the new Brazilian elite. At first glance, the acceptable face of Indianism serves to mask the true nature of the text, but beneath this cover, Floresta's Indian in fact enhances the subversive force of her attack on Brazil's monarchical hegemony by appropriating and deconstructing the establishment's own discourse of self-justification.

Downplaying the underlying political purpose of the poem, which necessitates a wholly artificial and slanted construction of the Indian, Duarte looks to *Lágrima* for evidence of Floresta's understanding of the plight of the contemporary Indian. Instead, I would contend, we must turn to her later writings, both social commentary and *ufanismo*, to draw conclusions regarding the writer's perception of the 'real' Indians and the position she envisaged for them in nineteenth-century Brazilian society. What we find reveals some interesting contrasts and correlations with her Indianist text.

The Indian as a social 'reality'

Whilst *Lágrima* is Floresta's only text that might be identified with the Indianist movement, references to the contemporary indigenous population and a concern for their fate appear in several of her texts. These references are generally brief and certainly never amount to a significant focus. The work in which Floresta devotes most space to a consideration of the native Indian population is *Opúsculo Humanitário*, with four of its sixty-two chapters dealing with the subject. However, this is the very last issue to be addressed in an extensive text that deals with a wide range of the writer's concerns, suggesting that the Indian was more of an afterthought than a priority. It is certainly clear that across all Floresta's works the plight of the native Indian receives considerably less attention than the condition of the black slave and the pernicious effect of slavery on society. Not only is *Opúsculo* her only text to discuss the contemporary Indian at any length, it is also her only Brazilian publication to do so; all other references, however brief, appear in works which were written and published in Europe.

In common with *Lágrima*, Floresta emphasises the abuses suffered by the Indian population at the hands of the colonisers and their ongoing mistreatment in the newly independent nation. In *Opúsculo* she quotes at length from a recently published work which includes detailed descriptions of the cruel treatment of Indians that the author had witnessed on his travels in the province of Minas Gerais, including enforced labour, the sexual abuse of Indian women and the extermination of an entire community by deliberate infection with measles (*Opúsculo*, pp. 154–5). Floresta herself goes so far as to suggest that the aboriginal population 'em pouco desaparecerão talvez inteiramente do solo brasileiro' (p. 150). In 'Viagem Magnética', a brief, *ufanistic* description of Brazil's natural resources and one of the five essays in *Cintilações de uma Alma Brasileira*, published in Florence in 1859, she describes 'os infelizes aborígines, aos quais os homens da civilização tudo arrebataram, e obstinam-se ainda a perseguir até dentro dos últimos recessos de suas inacessíveis florestas' ('Viagem', p. 165). Here, as in *Lágrima*, we find the popular Indianist idea that it is only hidden away in the natural surroundings of the forests that the native Indian finds peace, an idea reiterated also in *Opúsculo*, where those who are not 'de mais em mais entranhado em nossas florestas', must live in 'mesquinhas e desorganizadas aldeias' (p. 143).

However, unlike the Indianist construction echoed in *Lágrima*, in which the sanctuary of the forest is the only option for the Indian, in *Opúsculo* Floresta in fact suggests that there is an alternative future in which the Indian can participate actively as a valuable citizen of the nation. She makes it clear that the 'civilisation' and integration of the native population was and is a positive and necessary endeavour, both for the Indian and for Brazil. She states that the Indian people have the right to 'melhor sorte e os elementos necessarios para, bem dirigido, conosco marchar na via do progresso civilizador!' (*Opúsculo*, p. 145), and suggests that the government must take steps to facilitate the civilisation of the Indians, calling for 'medidas enérgicas para substituir, à perseguição e barbaria havidas com esses infelizes, maneiras conciliadoras e humanas' (p. 152). She believes that the uncivilised, abused Indian is of no benefit to the nation, but a proper education would 'arrancar essa pura, digna porção do povo brasileiro à vida em que vegeta e torná-la útil' (p. 156). More than this, Floresta implies that the failure of this civilising mission is to blame for the introduction of slavery and all the social ills which she, and so many of her contemporaries, attached to it:

> Negligenciando-se a civilização dos selvagens, tem-se não somente tirado ao Brasil os seus mais legítimos e empenhados defensores, mas também, a todos os seus filhos, a vantagem de serem servidos por braços livres dos que, nascendo em nosso mesmo solo, não nos teriam por sem dúvida transmitido vícios estranhos, inextinguíveis calamidades. (p. 153)

Central to this process of 'civilisation' is, of course, the catechesis. Floresta's later texts reveal more clearly a position she had hinted at rather than stated in *Lágrima*, as discussed above. Whilst she acknowledges that terrible abuses have been committed in the name of religious conversion, she believes that such a conversion is an essential part of the civilising process and of immense benefit to the Indian. In fact she describes the arrival of the Portuguese in the following terms: 'onde os homens da civilização vieram com a religião do Cristo oferecer-te as suas vantagens para fazer de ti um povo melhor' (*Opúsculo*, p. 144). However, this is only a description of the ideal theory; Floresta makes it clear that the reality of abuse and enslavement was completely unchristian, writing of the pre-Columbian Indian, in a sentence in which italics speak louder than words, 'sua sorte era preferível à que depois lhes trouxe o *cristianismo* de seus vencedores' (p. 147). Floresta praises Anchieta and the Jesuit *aldeias* for their paternal care and education of the Indian and she laments their demise (p. 145). She goes on to spell out her position more clearly, writing that the Indian will be justified in resisting 'enquanto os nossos civilizadores cristãos não quiserem compreender que somente pala-vras persuasivas e práticas evangélicas – e não o ferro, o veneno, e a licença – devem empregar para a civilização dos restos dessa grande e nobre raça' (pp. 155–6).

Floresta not only indicates that, with proper guidance, the Indian can partici-pate fully in Brazilian nationhood, she also gives examples of those who have already proved their patriotism. She lists several Indian leaders 'que, fiéis aos seus ingratos aliados, tantos e tão relevantes serviços prestaram à causa da civilização' (p. 145). Curiously, among the list is Antônio Filipe Camarão, contradicting Floresta's earlier criticism in *Lágrima*, in which she condemns this Potiguar ally of Martim Soares, the Portuguese pacifier of Ceará, as a renegade (quoted above on p. 105). She defends the good character of the Indians, condemning those who have misrepresented them as being incapable, disloyal and cowardly, including in her criticism 'alguns dos nossos escrevin-hadores' (p. 145) in a possible allusion to some early and pre-Indianist writers. The Indians are described as noble, pure and innocent, and it is suggested that they are driven to violence only in defence of their families (p. 155).

In *Lágrima* Floresta clearly establishes the Caeté's claim to the land in the face of Portuguese invasion; in *Opúsculo* this claim is much more ambig-uous. Whilst the Indian still has an undeniable right to Brazil's riches, those riches are no longer presented as being his alone. Although the colonisers are initially introduced as 'usurpadores' (*Opúsculo*, p. 143), this position is not maintained through the text. The Christian values of the Old World are put forward as the ideal state for the Indian, and those natives who fought alongside the Portuguese to expel the Dutch are exalted: '(d)essa raça que cooperou para que o Brasil não fosse então arrancado ao povo que o havia descoberto' (p. 149). Here it would appear that the Portuguese who 'discov-ered' the land are given the strongest claim to it. This contrast between *Lágrima* and *Opúsculo* highlights the nature of the Caeté's role in the earlier text, in which he is the figurative representative of the 'true' Pernambucan, nativistic and federalist in sentiment, whose claim to ownership of the land legitimates the popular struggle against the 'Portuguese' elite. In a direct consideration of the social status of the contemporary Indian, as we find in *Opúsculo*, such radicalism is clearly impossible and counterproductive to the message of social improvement that Floresta sought to transmit. Unlike the symbolic Caeté, whose future is extinguished with the failure of the federalist project, the real Indian does have a future as a valuable citizen, but must be civilised and integrated into the essentially European reality of imperial Brazil if (s)he is to be of use to the nation.

However, what most sharply distinguishes Floresta's consideration of the Indian in *Opúsculo*, not only from *Lágrima* but also from most contemporary discussions of the aboriginal population, is her specific focus on indigenous women, and although she in fact goes on to discuss the situation of all Indians, she makes it clear where her particular interest lies (pp. 142–3). Floresta describes these women in much the same terms as she does white women, employing the same rhetoric and ascribing equivalent values. Early on, she states that Indian women are 'dignas, por suas virtudes inatas, de receberem educação moral e intellectual que as colocasse a par de nossas mulheres civilizadas' (p. 146), and she confirms that despite their lack of education and the abuse they have suffered, Indian women have provided examples of virtue and heroism that equal those of civilised women of all times and all nations. The example she gives of this heroism is the wife of Camarão, who fought alongside her husband against the Dutch and led a female battalion in the battle of Porto Calvo in 1637.[47] Floresta suggests that her bravery and constancy were greater than those of Joan of Arc (p. 149).

Unsurprisingly though, considering Floresta's developing ideas on women's role in society, she primarily constructs the Indian woman within the same domestic, relational identity, – as wife and mother – with which she configures her fellow white women. She paints a picture of the Indian woman as the ideal mother in past and present circumstances, constantly surrounded by her children and most importantly breast-feeding them herself, unlike many educated white mothers. She holds the Indian mothers up as an example for her compatriots to follow, describing them as 'ligadas dia e noite a seus filhinhos por mais fortes vínculos de natural afeição do que muitas mães da nossa sociedade' (p. 148). This positive comparison can also be found in her European writing in 'Viagem', where she writes: 'Esta é a mãe selvagem, mais tomada por sentimentos maternos, do que tantas mães civilizadas do grande mundo' (p. 165). Floresta even urges her readers to go and see these mothers: 'Ide vê-las, hoje mesmo, como nós as vimos, nos restos de algumas aldeias, ao norte e ao sul do Rio de Janeiro' (*Opúsculo*, pp. 147–8). Presented as a kind of exhibit to be visited and observed without interaction, this idealised image of the devoted mother serves merely as a symbol, a 'national emblem', as Ania Loomba describes it, 'called upon to literally and figuratively reproduce the nation'.[48] The symbolic role served by the Caeté in *Lágrima* is now displaced onto the generic Indian woman. Whilst the Caeté is an idealised original Pernambucan, Floresta uses the Indian woman as a potent symbol of patriotism as the mother of the nation, nourishing her child with complete dedication; she is a kind of Brazilian 'mother/land', the original mother of a good and healthy Brazil.

[47]   See *Opúsculo*, p. 149, note 193.
[48]   Loomba, p. 215.

For her example of the ideal wife, which inevitably accompanies the depiction of the perfect mother, Floresta turns again to history, or more specifically to popular Brazilian legend. The figure she chooses is Paraguaçu, the Indian wife of Diogo Alvares Caramuru, the hero of Santa Rita Durão's eponymous poem of 1781. Whilst the existence of Caramuru and his probably numerous Indian wives would appear to be based on historical events, successive retellings over several centuries had greatly exaggerated his significance and singled out Paraguaçu as 'a representative figure, an ideal symbol of the Indian convert and the embodiment of the Catholic ethic in the mestiço colonial family'.[49] Durão's interpretation of the legend, re-edited in the 1840s, in which Paraguaçu plays a secondary role, was to become 'the received version of the story'.[50] However, the early stages of the Indianist movement had produced an alternative interpretation in Ladislau dos Santos Titara's *Paraguassú*, published in 1835. In this epic poem, in which the Indian woman plays a symbolic role as mother of the protagonists involved in the struggle for independence which the poem charts, her Portuguese husband appears only in an explanatory note.

It is this nineteenth-century text by Santos Titara that echoes more closely the sentiments Floresta expresses in *Lágrima*, and in fact Durão's description of the Indians as generally barbarous and corrupt would appear to place him amongst those 'escrevinhadores' whom she condemns, as mentioned above. Yet the Paraguaçu Floresta adopts to exemplify wifely devotion is clearly Durão's whitened, neutralised heroine,[51] who converts to Catholicism and is baptised in the French court where she takes the name of her godmother Catherine of Medici. In fact, Floresta's Paraguaçu can scarcely be considered an Indian at all. She is described as 'civilizando-se ela mesma para amenizar-lhe [ao esposo] os dias, privado como se achava ele das comodidades européias' (*Opúsculo*, p. 148). However, she is clearly a devoted wife and perhaps more importantly, she is a devout Christian (i.e. Catholic) and a patriotic Brazilian. Floresta informs her reader that Paraguaçu helped her husband in his civilising mission and that after her baptism she returned to Bahia, where the couple continued 'no mútuo e constante empenho de utilizar aquela nascente colônia' (p. 148). It is evident from this example that in Floresta's view the good, patriotic Indian woman must embrace white Brazilian culture and turn her back on her Indian heritage.

Curiously, Floresta also borrows another Indian character from the Caramuru legend, this time as an example of spontaneous, self-sacrificing love. That character is Moema, Caramuru's spurned lover who swims after the

---

[49] Treece, p. 59.
[50] Treece, p. 59.
[51] In Durão's text, Paraguaçu is portrayed as being different from other Indians. It is even suggested that her skin tone is lighter (see Treece, pp. 64–5).

ship that carries him and Paraguaçu to France, drowning in the process. What is surprising is that in Durão's version, and other colonial accounts of the story, Moema is an extremely negative and threatening figure, symbolising the 'dangerous, dark sexuality of the Indian woman'.[52] In this instance Floresta distances herself from Durão's interpretation, in fact her portrayal of Moema, whom she describes as 'sensível e infeliz' (Opúsculo, p. 148), could not be further from the figure to be found in Caramuru. Treece observes that her defiant character 'survives into the Romantic tradition as an obstinate reminder of the failure to integrate the colonial empire through military and religious conquest'.[53] Whilst this more positive re-appropriation in nineteenth-century Indianist literature may have encouraged Floresta to make use of the figure of Moema, the description we find in Opúsculo in no way symbolises the evils or failings of the colonial project. Instead she is reduced to a passive and pathetic image of unrequited love, strangely at odds with Floresta's usual representation of active, useful womanhood.

Floresta's essentially idealised and objectified discussion of Indian motherhood, and in particular her use of figures from foundation myths to exemplify wifely devotion and self-sacrifice, are extremely significant. Her reliance on these fictitious characters, which she presents as if historically accurate, clearly indicates that she was unable to free herself from the figurative, mythical value ascribed to the Indian by the intellectual elite of the second reign. In the end the examples she gives are as removed from reality and as laden with symbolic significance as her Caeté. They paint a picture of the ideal wife and mother, not as a fair representation of the nineteenth-century Indian woman, but as a sanitised, fictionalised model for Floresta's educated white readers to admire and emulate.

After the chapter containing these lengthy examples, Floresta does turn her attention to a more practical consideration of the Indian woman's value to society, challenging the stereotypes of 'preguiça natural, falta de fé e repugnância por fixarem-se em qualquer lugar' (Opúsculo, p. 150). She states that she has seen indigenous women in the aldeias more occupied than the women of the poor classes in the cities, who themselves can hardly be called lazy (p. 150).[54] She also implies that her own family had at some time employed Indian servants when she writes 'elas são aptas para todo o gênero de trabalho e artefatos e, tanto as que tivemos a nosso serviço como as que se educaram entre nossa família, deram-nos sempre provas da mais constante

---

52 Treece, p. 65.
53 Treece, p. 65.
54 Curiously, she herself accuses lower-class Brazilian women of being idle in an earlier chapter (p. 124). It is unclear why she should now wish to imply that they are hard-working; such a contradiction suggests that Floresta is reluctant to overstate her white compatriots' inferiority to the idealised Indian women, although she has no qualms about describing the latter's superior maternal care.

dedicação' (p. 150), although this suggestion of first-hand knowledge could of course be a device to strengthen her argument. She observes that the Indian woman is generally 'dócil e boa' (p. 151) and that when this is not the case it is as a result of her mistreatment. Floresta goes on to compare them directly with the black slave women:

> As mulheres são não somente mais asseadas que as africanas e mais próprias a ajudar-nos a criar nossos filhos, servindo-nos com fidelidade e submissão, sem o servilismo e vícios das infelizes escravas, mas também susceptíveis das mais doces e nobres afeições. (p. 151)

Despite stating that they deserve an education equal to their 'civilised' (i.e. white) counterparts, it is clear that Floresta did not believe that indigenous women also deserved a status in society equal to that of white women. The position in which she envisages them is clearly beneath that of her readers, as loyal and submissive servants. This vision of social reality stands in stark contrast to the defiant and morally superior position in which she casts her Caeté, again emphasising his figurative, almost mythical purpose in *Lágrima*. Significantly, Floresta writes that the Indian woman is suitable to help 'us' rear 'our' children, indicating that, for all her recommendations for active Indian citizenship, she does not consider them to be part of that 'us' and therefore they are not even included in the partial claim to Brazilian nationhood afforded to white women. Her attitude towards the Indian could not be more clearly expressed than in the observation that 'de grandes virtudes são capazes e tão úteis nos podiam ser' (*Opúsculo*, p. 151).

In her consideration of both male and female Indians, it is significant that whilst Floresta defends the Indians' character and condemns the abuses they suffer, she fails to ascribe real value to their traditional way of life and belief systems. She can only view them from a standpoint that is white, Christian and essentially European in origin, and which defines itself as civilised. Despite being repeatedly presented as the original Brazilian, in order to operate as a useful, patriotic citizen and gain access to Brazilian nationhood the Indian must in fact embrace the 'civilized', Christian values of the 'usurpers'. Thus the indigenous population can symbolise Brazilianness, but can only conditionally belong to it. In Floresta's vision of useful citizenship, the original Indian, whose lost way of life she mourns in *Lágrima*, is indeed soon to disappear from Brazilian soil.

The description of the Indian in his traditional dress and natural surroundings, which we find in *Lágrima* and which is such an essential element in Indianist literature, is excluded from *Opúsculo*. However, it does appear in references to the indigenous population made by Floresta in her European texts. In 'Viagem' she provides a further idealised image of the native population, writing:

Na profundeza de alguma daquelas ainda virgens florestas, multiplicam-se
aos milhares várias raças que aproximam-se para unirem contra o comum
adversário, o povo civilizado [...]. Eu os vejo daqui, em seu estado natural:
os homens munidos de flechas pontudos, [...] as mulheres a caminhar
encurvadas sob a preciosa carga de suas crianças. ('Viagem', p. 165)

This image could be mistaken for a description of the Indian in the first
moments of colonisation; it is clear that Floresta does not attempt to portray
the complex reality of the nineteenth-century Indian, making only a brief
acknowledgement of their persecution. In fact, embedded, as it is, within an
account of Brazil's rich natural resources, the Indian appears as just another
example of the tropical flora and fauna which the essay describes. Thus, for
her European reader, the Indian is lost in the natural backdrop of lush vegeta-
tion and excluded from the image of Brazilian cultural and social life Floresta
simultaneously sought to portray.

An explanation for this limiting discourse can be found in the more substantial but equally *ufanistic* essay 'O Brasil', published in the same collection in
1859. In this text Floresta comments on the ignorance of Europeans regarding
the reality of Brazil and its inhabitants. She observes that most know only of
its scenery, animals and indigenous races, more or less accurately described
by foreign travellers ('O Brasil', p. 57). She recounts the surprise shown by
Europeans on meeting a white Brazilian (since most believe that 'todos os
Brasileiros devam ter o tom trigueiro das raças indígenas'), and the frequent
exclamation such meetings produce: 'Não é que pareça um Brasileiro!', on
which Floresta makes the sarcastic observation '(Que bela nota de senso de
humor, e de urbanidade!)' (p. 57).

It is probable that Floresta had herself encountered this reaction on a
number of occasions during her travels in Europe, which would account for
her evident frustration. However, her interest is more than personal; it is
clear that this ignorance regarding Brazil's social, intellectual and political
status concerned Floresta greatly and she takes pains to distinguish between
the stereotypical misconception of the native Indian with 'o lábio furado'
('O Brasil', p. 59) and the image of a civilised, westernised urban society,
which she wished to portray to her European readers. Her increasing sense of
patriotic purpose once writing in Europe (the subject of Chapter 6), explains
her reluctance to discuss the problematic position of the Indian in a society
which she preferred to present as civilised, Christian and white.

It is apparent that in all Floresta's depictions of the Brazilian Indian,
whether as timeless allegory or nineteenth-century 'reality', the pervasive
idealising discourse of the Enlightenment's noble savage and, more specifically, the tropes and traditions of Brazil's Indianist movement have a considerable influence on her approach. Whilst this influence confirms *Lágrima*'s
status as an Indianist text, it severely hampers her attempt to address the

genuine social condition of the indigenous population in contemporary society. However, beyond a consistent underlying idealisation, what we see are in fact three quite distinct constructions of the Indian with three very different purposes in mind.

In a text concerned with political ideals, the Caeté provides Floresta with the perfect representative of the Pernambucan people, and through his allegorical construction she can extend his right to land ownership and vengeance to the Praieira Revolt, and in turn sanctify the ideals and motivations of her real hero Nunes Machado. In *Opúsculo*, on the other hand, Floresta is concerned with the Indian's place in, and contribution to, society and the nation. The unifying nationalist/patriotic rhetoric within which she presents this text leads her to a generic 'Indian' people, denying the regional, tribal identity so central to *Lágrima*. Moreover, in her quest for a civilised Brazil, able to compete on an equal footing with Europe, the pure original Indian embodied in the Caeté is reconfigured as barbarous and must be civilised. Thus the fate of the allegorical and the genuine Indian are diametrically opposed. Whilst the Caeté remains culturally intact, he cannot survive physically; in fact he is already extinct. The Indian in *Opúsculo*, meanwhile, can enjoy an active, participatory existence in Brazilian society, but in the process his/her cultural identity is obliterated.

Finally, in Floresta's European essays she ostensibly comes full circle, yet the end result could not be further from the purpose to which she sets the symbolic 'hero' of *Lágrima*. Superficially, this third Indian has returned to the representation of the Caeté, but the Caeté's traditional, stereotypical garb served to remind the reader of his noble savage credentials and true Brazilian origins, and to differentiate him from the corrupt 'civilised' Portuguese. In this final construction, however, the Indian's clichéd appearance serves the opposite purpose, distinguishing him from the 'genuinely civilised', white Brazilian population. From internal emblem of national identity he has become the antithesis of a national identity constructed for and from Europe.

In the next chapter I will be looking at the writer's discussion of slavery and her attitude towards Brazil's black slave population. A comparison of her approach to the nation's two 'other' racial identities, both deeply problematic for the construction of the white, westernised society she sought to portray, reveals a number of fundamental differences which in fact highlight the relative extent of Floresta's engagement with the Indian population, however complex and stymied that engagement might be, in contrast with her fundamental exclusion of the slave from national identity and citizenship.

5

The Abolitionist

Since her death in 1885, Floresta's biographers have consistently identified her as an abolitionist, claims which are second only to her feminist label. Roberto Seidl suggests that she should be afforded 'o titulo incontestavel de precursora da propaganda das ideias e doutrinas abolicionistas'.[1] Rather more emphatically, Adauto da Câmara states that Floresta deserves to be 'inscrita no rol de Nabuco, Patrocínio, Luiz Gama, Rui, Tavares Bastos, José Boni-fácio, etc.'[2] Seidl also observes how it is precisely through her condemnation of slavery that Floresta's name became known again in Brazil at the end of the nineteenth century when positivists reproduced anti-slavery passages from her European works, claiming her as an abolitionist, and a disciple of Positivism, long before she was heralded as Brazil's first feminist.[3] However, it is not just her published writing which has earned Floresta the title of abolitionist. Biographers have also afforded considerable significance to the undocumented 1842 meetings, discussed on page 5 in the Introduction, at which Floresta is said to have spoken in favour of abolition. Constância Lima Duarte observes that it is this title of 'abolicionista', together with that of 'defensora dos direitos das mulheres', 'que mais lhe granjeou estima e admiração dos estudiosos'.[4] This chapter will look at Floresta's many varied discussions of slavery and consider whether such claims regarding her status as an abolitionist are justified.

I will be looking at each of the many texts, or passages, in which Floresta discusses Brazilian slavery, in order to identify the discursive and social influences which shaped her approach, showing how her position regarding slavery and emancipation shifted subtly over the course of her writing, due in part to her encounter with European abolitionist sentiment, since she was writing at a time when very few people in Brazil gave any thought to the subject. However, I will also highlight the way in which Floresta addressed different audiences and different aspects of the debate on slavery, drawing on a range of abolitionist, anti-slavery and justificatory discourses

[1] Seidl, p. 38.
[2] Câmara, *História*, p. 51.
[3] Seidl, p. 41.
[4] Duarte, *Vida e Obra*, p. 130.

depending on the context, and frequently contradicting herself, even within the same text, thus complexifying and calling into question any uniformly abolitionist reputation.

I will conclude the chapter with a gendered analysis of Floresta's writing on slavery, assessing the extent to which she engages with various gender-specific issues of slavery, such as miscegenation, maternity and family life, along with sexual abuse and the sexualisation of the slave woman. I will compare Floresta's specific depiction and discussion of slave women with the tropes commonly found in British and American women-authored anti-slavery discourse, and with the writing of her only Brazilian contemporary, Maria Firmina dos Reis. The symbiosis of feminist and abolitionist writing has been well documented in nineteenth-century discourse in Britain and the USA, and with this in mind I shall look at how Floresta's 'feminist' views interact with her approach to slave women.

Although the primary concern of this chapter is to evaluate the validity of Floresta's reputation as an abolitionist, a certain insight into her wider attitude towards the black race might be expected to emerge from her discussions of slavery. What is important to note here, if only to contextualise her comments on slavery, is that at no point in her work does she allude to Brazil's pre-existing free black and mulatto population, despite the fact that by the first national census in 1872, they outnumbered the white population.[5] This, I would suggest, is indeed a silence that speaks a thousand words, and I will attempt to tease those words out over the course of the chapter.

A considerable number of Floresta's works feature in this chapter, reflecting the writer's persistent concern for the issues of slavery. The subject appears in her Indianist poem, in social commentary, *ufanismo*, travel writing and even in a deeply personal elegy to her recently deceased mother, although only one text, the short piece of fiction 'Paginas de uma vida obscura' (1855), deals exclusively with slavery and therefore receives the most detailed analysis. Within this range of genres it is hardly surprising that Floresta adopts a variety of discourses to suit the purpose and readership of each text.

Although the term 'abolitionist' is one which has, posthumously at least, always been applied to Floresta and her work, it is important to note that slavery is not a subject she addressed in any of her early works, in which her focus was almost exclusively that of female education. What makes Floresta's participation in the development of anti-slavery discourse in Brazil so unusual, other than the fact that she is one of very few women to address the subject at all, is that she in fact begins to discuss the institution, its pernicious effects and inhuman conditions in 1853, at precisely the moment when political and social attitudes were most staunchly conciliatory and pro-slavery in the

---

[5]   See Thomas E. Skidmore, *Brazil: Five Centuries of Change* (Oxford: Oxford University Press, 1999), p. 57.

immediate aftermath of the end of Atlantic slave trading in 1850.[6] This fact can only be explained by her trip to Europe. Before this evidently influential experience Floresta had, however, touched on the subject of the international slave trade. Curiously, that brief comment appears in her Indianist poem *A Lágrima de um Caheté* (1849), discussed in the previous chapter.

Writing in Brazil

During a lengthy description of the virtues of her Caeté hero, Floresta includes the following information:

> Era um homem sem mascara, enriquecido
> Não de ouro roubado aos eguaes seus,
> Nem de miseros africanos d'alem mar,
> As plagas Brasileiras arrastados
> Por sedenta ambição, por crime atroz! (*Lágrima*, p. 9)

Within the context of Indianist writing, this is a surprising and interesting allusion to slavery. Critics have observed the all but total absence of reference to black slavery in Indianist literature of the 1800s, whilst Indian slavery was widely covered.[7] When it did appear, it was to maintain the popular stereotypes of the inherently weak black contrasting with the indomitable Indian spirit.[8] In Floresta's poem, however, the dichotomy lies between the Indian and the white slave trader, and not between the Indian and the black slave, who are both portrayed as victims of the coloniser's cruelty and greed.

Whilst a comparison with other traditional Indianist texts reveals this considerable discrepancy, a consideration of both the political circumstances of the moment and the underlying purpose of the poem, as discussed in the previous chapter, sheds new light on Floresta's motivations for including a mention of slavery in the poem. *Lágrima* was written during a crucial period in the gradual demise of the African slave trade at the end of the 1840s. The Brazilian government was finally taking steps to eradicate the illegal but flourishing traffic and the British were applying a huge amount of pressure, employing aggressive tactics that were deeply resented by politicians and public alike in Brazil. After the failure of the 1848 bill, anti-slave-trade sentiment had grown rapidly and Floresta was writing *Lágrima* in the midst of a considerable public debate.[9] It is clear that her description of Africans being

---

[6] See, for example, Robert Brent Toplin, *The Abolition of Slavery in Brazil* (New York: Atheneum, 1972), p. 41.

[7] See, for example, Treece, p. 14.

[8] A clear example of this differentiating discourse can be seen in Gonçalves Dias's poem 'Tabira', published in his *Segundos Cantos*, in 1848 (*Dias*, p. 22).

[9] See Leslie Bethell, *The Abolition of the Brazilian Slave Trade: Britain, Brazil and*

'as plagas Brasileiras arrastados' (p. 9) is a specific reference to the international slave trade and not to the institution of slavery per se. With these few lines Floresta was taking the opportunity to make clear her own position in favour of the abolition of the trade.

However, there is more to this passing description than a simple condemnation of the slave trade. It was in fact the failure of the bill introduced by the Liberal cabinet to put a stop to the trade, in the autumn of 1848, that led directly to the federalist Praieira Revolt celebrated in *Lágrima*. The postponement of the bill provoked the resignation of the Liberal cabinet, and rather than arrange elections, Pedro II chose to appoint a Conservative government in its place. It was this abrupt and arbitrary loss of power, at a local as well as national level, which led the Praieira faction in Pernambuco to revolt.[10] Thus, at a national political level the issue of the slave trade was closely related to the uprising, and by stating her support for the abolition of the trade, and by extension her support for the defeated Liberal bill, Floresta was also confirming her support for the ousted Liberal factions behind the revolt.

Moreover, within the context of *Lágrima*, the white man who provides the negative contrast to the virtuous Caeté is explicitly Portuguese. When applied to the slave trader this construction would have had a particular resonance for Floresta's readers. One of the principal motivations behind the growing support for the effective abolition of the Atlantic trade was a hatred of the slave traders, who were blamed for all the associated problems of the traffic, both internal and international. This hatred was only exacerbated by the fact that the majority of traders were Portuguese nationals. In 1850 the British consul in Rio de Janeiro observed: 'political hatred is ... mixed with the wish to abolish slavery [*sic*] [...]. They hate the Portuguese party and the influence which, as foreigners, they have assumed in the country.'[11] This vilification of the Portuguese was central to the rhetoric of *nativist* uprisings such as the Praieira Revolt.

In her discussion of the Praieira Revolt and the persecution of the native Indians, Floresta's villains must be cast as Portuguese by dint of their political persuasions rather than their place of birth; within the context of the slave trade, however, Floresta has a genuine example of Portuguese villainy. By tapping into this popular discourse within the slave trade debate she also gains extra ammunition against the anti-federalist, metaphorical 'Portuguese' that the poem condemns. More importantly, she makes it clear to her reader that the 'true Brazilian' does not, and would never, engage in the evils of slave trading. At a time when the unchecked traffic of slaves was a source of increasing shame to the nation and the cause of considerable international

the Slave Trade Question, 1809–1869 (Cambridge: Cambridge University Press, 1970), pp. 292–313.

   10   Barman, pp. 230–4.
   11   Quoted in Bethell, p. 314.

pressure and isolation, Floresta acknowledges the slave trade debate as an issue of national pride and seeks to dissociate such activity from the truly independent, civilised Brazil which she hoped for. In her many subsequent discussions of domestic slavery, we frequently find this anti-Portuguese rhetoric employed to blame Portugal for the existence of slavery in Brazil and to distance the stigma of the institution from the new Brazilian national identity under construction at that time.

Shortly after the publication of *Lágrima*, Floresta left Brazil to spend two years in Europe, an absence which in fact coincided with the final demise of the Atlantic trade. In previous chapters I have discussed the profound effect that Floresta's visit to Europe had on her writing on a range of subjects, but perhaps the greatest change can be seen in her increased awareness of and concern for the issue of slavery. From the briefest of passing references in just one of the five surviving works she published prior to her departure in 1849, after her return the subject of slavery assumes a significant position in her work. Floresta published five known texts after 1852 and before her definitive return to France in 1856; three of them, *Opúsculo Humanitário* (1853), 'Passeio ao aqueducto da Carioca' (1855) and 'O pranto filial' (1856), contain significant criticisms of slavery whilst a fourth, 'Páginas de uma vida obscura" (1855), is dedicated entirely to the subject, depicting the tragic and difficult life of a slave. This sudden shift in emphasis is clearly no coincidence. Floresta would have encountered strong abolitionist sentiment during her time in Europe and would undoubtedly have heard her own country, together with the United States, condemned as the only remaining independent slaveholding nations.[12] Floresta's writings after 1852 reveal a much greater awareness of intellectual movements and pressures beyond Brazil's borders. She shows a deep concern for foreign perceptions of her country and this concern is particularly apparent in her treatment of slavery.

The text in which this new self-conscious tone can be heard most clearly is *Opúsculo*, her first publication after returning to Brazil. Although Floresta presents the book as an appeal for improved female education (*Opúsculo*, p. 29), she in fact includes a range of subjects relating to Brazil's social condition, including slavery, which comes under discussion a number of times through the course of the text. At first glance Floresta appears to take a strong stance against slavery. At various moments she condemns the institution in powerful terms: she describes it as a 'barbaro prejuízo' (p. 117), a 'negra mancha' and a 'cancro moral minando-lhe [ao nosso povo] as mais excelentes qualidades d'alma' (p. 132). It is both unchristian and uncivilised (pp. 97 and 117). However, these descriptions ultimately begin to reveal a rather less humanitarian motivation than the moralistic tone might suggest. Throughout

---

[12] In fact, Floresta informs her reader that she heard just such condemnations (*Opúsculo*, p. 52).

her work, Christian virtue and civilisation are the qualities Floresta most admires, and wishes to see fostered in Brazil. From her description of slavery obstructing the process of civilisation and eating away at the moral values of society it becomes apparent that her primary concern lies with the well-being of Brazilian society, rather than with the well-being of the slave.

By adopting this rhetoric of the negative, corrupting influence of the slave system, Floresta echoes the prevailing anti-slavery arguments of her day. Celia de Azevedo charts the persistent belief that 'a escravidão constituía a fonte de todos os males do Brasil'.[13] Household slaves were perceived as a particularly grave threat, due to their intimate cohabitation with their master's family. A newspaper article published in Rio in 1850 called for the employment of free, white servants for domestic service, but did not question the use of slave labour in other areas: 'queremos, por ora, negros escravos ou livres, para o serviço externo, mas que não venham residir em nosso seio de família e emprestar-nos suas idéias acanhadas perniciosas e aviltadas pela immoral escravidão'.[14]

Floresta evidently shares this deep concern about the pernicious influence of domestic slavery, taking several pages to describe the 'tristes inevitáveis resultados do constante viver dos meninos em contato com escravos' (p. 97). She also quotes (on pp. 99 and 140) from two recently published French works which are both deeply critical of Brazilian society and identify slavery as one of the primary causes of the nation's degeneracy. Her inclusion of these foreign texts may in part reflect the lack of contemporary anti-slavery discourse within Brazil, but it seems more likely that, having been prodded herself into addressing the issue of slavery by her encounter with such critical attitudes, Floresta hoped to provoke a similar reaction in her readers by shaming them with 'civilised' European criticism. This is in fact a tactic Floresta employs quite explicitly elsewhere in *Opúsculo*.[15]

In fact, in displaying such concern for international opinion, Floresta is again reflecting and even pre-empting and contributing to the development of another common anti-slavery discourse within Brazil, which focused on Brazil's reputation and standing in the international community. Foreign pressure had played a significant part in the eventual abolition of the Atlantic slave trade with the recognition that only thus could Brazil 'secure respect

[13] Célia Maria Marinho de Azevedo, *Onda Negra, Medo Branco: O negro no imaginário das elites – Século XIX* (Rio de Janeiro and São Paulo: Editora Paz e Terra, 1987), p. 42.

[14] *O Americano*, 02/01/1850, quoted in Giacomini, p. 146. In this instance it is clear that the writer's argument is racially motivated, as he/she does not want free or captive blacks in service within the home, whilst Floresta's concern is with the corruption inherent only to slavery, not with the notion of racial inferiority.

[15] With regard to the use of wet-nurses, for example, Floresta writes that if Rousseau put French mothers to shame, how much worse should Brazilian mothers feel? (p. 93).

for her national sovereignty'.[16] In the decade after this event, when Floresta was writing, such pressure fell away, but by the mid-1860s and the end of the American Civil War, Brazilians began to be increasingly aware of their isolated position as the last independent slaveholding nation, and the subtle pressure of moral condemnation grew steadily. There was a growing perception that the world was 'judging us barbarians and savages', in the words of one senator.[17] An anonymous writer in 1871 wrote: 'Slavery has been the black mark on our civilization,'[18] a sentiment which echoes Floresta's position closely. Writing almost two decades earlier, Floresta had revealed the voice of personal experience when she described slavery as 'manchando-a [nossa sociedade] perante as sociedades da Europa, onde mais de uma vez tivemos de corar, ouvindo incluir os brasileiros na censura em que ali incorrem, e horror que inspiram, os povos traficadores da espécie humana' (*Opúsculo*, p. 52).

Like many of her contemporaries, Floresta blames Portugal for Brazil's continuing slave system, making an apparent allusion to Portuguese involvement in the by then defunct slave trade: 'Os prejuízos de Portugal estenderam-se sobre as vastas plagas do Brasil [...] pois que tiveram de envolver nossa límpida atmosfera no tenebroso manto da escravidão, que Portugal repelia de seu seio e que seus filhos traziam a infestar a nossa sociedade' (p. 52). The idea that Portuguese colonisation lay at the root of Brazil's social and political malaise was a widespread and long-lasting concept, and one that Floresta goes on to employ in almost all her discussions of slavery in Brazil and Europe.

Where Floresta diverges from the majority of her contemporaries engaged in both the pro- and anti-slavery debate, is in her avoidance of theories of racial inferiority. The concept of the inferiority of the African had been commonplace in previous centuries, but in the nineteenth century this idea was increasingly supported by scientific theories of racial difference originating in Europe and the United States.[19] Early emancipationists still suggested that the apparent mental and moral 'inferiority' of the Africans might be a result of their condition as slaves.[20] However, by the 1850s the rhetoric of scientific racism was gaining ground, and contributed to the emergence of an *imigrantista* project, which began in São Paulo in the late 1840s,[21] that called for a policy of European immigration and sometimes the repatriation of freed slaves to Africa in an attempt to dilute the degenerate influence of the

---

16   Bethell, p. 319.
17   Quoted in Toplin, p. 42.
18   Quoted in Toplin, p. 43.
19   Azevedo, pp. 56 and 60.
20   Azevedo, p. 42.
21   Azevedo, p. 60.

black population, an idea which in turn led to the concept of *branqueamento*. Within this vision, the black race could be blamed for white Brazil's poor development and cast as the oppressor of Brazilian society, rather than the victim. Viotti da Costa observes that most white Brazilians, including those who opposed slavery on economic and political grounds, believed in the 'moral inferiority, and political and social incapacity of the African race'.[22]

Floresta, however, clearly aligns herself with the early emancipationists, making evident her belief that the brutal conditions of slavery were responsible for the slaves' moral degeneracy. She condemns the hypocrisy of those who judge a slave more harshly than their own peers:

> Não se refletindo que o embrutecimento dos escravos, privados de toda a educação moral e religiosa, deve excusá-los de grande número de suas faltas, não se lhes tolera a mais ligeira desobediência, quando por toda a parte vêem eles os que receberam educação cometerem, em grande escala, graves desobediências quer para com seus pais quer para com as leis do Estado. (p. 115)

She explicitly condemns those who lose 'o sentimento de sua natureza, julgando-se de uma raça privilegiada, superior a todos os seus semelhantes' (p. 118) and who 'crêem comprar no homem ou na mulher sujeitos ao tirânico jugo da escravidão um animal de carga' (p. 116). In fact, she is at pains to stress the slaves' humanity, saying that it is time to teach young people that 'entre esses infelizes [...] existem mães, filhos, irmãos etc.' (p. 116). In this instance Floresta uses family relationships to humanise the slaves, although this message is curiously at odds with the dehumanisation of slave mothers to be found in her discussion of wet-nursing elsewhere in *Opúsculo*, an issue that I shall return to later in the chapter. A similar tension can be seen in Floresta's discussion of slave morality. Having earlier stressed the corrupting influence of contact with degenerate domestic slaves, as discussed above, she then goes on to point out the slave's capacity for moral virtue, writing: 'sob o invólucro grosseiro do preto bate muita vez um coração nobre, generoso e capaz das maiores virtudes que honram a humanidade' (pp. 115–16). Even in this ostensibly positive depiction, however, her use of the word 'grosseiro' reveals an element of the inescapable racism upon which all discourse on slavery was founded.

It is possible that this image of the noble and virtuous slave, which Floresta attempts to portray, is partly inspired by Harriet Beecher Stowe's famous American anti-slavery novel *Uncle Tom's Cabin*, a work Floresta praises and draws examples from in *Opúsculo*. Stowe's text, which first

---

[22]   Emilia Viotti da Costa, *The Brazilian Empire: Myths and Histories* (London: University of Chicago Press, 1985), p. 137.

appeared in serial form in the *National Era* in 1851, was published as a book in March 1852. The novel's success was massive and instant; within six months it had sold one hundred and fifty thousand copies in the USA and was immediately translated into a number of languages.[23] As Peggy Sharpe observes, the fact that Floresta had read and was drawing influence from such a recently published work reveals her keen interest in current literary and cultural affairs.[24] That *Uncle Tom's Cabin* had a significant influence on Floresta's thinking is evident, not only from the effusive praise she bestows on the book and its author in *Opúsculo*, but also from the publication two years later of 'Paginas', a short story inspired directly by the character of Uncle Tom, which I discuss in detail below. Her praise for Stowe's novel in *Opúsculo* also suggests that Floresta expected her readers to have heard of the text, and she urges them to read it, and make their children learn from it too (p. 42).

Within the context of *Opúsculo*, with its primary focus on women's education and behaviour, it is clear that her interest in *Uncle Tom's Cabin* is as much due to its female author as to its anti-slavery message. She writes: 'Mrs Stowe é o verdadeiro tipo da americana e o mais perfeito modelo que se pode apresentar a todas as mulheres' (p. 41). She uses the writer and her work to illustrate the education and intelligence of North American women and praises the book for its style, sentiment and, most importantly, for its Christian message. It is not surprising that such a devoutly Christian, moral book, written by a woman, who was herself a wife and mother, would have been of great interest to Floresta. The massive repercussions of the novel offered clear evidence that a woman could indeed influence popular and political opinion, as Floresta sought to do with her own publications, without abandoning the domestic role and feminine virtues which she advocated.

Like Stowe, Floresta does not make a direct appeal for action to bring about the end of slavery. She appears to consider this end to be a happy inevitability, informing her readers that 'é mister habituar nossos filhos para esse feliz porvir, em que todo o trabalho será feito por braços livres, porvir de grandeza e de glória' (p. 133). However, it is unclear what timescale she envisages for this natural process of emancipation to occur, only that 'graças aos progressos da civilização moderna, a voz da humanidade [...] conseguirá banir [a escravidão] da face de todo o mundo cristão' (p. 117). What is clear is that Floresta does not identify, for herself or her readers, an active role in bringing about the end of slavery. On the contrary, she appears to advocate an attitude of resignation, suggesting that her readers can have no effect on the status quo, which lies in the hands of the government. She urges mothers to

---

[23] Ann Douglas, 'Introduction: The Art of Controversy', in *Uncle Tom's Cabin, or Life Among the Lowly*, Harriet Beecher Stowe (Harmondsworth: Penguin, 1986), pp. 7–34 (p. 9).

[24] *Opúsculo*, p. 41, footnote 95.

teach their children to look at slaves 'como nossos semelhantes e, por conseguinte, dignos de nossa comiseração no estado a que os reduziram nossos maiores' (p. 116).

This is, of course, a naively simplistic and unfeasible recommendation, since a slave could only be considered a 'semelhante' when he or she was no longer a slave. Floresta at no point suggests that her readers should free their slaves, despite recommending the example of George Shelby in *Uncle Tom's Cabin* (for his 'sentimentos que devem distinguir o verdadeiro cristão' [p. 43]), who does just that. She seems unable to acknowledge that every slaveowning family contributes to and is complicit with the institution that she is condemning. Instead she appears to lay the responsibility entirely at the doors of the government, although even then she makes little more than veiled criticisms and at no time calls for direct political action. Meanwhile, the most she can recommend to her readers is that, as Christians, they should 'caridosamente dirigir' their slaves (p. 116), thus implying that kind and careful guidance is a valid substitute for liberty.

It is important to remember that Floresta does not here address the subject of slavery as a distinct social or political issue, including it instead in her consideration of other social ills such as poor education and the neglect of maternal duties, or as part of a wider picture of social degeneration. This is largely due to the fact that her motivation for writing *Opúsculo* was her concern for women's education and not her concern regarding slavery. This is immediately apparent when reading the text, as her discussions of slavery are limited to those aspects of the institution which she perceives as affecting the formation and education of the young, predominantly the influence of household slaves. Moreover, she fails to draw parallels between the effects of slavery and other social phenomena that she observes. For example, despite repeatedly observing the widespread idleness and disdain for work to be found amongst Brazil's poorer classes (e.g. pp. 113, 124, 126), Floresta does not link this attitude to the nation's dependence on slave labour, nor, when she comments that skilled and able immigrants do not settle in Brazil (p. 80), does she acknowledge that it was slavery, more than any other factor, that repelled immigration. It is apparent that Floresta's concern regarding Brazil's slave system only manifests itself in terms of its moral effect on the slave and, primarily, on the slaveowner, a focus that mirrors the overwhelmingly moral orientation of her approach to women's behaviour and education, as discussed previously.

When contrasted with *Lágrima*, *Opúsculo* is an extremely conciliatory text throughout: at no point does it reveal the strength of language or emotion to be found in Floresta's federalist poem and this contrast is particularly stark when considering those passages in *Opúsculo* which discuss slavery. This conciliatory tone is even more apparent in Floresta's next publication, 'Paginas', the short piece of fiction inspired by Beecher Stowe's novel, which was published in serial form in the fortnightly Rio journal *O Brasil Ilustrado* between March and June of 1855. It is of fundamental importance in an analysis of Floresta's position regarding slavery, not least because it is her only work devoted solely to a consideration of the subject. More importantly though, it is also in 'Paginas' that we see most clearly laid out the many conflicts of interest and contradictions which beset her engagement in the slavery debate and which eventually prevented her from constructing a coherent argument either for or against slavery. Such contradictions were by no means peculiar to Floresta, as Constância Lima Duarte points out. They were in fact 'presentes também no pensamento liberal da época e se refletiam nas ambigüidades tão freqüentemente apontadas'.[25]

The text is an account of the life of an African slave called Domingos and the various predominantly unhappy events that befall him. He has four successive masters, three 'good' and one 'bad'. He confesses to a murder committed by his cruel master in order to save him from prison, and is rewarded, not with his promised freedom but by being sold. He falls in love, but is separated from this love when her owner moves away, and is eventually reunited with her only in time to see her die, weakened by her broken heart and the cruelty of her mistress. He has a son and then sees the boy's mother sold away; some time later the child also dies. Throughout these many tragedies Domingos remains a hard-working and faithful slave and a devout Christian. He rejects the options of revolt and escape, believing his life as a slave to be ordained by God and his happiness to lie in the afterlife.

Unlike Floresta's Indian hero in *Lágrima*, whose encounter with a number of explicitly allegorical figures emphasises his own allegorical function in the poem, Floresta portrays her slave 'hero' as a real person. More than this, she attempts to convince the reader that the narrative is a factual account of the life of an actual slave. She does this by including a number of specific details, such as dates and addresses, and also by including herself in the text as a first-hand witness (e.g. p. 46). Although many readers may not have realised it, she drew considerably on events and locations in her own life. Domingos' life as a slave begins (at the age of ten) in 1810, the year of Floresta's birth; he moves to Porto Alegre and Rio at approximately the same time she did, and whilst in Porto Alegre, he takes his owner's child to a school in the Rua Nova, where Floresta's biographers suggest she may have run a school for girls.[26] However, as the narrative develops, it becomes increasingly clear that Domingos, far from being a 'real' slave, is in fact an extremely idealised figure, a point I will return to below.

Slave narratives, often accompanied by supporting letters confirming their truth, had been commonplace in American anti-slavery magazines since the

25 Duarte, *Vida e Obra*, p. 150.
26 See Duarte, *Vida e Obra*, p. 145.

1840s, and the genre's origins stretch back to 1789 and the publication in London of *The Interesting Narrative of the Life of Olaudah Equiano*;[27] but no such parallel movement has been identified in Brazil, and Duarte asserts that the subject matter was 'ineditado'.[28] However, whilst Floresta may have been among the very first to compose such a narrative in Brazil, the very existence of the text is clearly due in large part to the international success of Stowe's *Uncle Tom's Cabin*. Floresta openly acknowledges this relationship, describing Domingos as 'o *Tom* brasileiro' (p. 63). It is apparent that Floresta not only expected her Brazilian readers to be familiar with the American novel, but also hoped to gain their acceptance and approval by identifying her own work with such a hugely successful book. We already know, from the homage she paid to Beecher Stowe in *Opúsculo*, that *Uncle Tom's Cabin* had a considerable influence on Floresta's thinking and writing, and in 'Paginas' we see the culmination of this influence with a piece of fiction that draws directly and heavily from Stowe's famous work. In fact, it is extremely difficult to imagine that 'Paginas' would ever have been written, much less published, without the prior success of *Uncle Tom's Cabin*. The ways in which Floresta's text both echoes and diverges from its American inspiration are therefore immensely significant and revealing.

It is probable that this explicit link with *Uncle Tom's Cabin*, widely recognised as the great anti-slavery novel of the nineteenth century, is one of the reasons why 'Paginas' has traditionally been identified as an anti-slavery text, and it is certainly true that the narrative presents itself as such. In the early pages we find slavery introduced as 'esse monstruoso parto do despotismo, esse infame libello dos povos christãos' (p. 15), immediately establishing a strongly critical tone. Moreover, 'Paginas' draws on a number of classic anti-slavery discourses, which feature constantly throughout the work. However, beyond these early condemnations, the text's myriad contradictions begin to reveal themselves, undermining many of the anti-slavery positions Floresta claims to adopt in the text. Indeed, her engagement with the slavocratic ideologies of religious justification, Christian resignation and complicity make this anti-slavery label hugely problematic.

Before considering the ways in which Floresta's anti-slavery message is compromised, it is important to identify precisely those discourses which have earned 'Paginas' its anti-slavery reputation. Firstly, very early in the text Floresta makes it clear that there should be no place for slavery in the free, independent Brazil and condemns the hypocrisy of those who propagate it:

---

[27]   Douglas, pp. 32–3; Sonia Hofkosh, 'Tradition and *The Interesting Narrative*: Capitalism, Abolition and the Romantic Individual', in *Romanticism, Race, and Imperial Culture, 1780–1834*, ed. Alan Richardson and Sonia Hofkosh (Bloomington: Indiana University Press, 1996), pp. 330–43 (p. 332).

[28]   Duarte, *Vida e Obra*, p. 144.

A escravidão [...] foi sancionada pelos mesmos homens, que tudo havião sabido sacrificar para libertar-se do jugo de seus oppressores, e assumirem a cathegoria de nação livre! Elles que acabavão de conquistar a liberdade não coravão de rodear-se de escravos! Anomalia de um grande povo apresentada em caracteres de lagrimas e de sangue á face da civilisação moderna para rebaixal-o aos olhos da philosophia, e da humanidade. ('Paginas', p. 15)

This condemnation also once again reveals Floresta's constant concern regarding the image which her newly independent nation projected to the 'civilised' world.

A central theme of the text, and an important anti-slavery discourse, is the condemnation of the cruelties so often associated with the slave system. Floresta highlights the fact that the abusive slaveholder is the norm, stating that her hero's first owner is 'avaro e endurecido, como são quasi todos os senhores no systema anti-humanitario da escravidão', whilst benevolent, philanthropic masters are 'raros oasis no grande e arido deserto da escravidão' (p. 15), an assertion that is undermined by the narrative, in which three of Domingos' four masters are 'benevolent'. Parallel to this criticism of the cruel treatment of slaves is the belief, expressed repeatedly in 'Paginas', that it is the harsh conditions of slavery that lead to moral, physical and intellectual degeneracy among the slaves. For example, Domingos' true love, Maria, is described as attractive and intelligent, but, we are told, education would have brought out the good qualities of her heart that slavery has smothered (p. 46). Likewise we are told that the mother of Domingos' son

era uma alma fraca que não havia podido, como a do nobre Negro, permanecer intacta da abjecção a que geralmente conduz um longo captiveiro. [...] a pobre escrava havia percorrido toda a escala dos soffrimentos que nas almas mediocres degenera quasi sempre em vil torpor e em abnegação de todos os sentimentos de dignidade pessoal. (p. 55)

By attributing slaves' faults to their condition as slaves and not to their race, Floresta is automatically taking up a position against the theories of scientific racism which were to be found increasingly at the heart of pro-slavery discourse at the time.[29] In fact Floresta goes even further, explicitly challenging those who believe race to be a determining factor in moral character: 'Homens, que acrediteis, que a côr, esse caracteristico da degeneração das raças humanas devida a influencias atmosfericas, deve influir nos sentimentos do coração, nas inspirações d'alma, e ser excluida da consideração da sociedade: attentai para esse eloquente quadro em que o negro se apresenta virtuoso; [...] grande; [...] sublime' (p. 31). However, as we saw previously

---

[29] Azevedo, p. 60.

in *Opúsculo*, this apparently positive, anti-racist affirmation is still coloured by a notion of degeneration associated with the African race. Floresta also declares a lie the notion that Africans are happier as slaves in Brazil than as free men in Africa, saying that those who make this claim have no shame because they are lying to humanity and their own consciences ('Paginas', p. 15), although Duarte rightly observes that the author's ethnocentric prejudices are revealed in her negative depictions of Africa as barbarous and pagan.[30]

One particular concern, which becomes a recurrent theme in the narrative, is the separation of family members. Domingos himself suffers this fate on two occasions, but more importantly it is used consistently to illustrate the cruelty of the slave system at that time. Floresta remarks, 'quem não tenha visto na misera escravidão o homem, a mulher a quem tiram a esposa, o esposo para vendel-os a um novo senhor' (p. 31). To bolster her argument in favour of protecting slave family ties, she takes pains to stress that such ties are valued by the slaves, stating that, 'no coração do negro superabunda tambem o amor de familia que algumas vezes falece no do branco' (p. 16). This comment is clearly intended to challenge the widespread belief at that time that blacks were promiscuous and unable or unwilling to forge lasting emotional ties, an argument used to justify the separation of family members.[31] Floresta's particular concern over family separation is not just a reflection of her personal interests. She was also contributing to the earliest awakenings of public and political interest in the conditions of slavery. In 1850 and again three years later a deputy had proposed a bill which recommended, among other things, a ban on the separation of married couples.[32] Whilst both attempts were dismissed outright, such a move is evidence of the first stirrings of a social conscience regarding slave conditions. That said, the impetus behind Floresta's concern for both slave families and the corrupting effect of the system on individual slaves may also lie with the influence of *Uncle Tom's Cabin*. Ann Douglas observes that it is precisely these two issues, the destruction of the soul and the destruction of the family, which also dominate Beecher Stowe's famous condemnation of slavery.[33]

Whatever the influences behind Floresta's concern, it is clear that the primary aim of 'Paginas' was to help bring about an amelioration in slave conditions. She appeals to her white, slave-owning readers to treat their slaves more humanely, stressing the religious importance of showing kindness and

---

[30] Duarte, *Vida e Obra*, p. 160.

[31] See, for example, Robert Wayne Slenes, 'Black Homes, White Homilies: Perceptions of the Slave Family and of Slave Wmen in Nineteenth-Century Brazil', in *More than Chattel: Black Women and Slavery in the Americas*, ed. David Barry Gasper and Darlene Clark Hine (Bloomington, IN: Indiana University Press, 1996), pp. 126–46.

[32] Robert Conrad, *The Destruction of Brazilian Slavery, 1850–1888*, 2nd edn (Malabar, Florida: Krieger Publishing, 1993), p. 27.

[33] Douglas, p. 24.

compassion to slaves and giving several examples of good Christian owners. However this appeal to her readers' moral virtue comes a very poor second to her appeal to their fear of slave rebellion. Floresta was writing at a time when such fears were widespread and weighed heavily on the minds of the slaveholding elite.[34] She apparently seeks to tap into this fear, in an attempt to make her recommendations for a more benign system of slavery more palatable to a cynical society which, in the words of Robert Conrad, was 'not yet in a mood to alter the status quo'.[35] The text implies that those masters who treat their slaves well and, most importantly, educate and catechise them, will be rewarded with loyal, hard-working and virtuous servants, whilst those who treat their slaves inhumanely and allow them to remain spiritually ignorant bring upon themselves the constant threat of violence, rebellion or flight.

Duarte states that, accepting the existence of slavery as unalterable, Floresta concerns herself with improving social practices, 'sugerindo normas que a tornassem mais estável, produtiva e, ao mesmo tempo, menos violenta'.[36] What she does not acknowledge is that this more stable, productive system is entirely in the interests of the white elite and of no benefit to the slaves. Floresta's message is further clouded by the fact that Domingos in fact serves his cruel and abusive master with the same devotion and resignation with which he serves his kinder owners, a situation which seems to imply that as long as the slaves are devout Christians, it is not even necessary to treat them well.

Furthermore, in the account of Domingos' son it is made clear that he is sickly and dies in infancy because he was contaminated by his morally and physically weak mother, herself corrupted by the abuses of slavery. Although Floresta portrays this infant death as a further tragedy her hero must suffer, by blaming the mother's health rather than the child's condition as a slave, the obvious implication is that, had his mother been well treated and therefore healthy, the child would have lived to serve as a good and valuable slave. In a slave system plagued by extremely high infant mortality rates and therefore unable to sustain itself after the end of the Atlantic trade, Floresta in fact presents the good treatment of slaves as offering the possibility of a more robust perpetuation of slavery. Both these projected benefits of benevolent slave-owning clearly reveal that Floresta's concern lies more with the benefits to society and the nation as a whole than with the welfare of the slave population. Whilst it can be argued that such a slant was necessary to appeal to the white, slavocratic readers she hoped to influence, it seems probable that her own patriotic concerns also overrode humanitarian considerations. The

---

[34]   This is the 'medo branco' which Celia de Azevedo charts in her book *Onda Negra, Medo Branco*.

[35]   Conrad, *The Destruction of Brazilian Slavery*, p. 27.

[36]   Duarte, *Vida e Obra*, p. 150.

limited importance of humanitarian arguments had been, and would continue to be, characteristic of the Brazilian anti-slavery debate even in the final years of the abolitionist campaign in the 1880s, with political, economic and social concerns always taking precedence.[37]

Central to this conflicting discourse, which on the one hand seeks to condemn slavery whilst on the other describing a perfect means for the system's naively harmonious continuance, is the figure of Domingos himself with his unrelenting sufferance and exaggerated acts of dedication. Indeed, many of the text's contradictions lie within his characterisation. The most important aspect of Domingos' character is his Christian faith. In fact it becomes increasingly clear that this is essentially the only aspect of his character. He is a totally one-dimensional figure who appears to be motivated by religion alone. Viotti da Costa notes that religion was widely perceived as the best means of controlling and pacifying slaves, but also observes that 'for the most part [...] Christianity was little more than a veneer over African traditions and practices'.[38] A 'genuinely' pious slave would therefore have been a profoundly reassuring image for Floresta's slaveholding readers. Domingos is identified as a Christian from the first page, as a means of gaining audience acceptance: 'Christãos! Não motegeis; é a biographia de um verdadeiro christão que vamos escrever' (14/03/1855 [page number illegible]). The reader is also assured that he is noble and intelligent, and that he is 'um monumento vivo de fidelidade, de paciencia, e de abnegação christã' (p. 47). Floresta recommends that her readers learn from his example, suggesting that his race is not an issue: 'Que importa que aquelle que as [virtudes] praticou fosse um preto ou um branco' (14/03/1855). This is a significant fallacy because it clearly matters greatly that the subject is black: the kind of treatment that Domingos is required to endure and embrace would be unthinkable for a white subject. In fact, it is not even acceptable when the subject is an Indian. Floresta makes it abundantly clear in *Lágrima* that the Indian hero has God and man on his side in seeking vengeance for his mistreatment. It is only the black man who must adopt the role of passive victim, a position in which he is conveniently excluded from social or political agency.

Floresta also informs her reader on the opening page that Domingos was born free, and again appears to use this information to gain sympathy for his character and her unorthodox choice of hero. She writes: 'Ingratos! Não sensureis; é de um homem que nasceo livre, e a quem o poder do mais forte escravisou sem conseguir viciar-lhe a nobre alma' (14/03/1855). We later learn that Domingos is the son of an African chief and was captured at the age of ten. On the one hand it is possible to see how, in the light of the prohibition of the African slave trade but continuing acceptance of domestic

---

[37] See Bethell, p. 313, and Costa, *The Brazilian Empire*, p. 170.
[38] Costa, *The Brazilian Empire*, pp. 138 and 143.

slavery, a contemporary audience might see the enslavement of a previously free individual as more serious and in some way less legitimate than the status of one born into slavery. The unspoken significance of this position, however, is the notion that a slave who was not Christian and not born free would not be an appropriate or acceptable subject, and would therefore deserve neither pity nor acknowledgement.

More importantly, Domingos' free, African birth is not given a uniquely positive value in the text. On the contrary, on closer inspection it becomes apparent that it subtly serves to exclude him from the possibility of true Brazilian citizenship. In this, Domingos is by no means alone. Maria is also of African birth, 'natural do mesmo paiz que Domingos, fallando-lhe a linguagem da patria' (p. 46). Likewise the other slaves he encounters, 'rugião como leões entre as cadeias que os retinhão longe da patria e das familias' (p. 16). In fact it appears that in this and other texts Floresta was unable to engage with the concept of a genuinely Brazilian (born) slave. In *Opúsculo* the slave nurses are 'míseras Africanas' (p. 92), the lone slave in 'Passeio' sings about his lost youth and family in Africa, and the washerwomen in 'O Brasil' are from Nigeria and the Congo (p. 31). The only slave whom we know for certain to be of Brazilian birth, Domingos' son, is not allowed to survive.

Floresta tries to establish Domingos as a kind of 'everyslave' by portraying him performing a range of the typical tasks in which slaves were involved in the nineteenth century – mining, agriculture, domestic work and commercial/ errand-running duties.[39] She also subjects him to a number of the stereotyp- ical sufferings of slavery – the cruel master, racial prejudices, the separation from loved ones and the death of a child. In truth, however, Domingos is far from representing a real or realistic slave; on the contrary he is a completely simplified and idealised figure. As Duarte observes, there is no space for the 'human' in his characterisation, he functions solely as a slave, and moreover as an 'ideal slave', imbued with white Christian virtues.[40] Whilst Floresta suggests that these virtues of patience and resignation are in the best interests of the slave's spiritual well-being, it is clear that they are in fact in the best interests of the slave system. Domingos is, of course, the kind of slave any slaveholder would dream of owning, and if all slaves were like him, slavery could continue unchallenged forever.

Superficially, the purpose Domingos serves in the text echoes the func- tion of the Caeté in *Lágrima*. The 'noble slave' parallels the 'noble savage' and by emphasising this nobility, Floresta rehabilitates both the black and the Indian in the face of racial prejudice. However, whilst Floresta uses this moral superiority to empower the Caeté and establish his right to self-

---

39 Duarte, *Vida e Obra*, p. 145.
40 Duarte, *Vida e Obra*, pp. 151–3.

defence and vengeance, Domingos' moral superiority denies him access to
social agency and shores up his status of social inferiority and his position
as helpless victim. The telling difference between the two is that the Caeté
represents the true Brazilian, his race in *Lágrima* is purely symbolic. By
contrast, Domingos specifically represents the black population. His race is
defining and inescapable, and as a black man, and significantly an African, he
is denied the rights and privileges afforded to the Brazilian 'Indian'.

One important aspect of the characterisation of Domingos is that he is
frequently depicted setting a positive example to his fellow slaves, encouraging them to adopt his approach of acceptance and dedication (e.g. pp. 15
and 32) and he even admonishes them when they fail to perform their work
well (p. 56). In this Domingos differs noticeably from his North American
inspiration, for whilst Tom's resignation leads him to even greater suffering
than Domingos, he acknowledges that not everyone can follow his chosen
path. He actively encourages Cassy to escape, and even admits that there
was a time when he would have attempted to flee himself.[41] Domingos, on
the other hand, becomes, as Duarte observes, the 'porta-voz da ideologia
senhorial junto aos outros escravos'.[42] In fact it is from Domingos' own lips
that we hear some of the most powerfully pro-slavery notions: that the slaves
are themselves often the cause of their own mistreatment (p. 32) (although
Domingos himself unwittingly disproves this argument as he is punished
cruelly for his supreme devotion); that the slaves continue in captivity at
God's will as punishment for their fathers' constant wars in Africa (p. 15);
and that a good master 'é imagem de Deus sobre a terra' (p. 32).

It is this religious justification which affords the most explicitly pro-slavery
perspective in the text. The notion that slavery saved blacks from paganism
in Africa had been prevalent throughout Brazil's colonial era, most famously
expressed by the seventeenth-century Jesuit Padre Antônio Vieira. Although
this discourse can still be seen in use after independence,[43] it was rapidly
losing ground. Leslie Bethell notes that in a lengthy debate on the Atlantic
slave trade which took place in the Chamber as early as 1827, no deputy used
the 'time-honoured' arguments of religious justification and in fact a denunciation of such arguments produced enthusiastic applause.[44] Floresta makes
some attempt to counter this sort of justificatory discourse by condemning
those who suggest that Africans are better off in Brazil as slaves than in
Africa as pagans (p. 15), yet in truth this condemnation was largely obsolete

---

[41] Harriet Beecher Stowe, *Uncle Tom's Cabin, or Life Among the Lowly* (Harmondsworth:
Penguin, 1986), p. 562.

[42] Duarte, *Vida e Obra*, p. 146.

[43] Robert Conrad cites a British writer who observes the use of this religious defence of
slavery in 1852 (pp. 27–8).

[44] Bethell, p. 63.

by 1855 as it only applied to the already illegal and eradicated Atlantic slave trade and not to domestic slavery.

Duarte identifies similarities between the depiction of Domingos in 'Paginas' and the work of Antonio Vieira, who famously established the link between slavery and calvary, suggesting that 'ser escravo é ser Cristo'.[45] However, in light of Floresta's aforementioned criticism and the fact that such religious pro-slavery arguments were losing favour, I would suggest that the inspiration for Domingos' Christ-like resignation can be wholly attributed to the influence of *Uncle Tom's Cabin*. Tom's final act in forgiving his master as Legree beats him to death leaves the reader in no doubt as to the parallels Stowe sought to draw between her hero and Christ, and Floresta is even more explicit in comparing Domingos to Jesus, stating simply that 'o nosso heroe negro imitava a J.C.' (p. 31). It is significant, therefore, that Floresta chose not to follow Stowe in giving Domingos a cruel and agonising death comparable with Christ's sacrifice. This omission is in keeping with the generally sanitised nature of the text, which contains no depiction of physical abuse and, for the most part, little more than allusions to the emotional cruelties of captivity, family separation and premature death.

The predominantly humane picture which Floresta paints of slavery in Brazil is strangely at odds with her early assertions that the majority of slave-owners are hard and greedy (p. 15). In fact only one of Domingos' four owners falls into this category, and whilst Maria dies as a result of the effects of slavery, it is primarily due to a broken heart after her separation from Domingos, a tragedy which Stowe's characters are all strong enough to survive physically, if not morally. By affording Domingos a peaceful death in a caring hospital, with a kindly and devoted master in attendance, the significance of his self-sacrificing life is lost and the powerful indictment of the slave system with which *Uncle Tom's Cabin* ends is entirely absent from the Brazilian text. More significantly, whilst both Stowe and Floresta stress the importance of the slaves' souls over their bodies, and Tom and Domingos both espouse the values of Christian resignation equally, it is in Domingos' assertion that the slaves are being punished by God for the sins of their fathers that Floresta deviates from her American contemporary, and strays into the domain of pro-slavery discourse.

However, this religious discourse is by no means the only factor contributing to the pro-slavery undertones of the text. On inspection, several aspects of the narrative contain an implicit acceptance of the slave system and, taken as a whole, the text fails to present any real challenge to the status quo. In what is perhaps the most extraordinarily complicit passage in 'Paginas' Floresta praises Domingos for his devotion to his master: 'Bom, excellente negro, alma sensivel e grata! Tu crias, como os poucos que se te assemelhão,

---

[45] Duarte, *Vida e Obra*, p. 148.

que nunca se paga assaz o bem que se recebe embora se dê uma vida de dedicação áquelle de quem o recebemos!' (p. 55). As Duarte asks, what exactly
does Domingos owe his master? She observes that at this and other moments
'o texto revela [...] sua dívida para com o pensamento da classe dominante',[46]
but it is more than this. It is clear that Floresta wished to encourage her slaveholding readers to treat their slaves better by showing the good behaviour
which would be their reward, but by suggesting that the slave is thereby
indebted to his/her master she implies that the humane treatment of slaves
is not a moral obligation, but a favour bestowed in a spirit of generosity. In
this way Floresta also inverts the relationship between the elite and the slave
population, negating the immeasurable contribution of four centuries of slave
labour to Brazil's economic development, a contribution which in reality left
the white elite indebted to, and hugely dependent on, slavery.

   Another central issue in the narrative which delivers an implicit pro-
slavery message is the fact that Domingos is never freed by any of his
masters. Whilst in this he is no different from Tom, in the American text
Tom's condition is juxtaposed with the successful escapes of George Harris
and his family and of Cassy and Emmeline, whilst at the close of the novel
we see George Shelby free all the slaves on his Kentucky farm. By contrast,
no slave in 'Paginas' gains his/her freedom, by legitimate or illicit means, and
more importantly Floresta makes no criticism of this fact. Stowe includes the
white, slaveowning character of St Claire as an example of, and a wake-up
call to, those slaveholders whose good intentions were thwarted by their own
incapacitating apathy. Floresta appreciates this message in *Uncle Tom's Cabin*,
but is unable to express it in her own work. She is critical of the 'descuidoso
philantropo *St. Claire*' (p. 63), but when the very same fate befalls Domingos
with his first owner, who likewise promises to free him but dies first, she
blames misfortune, rather than negligence, stating only that 'a sorte fatal [...]
permittio que esse homem philantropo da resumida classe dos senhores [...]
morresse subitamente antes de realisar o seu projecto' (p. 15).

   Domingos' third master is similarly excused for his failure to free his
faithful servant. The family is French and Floresta is keen to inform the
reader that they conserve 'os usos de sua nação' (p. 31) and therefore always
employ servants, except, that is, for Domingos. However, although Floresta
portrays the owner as a generous and civilised man, when he returns to
France he chooses to sell his only slave rather than free him. The reader is
told that 'Domingos não podia esperar de seu senhor, á quem ha pouco tempo
pertencia, um acto de philantropia em seu favor' (p. 31) and is reassured of
the man's generosity in allowing Domingos to choose his next owner. The
Frenchman's active participation in slave commerce could easily be seen as
an example of the corrupting influence of Brazil's slave system on the Euro-

---

[46] Duarte, *Vida e Obra*, pp. 152–3.

pean ideals which Floresta claimed to value and admire so greatly; but she chooses not to present it as such, assuming instead that the character's nationality is enough to vouch for his anti-slavery principles and recommending the example he sets in his 'benevolence' towards Domingos.

It is the unfortunate slave's fourth and final owner who is most generously defended, however. This man, with whom Domingos stays for the rest of his life, is consistently described as a charitable, just and paternal master, who cares deeply for the well-being of his slave and comes to view him as a friend and confidant, particularly after Domingos saves his life. Yet at no time does this 'good' man express any desire to free him. Despite this obvious failing, Floresta seeks to make a clear distinction between her noble master and Stowe's St Claire, writing, 'lá o escravo negro christão havia sobrevivido ao branco senhor, negligente em recompensa-lo e honrar a sua memoria eternisando as suas virtudes!' (p. 63). She cannot acknowledge that by failing to free Domingos, her Brazilian master is equally negligent in compensating his slave. Floresta seeks to nullify this omission by portraying the relationship between master and slave as one of friendship between equals. She makes this very clear throughout, informing the reader that 'Domingos não foi mais olhado como escravo' (p. 47). In fact, we are told that the two characters almost immediately 'se apercebessem da unanimidade dos sentimentos caridosos que a ambos animavão, sentimentos que tendem a impellir o negro e o branco para a igualdade moral conforme a estabeleceu J.C. entre todos os filhos de Adão, morrendo por todos os homens em geral' (p. 32).

The suggestion that equality or even superiority can be achieved through adherence to the Catholic faith is a constant theme throughout the text. The reader is reminded, in a passage very reminiscent of *Lágrima*, that 'o selvagem da naturesa póde civilisar-se e ser capaz de praticar todas as virtudes christãs, mas que do selvagem da cidade, que nutre os instinctos da fera, nunca se conseguirá fazer um bom christão' (p. 16), suggesting that a black slave can elevate himself above a free white. Floresta also refers to Domingos' final owner as 'o seu semelhante' (p. 47), yet this discourse is clearly a fallacy. As Duarte observes, it is only the possibility of spiritual equality which is on offer here – any other form of equality is unthinkable.[47] Moreover, in practical terms Domingos clearly has nothing in common with his master. What appears at first glance to be an emancipating discourse, and is certainly presented as such by Floresta, is in fact deeply divisive and justificatory. By placing such importance on spiritual equality, which could be achieved regardless of the bonds of slavery, Floresta completely devalues the social and political rights that slaves aspired to, and by implying that this spiritual equality somehow overrides slavery and negates the need to grant a

---

47 Duarte, *Vida e Obra*, p. 147.

slave genuine freedom, she provides the perfect excuse for the slave system to remain unchallenged.

In the midst of this overwhelmingly complicit discourse, Floresta offers her readers one brief glimpse of the opposing position. In what is undoubtedly the most interesting passage in the text, Domingos meets and holds a conversation with a slave who curses all slaveholders and forcefully condemns the injustices of a system which expects a slave to remain loyal to a master regardless of the treatment he receives, and which punishes crimes perpetrated against whites whilst condoning the same acts when the victim is a slave. He describes the cruel conditions in which he is kept, suggesting his treatment is worse than that of a beast of burden. He also highlights the hypocrisy of slaveholders who claim to be Christian, saying 'Christianismo! [...] Praticão-o os nossos tyrannos? Sentimos nós outros victimas de seus crueis caprichos, de seu brutal dominio, influencia alguma em tal conducta havida comnosco, dessa religião que dizem professão e de cujo ensino e verdades deproposito nos privão?' (p. 40). Whilst this anonymous slave makes no mention of rebellion or flight, it is clear that he does not share Domingos' belief in Christian resignation. In fact, he has either totally lost his faith, or has never been catechised, and thus represents the complete antithesis of Domingos' character.

Duarte appears to suggest that this slave allows Floresta to express her own condemnation of the institution of slavery, and more importantly that the arguments used serve to effectively challenge Domingos' position. She writes: 'Diante da força contundente da denúncia presente nas palavras do opositor, mais evidente se torna a debilidade da argumentação de Domingos, que se limita a repetir mecanicamente os ensinamentos cristãos necessarios a um comportamento resignado.'[48] The inherent weakness of the argument for Christian resignation is an accusation which has also frequently been levelled at Beecher Stowe's novel. As Ann Douglas points out, however, this is very much the interpretation of a modern reader. She suggests that 'Uncle Tom and Little Eva appear ridiculously exaggerated only to constrictedly secular minds'. Within the deeply religious context of the time and of Stowe's own faith, her portrayal of Uncle Tom is far from being a portrayal of weakness. Douglas observes, 'Uncle Tom's docility is docility only in the sense that Stowe considers it "feminine", but it is "feminine" only in that it represents adherence to spiritual values – and this adherence, for Stowe, is strength.'[49] Floresta's own devout Catholicism is abundantly clear throughout her work, as discussed in previous chapters. I would therefore contend that Floresta, like Stowe, would have seen the kind of saintly resignation exemplified by Tom and Domingos as a mark of great spiritual strength and nobility, not as a sign of weakness.

[48]   Duarte, *Vida e Obra*, p. 154.
[49]   Douglas, pp. 24 and 25.

Therefore, rather than serving to give voice to the author's own anti-slavery views and reveal the weaknesses inherent in Domingos' defence of Christian resignation, I would suggest that the purpose of the unhappy and angry slave in the text is in fact to illustrate once again the dangerous effects of the mistreatment of slaves. The slave's negative attitude is juxtaposed with Domingos' contentment at that time and his resulting enthusiasm for his work. The mistreated slave also refuses to recognise the goodness of any owner, including Domingos' master, a position which clearly does not reflect Floresta's own view, as she makes it clear elsewhere in the text that he is indeed a good man and an example to be followed. Most importantly, the slave is spiritually debilitated by his mistreatment, rejecting the Christian faith because the only example he sees is that of his supposedly Christian, abusive masters. The fact that this unfortunate slave cannot be persuaded by Domingos' arguments is not a reflection of the weakness of those arguments, as Duarte implies.[50] Rather, it is an indication of the destruction of the soul brought about by physical and spiritual neglect. It is apparent from this passage that Floresta shared Stowe's concerns about the damage that the cruelty of the slave system inflicted on the spiritual health of the slaves, as much as, if not more than, its effect on their physical well-being.[51]

In seeking to emphasise the significance of 'Paginas' and perhaps to reaffirm the text's position in the canon of anti-slavery literature, Duarte presents the encounter between Domingos and the unhappy slave as an important departure from *Uncle Tom's Cabin*. She writes 'o romance Americano não representa o escravo *revoltado* se opondo a Tomás. Os que se lhe opõem o fazem apenas por apatia ou desespero, nunca por consciência do próprio destino de oprimido. Neste aspecto, "Páginas de uma vida obscura" avança bem mais ao dar voz também a este escravo.'[52] However, this conclusion is extremely difficult to support when the two works are compared side by side. As Duarte herself observes, Floresta's unhappy slave condemns the cruelties of slavery but falls short of condemning the existence of the institution itself. In fact he makes no attempt to question the legitimacy of the system, apparently accepting unquestioningly both his status as slave, and the white man's right of ownership. The limited nature of his criticisms severely reduces the anti-slavery tone of his presence in the text, and calls into doubt Duarte's suggestion that he is conscious of his own 'destino de oprimido'. Can he be said to be truly conscious of his oppression if he fails to identify the injustice inherent in the system which oppresses him? In truth it would appear that he is conscious only of his mistreatment – of his hunger, pain and the loss

---

50   Duarte, *Vida e Obra*, p. 154.
51   Ann Douglas observes that 'the gravest charge Stowe levelled against slavery was that it could kill the soul in slaves [...] and in masters' (p. 24).
52   Duarte, *Vida e Obra*, p. 158.

of his family. In this way he differs very little from the slaves Tom interacts with in Stowe's novel, a clear example being the character of Cassy, who also describes the appalling treatment she has received (including separation from her family), and who has also lost her faith as a result.

Moreover, to suggest that *Uncle Tom's Cabin* does not give voice to 'o escravo revoltado' is to overlook the character of George Harris. The fact that his passage through the narrative does not coincide with Tom's in no way reduces his importance, and it is his presence in the American novel, more than any other aspect, which distinguishes the two texts and highlights the pro-slavery undertone of 'Paginas'. George Harris is a slave who is genuinely conscious of his oppression in the widest sense. He is not just another voice detailing the abuses of a cruel master; instead he offers a forceful and eloquent defence of liberty. More importantly, he believes, and through him Stowe reveals her belief, that he has the right to challenge his oppression by escaping. It is particularly significant that the heart-felt appeal which George makes to Mr Wilson convinces the kindly slaveholder that George is right to flee and even inspires him to give the fugitive some money to help his escape.[53] In this passage Stowe makes it clear to her readers not only that she condones slave runaways, but also that such acts might justifiably be aided and encouraged.

Duarte suggests that Floresta does 'por vezes mostrar-se compreensiva e até justificar a revolta', and that the text juxtaposes Domingos' character with examples of angry, rebellious slaves, although she acknowledges that the narrative tends to favour the silent resignation of Domingos.[54] I would contend, however, that 'Paginas' is far more one-sided than this. Floresta makes no mention of revolt or rebellion of any kind, and only one brief comment to suggest that she sympathised with slaves who tried to escape, when she tells the reader that Domingos longed to be free but he did not wish to achieve this 'por nenhum meio ignobil, se todavia a fuga de um escravo para subtrahir-se ao tyrannico despotismo de um senhor venal póde ser julgada acção ignobil perante juisos rectos e imparciais' (p. 16). Despite this apparent understanding, not one slave is portrayed even attempting to flee and Floresta is so full of praise for Domingos' loyalty to his various masters that it is clear where the writer's approval lies. In fact, she depicts Domingos embracing his condition and his duties so enthusiastically that the reader is left doubting whether he actually wishes to be free at all.

The imbalance of Floresta's text in comparison with Stowe's novel is most clear in its lack of developed slave figures. *Uncle Tom's Cabin* is full of well-developed and carefully observed characters whose means of dealing with or escaping their condition as slaves varies widely. Uncle Tom himself is by no

53   Stowe, p. 188.
54   Duarte, *Vida e Obra*, p. 153.

means the novel's only hero. 'Paginas' is, of course, a far shorter work which in no way allows for the depth of characterisation or breadth of narrative to be found in Stowe's vast novel. However, Domingos is the only developed character in the text, and even he is constructed very one-dimensionally, with the sole purpose of exemplifying the perfect slave, as discussed above. In the American novel Tom's model of resignation is interwoven with the rebellious examples of Cassy and George, and equally importantly with the character of Eliza Harris, who remains a devout Christian throughout the novel, despite running away. In Eliza's character Stowe shows that escape and piety are not incompatible. Domingos, on the other hand, has no such counterfoil and thus comes to represent the only acceptable model of slave behaviour according to Floresta.

Floresta's decision not to reflect any of Stowe's other slave characters in her narrative is an indication that she was unwilling to condone the kind of positive action which they represent. In *Uncle Tom's Cabin* we see not only the successful escape of a number of slaves, but also the lengths they are prepared to go to in order to achieve this, such as George's (and his Quaker friends') willingness to shoot at their pursuers, and what Ann Douglas describes as the 'tacit terrorism' which Cassy employs against the evil Legree.[55] Moreover, Stowe does not portray Tom as passive victim, far less as complicit with the system which oppresses him. He disobeys Legree by refusing to beat his fellow slaves or reveal the whereabouts of Cassy and Emmeline, and his death is itself a final act of defiance. Domingos, on the other hand, is denied any opportunity to oppose his own oppression, and dies lamenting the fact that he cannot go on serving his master, in a scene of complicity which contrasts sharply with the victory of faith over slavery represented by Tom's death. For all their supposed similarities, in reality Tom and Domingos serve very different purposes in their respective texts.

A final example of how the apparent similarities between the two texts mask their different messages can be seen in the juxtaposition of national independence and continuing slavery, a moral contradiction that both Floresta and Stowe observe. Both authors comment on the hypocrisy of the leaders of a nation who fought for and take pride in their own liberty, but continue to maintain their fellow men in captivity. Floresta writes:

> A escravidão [...] foi sancionada pelos mesmos homens, que tudo havião sabido sacrificar para libertar-se do jugo de seus oppressores, e assumirem a cathegoria de nação livre! Elles que acabavão de conquistar a liberdade não coravão de rodear-se de escravos!! (p. 15)

However, whilst she criticises the white elite for perpetuating slavery, Floresta

---

55 Douglas, p. 19.

is unable to make a direct connection between white Brazil's struggle against its Portuguese oppressor and the slaves' struggle against their elite Brazilian oppressors.

Stowe, on the other hand, sees this parallel clearly, and uses it to justify her characters' actions. George Harris declares 'I'll fight for my liberty to the very last breath I breathe. You say your fathers did it; if it was right for them, it is right for me!'[56] *Uncle Tom's Cabin* may not be overtly abolitionist, but instances like this reveal Stowe's belief that slavery must end, a belief which Floresta fails to express in 'Paginas'. Whilst she saw independence and federalism as noble causes which justified the violence that accompanied them (a view she expresses clearly in *Lágrima*), she is unable to see the destruction of slavery in the same light. In the end she is able to advocate nothing more than a benign system in which the slaves are spared the worst cruelties but which is essentially more secure and productive for the slavocracy.

As the only work published by Floresta which deals solely with the subject of slavery, 'Paginas' must be seen as a central text when considering Floresta's position within the slavery debate. However, the text's ambiguous and often contradictory message means that it sits uncomfortably within her traditional, monolithic construction as abolitionist. This conflict is apparent, for example, in Adauto da Câmara's 1941 biography of Floresta. In a short chapter entitled 'Abolicionista', which looks at her writings on the subject of slavery, Câmara makes no mention of 'Paginas', instead referring to the brief, but more explicitly anti-slavery, comments which Floresta makes in *Opúsculo* and later European publications.[57]

In her much later study Duarte acknowledges many of the text's shortcomings, as indicated above, but continues to view it as an anti-slavery piece. She is keen to emphasise its 'avanços teóricos',[58] yet in advocating a more humane system and challenging racial prejudices Floresta is reiterating ideas expressed by José Bonifácio de Andrada e Silva and others in the 1820s, and in fact falls well short of making an appeal for emancipation equivalent to that found in Bonifácio's famous address to the Brazilian Assembly.[59] Based on the overt condemnations of slavery found in the opening pages of the text, Duarte suggests that Floresta's intention in writing 'Paginas' was to denounce slavery, but that her portrayal of Domingos contradicts this intention.[60] However, Robert Conrad observes 'the Brazilian practice of prefacing

---

[56]   Stowe, p. 187.
[57]   Câmara, *História*, pp. 51–3.
[58]   Duarte, *Vida e Obra*, p. 162.
[59]   'A necessidade de [...] emancipar gradualmente os actuaes cativos é tão imperioso, que julgamos não haver coração brasileiro tão perverso, ou tão ignorante que o negue, ou desconheça' (José Bonifacio de Andrada e Silva, *Representação á Assemblea Geral Constituinte e Legislativa do Imperio do Brasil sobre a Escravatura* (Paris: Typ. De Fimin Didot, 1825), pp. 1–2).
[60]   Duarte, *Vida e Obra*, p. 141.

pro-slavery arguments with brief denunciations of an institution which even in Brazil was condemned in principle if not in practice'.[61] It seems that 'Paginas' could in fact be included in this category because, after briefly introducing slavery as 'esse monstruoso parto do despotismo' (p. 15), the text reveals itself to be overwhelmingly complicit with all but the worst abuses of the slave system.

'Paginas' was written when the slave system in Brazil was still reeling from the effective abolition of the Atlantic trade in 1850 and domestic slavery was fiercely defended by the majority of politicians and the public. Floresta was therefore one of a small minority of voices raising objections to the cruel treatment of slaves at that time. Moreover, by asserting that poor behaviour and moral weakness in slaves were a result of their condition as slaves rather than their nature, she sets out to challenge prevailing racial prejudices fed by the increasingly popular doctrine of scientific racism.[62] With this in mind, 'Paginas' should be acknowledged as an important work in the development of a critical discourse on slavery, and the text clearly deserves to be counted within the development of a social conscience regarding the slave system, but these appeals for a more humanitarian approach are not sufficient to earn 'Paginas' the title of anti-slavery writing. On the contrary, Emilia Viotti da Costa could be referring to 'Paginas' when she writes:

> Pictures of the faithful slave and the benevolent master – pictures fixed in Brazilian literature and history – represent not so much the actual behaviour of slaves and masters, but myths created by a slaveholding society to defend a system which that society regarded as indispensable. They affected people's behaviour only in as much as any other idealisation does.[63]

The pro-slavery undertones of 'Paginas' must also call into question the likelihood of the claim that Floresta held abolitionist meetings in Rio in 1842. In the light of her subsequent writings and the socio-political context of that time (when the government was finally coming under serious pressure to enforce the ban on the still virulent international slave trade), it seems probable that if these meetings did indeed take place, she was in fact addressing the subject of the abolition of the Atlantic trade, not of slavery as an institution.

After the appearance of 'Paginas', Floresta went on to publish two further short pieces of prose in the same journal, both of which contain references to slavery, although the subject is no longer the focus of her writing. On the contrary, these two texts have very different purposes, one being Floresta's first attempt at *ufanismo* in a description of the natural and cultural delights

61   Conrad, *The Destruction of Brazilian Slavery*, p. 9.
62   Azevedo, p. 60.
63   Costa, *The Brazilian Empire*, p. 137.

of Rio, and the other an elegy to her mother and a eulogy to maternal virtue. Neither of these pieces require or lend themselves to the inclusion of slavery as a subject matter, and the fact that Floresta chose to include a reference to slaves, although only briefly, is therefore an indication of the extent to which the issues relating to slavery interested and concerned her.

The first of these texts is a short piece entitled 'Passeio ao aqueducto da Carioca', which appeared in *O Brasil Ilustrado* in July 1855. Although the piece contains only a few brief paragraphs on the subject of slavery, we can identify a number of the discourses Floresta had previously employed in 'Paginas'. This work is written as a tourist guide, leading the visitor to Rio around some of the city's famous sights and calling attention to its modern development as well as the beautiful scenery surrounding the city. However, on this 'guided tour' Floresta comes across a solitary old slave and we again encounter the idea that slavery is an eyesore, an ugly anomaly which mars the otherwise harmonious image of a liberal and civilised Brazil that she seeks to portray, a point which Floresta had previously made in 'Paginas' (p. 15). This is a discourse she later employs consistently when writing for a European readership. She is keen to point out the hypocrisy of a nation that allows slavery to continue 'no seio de um grande povo tão ufano de suas *livres* instituições!' ('Passeio', p. 70). She also emphasises the cruelty of the situation, describing 'o infeliz escravo, quasi exhausto de forças, obrigado ao trabalho de cavouqueiro debaixo dos raios de um sol abrasador' (p. 70).

The unfortunate slave is singing a song in which he remembers his happy life in Africa and laments his subsequent misfortune. We learn from his song that he was separated from his wife and children, a typical motif of the cruelty of the slave system previously seen in 'Paginas'. However, we also learn from the song that the slave, like all Floresta's slaves, is of African birth, and he considers Africa to be his real home. Once again the slave is denied full Brazilian status and distanced from national identity. We also learn that he is Christian, and more importantly that he is resigned to his fate. In fact, although we are given no insight into his character, this information alone makes it clear that he is cast in the same mould as Domingos. He does not speak of rebellion or escape, instead praying to God to give him the strength to carry on working. Floresta also prays to God, but not for an end to slavery, only for the 'regeneração dessa infeliz raça' (p. 70). Neither does she make any appeal to the government or her readers to fight against the continued existence of the slave system. Once again she limits herself to a criticism of the cruelties involved, and creates a slave who is simultaneously complicit with slavery and excluded from Brazilian identity.

The second text, published the following year (1856) and entitled 'O Pranto Filial', is a deeply personal piece of writing in which Floresta reveals her profound grief. It is also a celebration of the love between a mother and her daughter and, more specifically, a homage to the maternal virtues of Floresta's own mother, and therefore an opportunity for Floresta to once again stress the importance of the role of mother for every woman. The incongruous textual setting does not allow for the familiar arguments employed by Floresta in previous works and, curiously, what emerges is a discourse that is rather more sympathetic and understanding of the slaves' situation, and which appears to be founded on a more genuine conviction regarding their equal human status.

During the latter part of 1855 Floresta had worked in one of the capital's hospitals, nursing the victims of the latest outbreak of yellow fever to hit the city. In 'Pranto' she describes the suffering which she saw there, writing: 'testemunhei [...] a dissolvição rapida e dolorosa das faculdades vitaes do homem livre e do homem escravo!' (p. 142). In sickness the free man and the slave are reduced to equals, both suffer the same effects of a disease which does not acknowledge status. Moreover, Floresta recognises that whilst the free man's hopes fade with his life, the slave's hopes grow stronger as he nears 'a morte que o hia libertar de um jugo atroz, sob o qual em vão lutava, extinguindo as forças durante a sua difficil peregrinação na terra! ...' (p. 142). This comment contrasts starkly with Floresta's position in 'Paginas', discussed above, in which she denies Domingos the escape which death represented by portraying him as reluctant to die (p. 63). She also now implies that the slave may not have accepted his condition, but instead struggled against captivity, something which she is unable to condone in 'Paginas', but which is by no means expressed in negative terms here.

In the above quotation Floresta likens slavery to a disease which weakens the slave, as yellow fever weakens the free man. Whilst this is an idea we find in 'Paginas' regarding the corrupting effect on slave morals, slavery was more often criticised for weakening the slaveholding society, and the corruption of the slaves themselves was discussed primarily as a risk to that society, as Floresta herself suggests both in 'Paginas' and, more explicitly, in *Opúsculo*. In 'Pranto', however, the dying slave is viewed as an individual, and the effect slavery has had on him is presented as a personal tragedy, not a social threat. Floresta goes on to tell how she wept as she closed the eyes of these unfortunate slaves' corpses, in an image of human compassion which again overrides the immense social divide between free man and slave, emphasising the slaves' humanity. For the first time Floresta does not refer to the slaves as blacks or Africans, making no racial or national distinctions. It is possible that her work with the sick did indeed bring her into close contact with a number of slaves and that this interaction inspired the subtle change in attitude which can be perceived in 'Pranto'.

However, in spite of this discourse of inclusivity, relative to her previous writings, Floresta still falls short of making an overt appeal for the end of slavery. Instead she can only express her distress at its continued existence and hope for an improvement in conditions, writing that she directs 'ardentes preces ao Eterno para que melhore a sorte de seus irmãos, nas terras onde o homem tolera escravisar o homem!!!' (p. 142). As we saw previously in *Opúsculo*, Floresta seems to imply that she, and therefore also her readers, cannot influence the situation, and that there is no chance of a rapid change in circumstances. On this latter point, Floresta is of course correct, and the fundamentally pessimistic tone of this brief passage reflects the political and social climate of the day, in which few voices were raised even against the worst excesses of the slave system and measures were in fact being taken to strengthen the institution.[64]

Writing in Europe

'O Pranto Filial' was in fact the last of Floresta's writings to be published in Brazil, or indeed in her native language, during her lifetime.[65] Within days of its publication on 31 March 1856, Floresta set sail once again for France, where she would settle permanently together with her daughter. None of her European texts repeat the pessimism found in 'Pranto', for now a new factor comes into play in her writing: the desire to show her nation to the rest of the world in the best possible light. Thus we begin to see the future end of slavery presented in an altogether different light, as a very real and close-at-hand prospect. It is also in her European writing that we begin to see a more clearly voiced abolitionist sentiment, reflecting the very different prevailing attitudes of her new readership. However, the influence of typically Brazilian discourse on slavery remains very apparent, leading Floresta to employ arguments which at times are ill-suited to her European readers. The first references to slavery in her European work are to be found in her two *ufanistic* essays, 'O Brasil', and 'Viagem Magnética', both of which appeared in the collection *Cintilações de uma alma brasileira*, published in Florence in 1859.

In the first, and most overtly *ufanistic* of these pieces, 'O Brasil', Floresta paints an overwhelmingly positive picture of her nation, describing not only the rich natural resources, but also the modern urban centres and the culture and education of the Brazilian people. She is also keen to emphasise the political development of the nation, writing that Brazil enjoys 'uma plena liberdade à sombra de sábias e amenas leis, conformíssimas à índole humanitária de seus cidadãos' ('O Brasil', p. 61). Such a description gives the impression that Floresta completely overlooks the issue of slavery, an institution whose position at the heart of Brazilian society clearly contradicts this vision of liberty and humanity. However, Floresta cannot completely ignore the subject. Writing for such a profoundly anti-slavery European audi-

---

[64] See Conrad, *The Destruction of Brazilian Slavery*, pp. 27–8.
[65] In fact it was not until 1982 that the first of her European works was translated into Portuguese and published in Brazil.

ence, this would be too great an omission. Instead she once again sets out to emphasise that slavery is an anomaly, the one dissonant factor which spoils her nation's image and reputation: 'tão rico e belo país, mas onde ainda se tolera, entre suas livres instituições, a oprobriosa lei da escravidão' (p. 33). The existence of slavery is a 'lastimável e reprovável contraste com o grande amor pela liberdade que reina entre o povo' (p. 33). This emphasis on the incongruity of slavery echoes the descriptions found in 'Paginas' and 'Passeio', except that we no longer see a criticism of the hypocrisy inherent in the maintenance of slave labour in a supposedly 'free' nation, as found in her texts published in Brazil. Whilst in these earlier works Floresta wished to challenge her Brazilian readers' complacency towards slavery, in 'O Brasil' she does not want the European reader to question her assertion that Brazil is in fact a civilised and liberal nation.

To this end Floresta once again employs the familiar tactic of blaming the Portuguese, stating that slavery was 'aí instituída pelos seus primeiros conquistadores de além-mar' (p. 33). She also observes that European countries have their own vices, for which they should in fact be judged more harshly because they are old, experienced nations (p. 39). Thus Floresta subtly reverses the notion of political hypocrisy which she had previously levelled at her own nation, implying that European countries are guilty of hypocrisy in condemning Brazil instead of addressing their own political and social shortcomings.

Floresta's description of slavery as 'oprobriosa' and 'reprovável', seen above, is in fact the only criticism of the institution to be found in 'O Brasil', and this language is very mild compared with the phrases such as 'barbaro prejuízo' and 'cancro moral' found in her earlier Brazilian works (*Opúsculo*, pp. 117 and 132). In 'O Brasil' she goes on to describe a scene in which slave washerwomen are working in a river, and although she acknowledges that their fate 'é muitas vezes confiada a senhores rígidos e egoístas' (p. 33), she in fact paints a very romantic image of these slave women which suggests a benign and harmonious system: 'Quem vê aquela sua extrema elegância, aquela comum alegria, e a cortês solicitude com que prestam seus serviços às famílias que aí se dirigem a passeio, não poderia jamais crer que essas seriam pobres escravas' (p. 33). There is no sign here of the corrupting influence of contact with morally degenerate slaves as described in *Opúsculo*, or of the cruel and inhuman treatment of slaves condemned in 'Paginas'. Instead Floresta suggests that there is no practical difference between slave and free labour, depicting happy workers in a scene the equivalent of which, she implies, one might witness in any other nation where slavery did not exist. Her aim appears to be to dispel the image of the horrors of slavery which fuelled European condemnation. Not only does she suggest that the slave washerwomen are content with their lives and status, she even pauses to appreciate the aesthetic value of the scene, describing it as 'um grato espectáculo pela franca e ingênua jocosidade de seus rostos pretos e expressivos, que mais se ressaltam com a brancura deliciosa de seus curtos saiotes' (p. 33). It becomes clear that Floresta is unable or unwilling to abandon the *ufanistic* tone of the text, even when discussing slavery, instead attempting to create an aesthetic space for the institution within the idealised, romanticised Brazil she seeks to construct for her European readers.

In the second of these essays, 'Viagem Magnética', we find perhaps the most explicitly pro-abolition argument expressed by Floresta, in which she condemns slavery in principle on moral grounds, as well as in practical terms for the harm it causes the nation. She declares that 'o espírito deste século, os verdadeiros interesses da nação, a moral e a humanidade imperiosamente reclamam a franquia da infeliz raça africana, oprimida pelo avaro despotismo de seus semelhantes!' (p. 171). She does not employ any of the positive imagery found in 'O Brasil', although she does once again emphasise that slavery is contradictory to the national character, writing 'Eu os vejo, estes desventurados indivíduos da raça africana, espalhados aos milhares em cada canto desta ampla região, calcar sob um belo céu o rico e livre solo brasileiro, arrastando atrás de si a pesada corrente da servidão: contra-senso escarnecedor das liberalíssimas instituições que governam esta bela nação!' (p. 171).

More significantly, she is keen to stress that steps have already been taken towards eliminating 'esta feia mancha que o Europeu deixou na América' (p. 171) and that the Brazilian people's natural love of justice and liberty will soon bring about total abolition. This analysis seems hopelessly optimistic in the light of the slavery debate in Brazil at that time, when the subject was largely ignored by politicians and public alike and laws were passed which gave more power to slaveholders. This reality is a far cry from the 'grito desdenhoso contra a opressão dos escravos' (p. 171), which Floresta suggests can be heard everywhere in her native country. However, this optimism is very much in keeping with the tone of the text, which is again predominantly *ufanistic*, although less explicitly so than 'O Brasil'. Here, rather than attempting to paint a benign picture of slavery, she tries to reassure the European reader that Brazil is moving rapidly towards abolition, and that most of the population oppose and are appalled by the existence of slavery in their country. In reality it would be another twenty years before such claims could legitimately be made, and thirty before slavery was finally abolished.

After the publication of her collection of essays, the next text to appear is Floresta's largest work, the journal of her travels in Italy and Greece, published over two volumes in 1864 and 1871 respectively. Here we find the same critical approach to the subject and, for the first time, very specific appeals for its end, but her condemnation of slave labour is still shaped by certain familiar Brazilian discourses. For the most part, Floresta now addresses slavery in generic terms rather than referring specifically to Brazilian slavery, in an apparent attempt to distance the subject from issues of national identity. She stresses that slavery exists in 'toda a América' (*Três Anos*, p. 257), a reference which can include Spain's final colonies as well as the USA. Moreover, by describing the 'milhões de infelizes escravos espalhados sobre a terra' (p. 223), and the continued oppression of blacks and whites in the New World and the Old (p. 258), she appears to extend slavery to metaphorically cover the politically and socially oppressed. With this technique Floresta deflects attention from her own nation's slave system whilst still making plain her condemnation of the institution.

Floresta also makes a point of condemning scientific theories of black moral inferiority, and the 'preconceitos mais absurdos e a atroz tirania' which this notion produces (p. 257). She stresses the many examples of 'devotamento, abnegação, coragem e heroísmo' that can be observed in Brazil's black population (p. 257). However, these characteristics are all noticeably un-threatening and are, in fact, identical to her portrayal of the complicit 'noble slave' in 'Paginas'. Furthermore, she challenges only the notion of moral inferiority and makes no attempt to demonstrate that black slaves possess the equivalent intellectual abilities which would afford them genuine social and political equality.

However, her position on the specific subject of Brazil's slave system is most clearly outlined in a lengthy passage which appears in the opening pages of the first volume. In this passage it is possible to identify many of the arguments employed by Floresta in her previous writings. The first and clearest of these arguments is that slavery is a source of shame to Brazil and damaging to the nation's international reputation. She introduces slavery as 'uma grande desgraça nacional, de que meu coração sempre se compadeceu profundamente!' (p. 41). It is unclear whether it is slavery itself or the shame it brings on Brazil which is the cause of Floresta's distress, although this becomes clearer when she goes on to urge her nation,

> Ó minha pátria querida [...] Sê consequente com as instituições livres que te regem, com a religião que professas: quebra, oh! quebra os grilhões de teus escravos! Por este ato de justiça e de filantropia, torne-te inteiramente digna da fama de generosa bondade que te atribuem aqueles que desconhecem tuas outras virtudes!' (p. 41)

Her appeal for abolition is clearly constructed as an act of patriotism and her primary concern is revealed to be the opinion of the international community. Whilst this concern was one of the driving forces behind the development of anti-slavery sentiment in Brazil, it did not, of course, feature in European condemnations of Brazilian slavery and is thus a meaningless piece of rhetoric to employ when addressing a European audience. As in 'O Brasil', Floresta stresses the anomalous position of slavery within an otherwise free and Christian nation. Intrinsic to this concern for Brazil's reputation, we once again find the assertion that Europe, and Portugal in particular, is to blame for the existence of slavery in Brazil. This is something that Floresta stresses vehemently here, reiterating the point three times on one page. Slavery is the 'funesta herança' which 'o espírito despótico do velho mundo transmitiu às plagas felizes da livre América!' (*Três Anos*, p. 41). Floresta is clearly suggesting that slavery is in fact completely alien to the New World, which is by nature free in a way in which, she implies, the Old World is not. By attributing slavery to Europe, she constructs the institution as an inherent part of the history and cultural identity of the Old World, whilst distancing it from Brazil's natural and national identity.

Floresta makes it clear that she is in favour of the abolition of slavery, describing it as 'esse grande passo na direção de tua [Brasil] verdadeira prosperidade' (pp. 41–2), but once again she presents abolition as being a wise choice for the benefit of the nation, not a moral obligation for the benefit of the slave, stressing the corrupting influence and the threat of violence slavery poses. She describes the institution as 'uma obra maldita pela ciência, pela religião e pela própria política. Embrutece a inteligência do proprietário, corrompe seu coração e, cedo ou tarde, sua propria carne', and observes that 'dela resultarão [...] terríveis represálias' (p. 42). It is clear from both these statements that her concern lies with the well-being of elite Brazilian society, not with the slaves. These arguments appear unnecessary and inappropriate in a text aimed at a European readership already convinced of the wrongs of slavery and far more concerned with its immorality than with the negative side effects for the slaveholder. Floresta does, at this point, claim to be addressing Brazilian slaveholders, yet she clearly intended the work to be published in Europe as she wrote it in French. Although she would have sent copies of *Três Anos* (and other works) to Brazil, its circulation is likely to have been limited to friends and family.[66] The vast majority of the text's readers would have been French. Floresta's continued use of the anti-slavery arguments traditionally employed to persuade Brazilian readers is therefore indicative of the extent to which her thinking was still shaped by the prevalent discourses of her own nation rather than the abolitionist sentiments she would have come into contact with in Europe.

Floresta goes on to condemn the pro-slavery faction in Brazil, urging the nation to ignore this 'voz desavergonhada da cupidez [...] [que] te engana, assustando-te, para melhor servires à sua ambição e à sua tirania!' (pp. 41–2). However, it is also clear that she does not advocate immediate abolition. She praises José Bonifácio, who was in favour of gradual emancipation and colonisation to replace the lost labour force, for recommending careful meas-

---

[66] Hand-written dedications tell us that the copy of the first volume in the national collection in Rio was given by Floresta to a cousin (whose name is largely illegible), whilst a copy of the second was passed on to the 'Ill° Sr Dr Sobragy' (?) by the writer's brother.

ures in the move towards abolition, and, in an apparent capitulation to the very pro-slavery arguments she had just condemned, she states that 'sábias medidas devem ser tomadas, digo-o, para evitar os resultados pretensamente perigosos da abolição da escravatura!' (p. 42). Moreover, the solution she envisages is extremely ambiguous. She suggests that the only way to avoid violent disorder is to 'transformar a escravidão em "domesticidade" [...] A solução da questão mais temível do novo mundo é, portanto, bem simples. Amai vossos negros e eles nos servirão, não como bichos, mas como homens livres e dedicados' (p. 42). Whilst this vision does, finally, allow the ex-slave a place in Brazilian society, the position she allocates them is still entirely submissive and shaped by racist thinking. In fact it is essentially no different from the final scenario in 'Paginas', in which the reader is assured that Domingos is no longer considered a slave, and continues to serve his master with dedication, in what is naively portrayed as a relationship of friendship between equals. Domingos, of course, remains a slave, and in this vision of 'domesticity' which we find in *Três Anos* it appears that the free black is also still a 'slave', by nature if not by name. In this I would suggest that the writer perhaps reveals the influence of Positivism on her thinking. Curiously, Duarte denies such an influence, stating that Floresta espouses 'a integração (não domesticação, como os positivistas) dos escravos na sociedade'.[67] Yet in the end it is precisely domestication that she advocates. She is never able to recommend a genuine integration of the slaves since she refuses to acknowledge their Brazilian identity.[68]

Floresta's final comments on slavery in Brazil are to be found in the French edition of her essay 'O Brasil', first published in Paris in 1871. This text has always been believed to be a simple re-publication of the essay contained within the collection published in Florence in 1859. However, a direct comparison of the two texts reveals several very interesting additional paragraphs. In particular, Floresta's praise for Brazil here takes on the explicit purpose of advertising her nation as a destination for economic migrants, a focus discussed in more detail in Chapter 6. She refers to various recent developments, but the event which interests her most, and which may well have been a direct spur to her publishing this amended text, is the passing of the Free Womb Law in September 1871. However, it appears that she may have rushed to press before fully understanding the facts of the law, either that or she is once again glossing over one of

---

67 Duarte, *Vida e Obra*, p. 198.

68 Floresta's emphasis on the black person's capacity for virtue, which she also stresses in *Três Anos*, also echoes Positivist notions. Comte characterised the black race 'primarily by the predominance of affectivity', which he eventually came to see as moral superiority (see Aron, p. 88). Like the moral superiority he ascribed to women, discussed in Chapter 3, this apparently positive definition did not bring with it active citizenship.

the less liberal realities of her nation, for she essentially claims the end of slavery, writing that this law 'a affranchi définitivement, dans tout le territoire brésilien la race noire esclave, avec des ménagements habiles de nature à assurer la protection des affranchis, la sauvegarde des intérêts des propriétaires et de ceux du trésor public' (*Le Brésil*, p. 49).[69] Moreover, in this final vision (shared by the vast majority of her Brazilian contemporaries) slave labour is to be replaced by European immigrants, whilst the massive freed black population just conveniently disappears, a 'solution' that confirms Floresta's fundamental inability to acknowledge the black population as part of Brazilian society and national identity.[70]

On the one hand, it is not difficult to see where Floresta's reputation as an abolitionist has come from. The writer began to address the subject of slavery and condemn its conditions and effects at a time when few of her contemporaries were doing so, pre-empting the emergence of a coherent anti-slavery discourse by at least a decade. She also makes full use of a range of anti-slavery arguments, including describing the cruelties of the system, its pernicious effects on society and the shame its continued existence brought upon the nation. All these lines of defence were to develop and become more commonplace in the years after the publication of 'Paginas', her most concerted writing on slavery, and it is even possible to speculate that the European horror and condemnation recounted by Floresta in *Opúsculo* may have directly contributed to the growing awareness of and concern for foreign opinion amongst the Brazilian elite. Floresta's contribution to the anti-slavery debate in Brazil cannot be denied. However, her early works also reveal a considerable degree of complicity with the justificatory, pro-slavery arguments used to shore up the institution. In the final analysis, despite its evident anti-slavery pretensions, her Brazilian-published writing on slavery is clearly compromised by the prevailing racism, complacency and dependence of the slavocracy in which she operated.

Even in her later European writing, where we do find an ethical, humanitarian condemnation of slavery, this approach is still overridden by a concern for the well-being of Brazilian society and her nation's international repu-

---

[69] This law, which liberated all children born to slave women after that date, but which effectively saw those children working as slaves for their mother's master until the age of 21, is widely perceived to have been an attempt to appease abolitionists and essentially to delay true abolition. Despite opposing it vociferously, beforehand, slaveholders quickly realised that it served them well, whilst abolitionists were equally quick to condemn the law, which would still see slavery continue well into the twentieth century (see Costa, *The Brazilian Empire*, pp. 165–6).

[70] Darién Davis notes how the end of slavery came to signify an escape from Brazil's African past, adding that 'even liberals who supported abolition did so not because they wanted slaves to be citizens, but because it was detrimental to their international image and their elite concept of nationhood' (*Avoiding the Dark: Race and the Forging of National Culture in Modern Brazil* (Aldershot: Ashgate, 1999), pp. 18–19).

tation, indicating that despite her contact with European liberal ideals, it was in fact the shame of European condemnation that continued to shape her arguments, combined with the growing 'desire to free Brazil from the problems of slavery', which Viotti da Costa identifies as the driving force behind the abolition movement.[71] Thus, for example, when Floresta stresses that the black slave's degeneracy is due only to his/her slave condition she opposes the growing theories of biologically determined racial inferiority, yet her own racial prejudices prevent her from converting this defence into a genuinely emancipatory discourse. Political and social equality are never on the agenda, only a romanticised spiritual equality that affords no real benefit to its 'recipient'.

The most important aspect of Floresta's portrayal of the slaves, which remains consistent throughout her work, is her continual insistence on their African birth and identity. More significant even than this fallacy, however, is the complete absence of the mulatto from her depiction of Brazilian society, both slave and free. Not only does she thus deny the constant sexual tension generated by white men having sex with their slave women, an issue I will discuss in more detail below, by ensuring that her imagined black population is absolutely distinct and absolutely black, she can also continue to refer to them as 'a raça africana' (as she does in *Três Anos*, p. 257), even when she cannot suggest that they were born in Africa. In this way she continues to cast the entire black population as somehow inherently not Brazilian, distancing and excluding them from national identity and citizenship. Floresta's exclusion of the black population reveals the fundamental influence of the racist, nationalist ideologies of her day. As Darién Davis observes, due to their perceived cultural and racial inferiority, 'Brazilian national identity would not, indeed could not, include blacks as equal participants in the nation.'[72] In the end, it must be recognised that Floresta operated within, and was severely limited and constrained in how far she could challenge the hegemonic, racist, patriarchal discourse that reinforced white, bourgeois constructions of Brazilian patriotism and national identity.

A consideration of the various arguments Floresta employs in her discussions of slavery certainly shows that the extravagant claims made by many of her biographers regarding her abolitionist credentials, outlined at the beginning of this chapter, are entirely unwarranted. Moreover, although a clear development can be charted through her work, I would contest Duarte's suggestion that in *Três Anos* Floresta reaches 'uma posição realmente humanitária'.[73] Historically, it was only in the 1870s and 1880s that Brazilian campaigners seeking the immediate end of slavery, often without indemnification, came

---

71 Costa, *The Brazilian Empire*, p. 170.
72 Davis, p. 15.
73 Duarte, *Vida e Obra*, p. 163.

to be identified as abolitionists. Previously, critics of the institution, who had favoured a gradual approach and the amelioration of slave conditions, seeking a compromise solution which would placate slaveholders, had been described as being 'anti-slavery' or emancipationists.[74] I would suggest that this important distinction should be considered in an evaluation of Floresta's writing, and that the expression of support for a gradual, measured end to slavery, which we find in *Três Anos*, definitively places Floresta in this category of 'emancipationist', but not 'abolitionist', in keeping with the period in which she was writing.

A gendered reading of Floresta's writings on slavery

An evaluation of Floresta's writings on slavery would not be complete without a consideration of her engagement with women slaves and the very specific issues and conditions that shaped their experience of slavery. A number of studies of the abolitionist movement in Great Britain and the USA have shown the importance of women in the movement, both as writers and campaigners, as well as the close links between abolitionist and feminist discourses, as women's participation in the public attack on slavery gave them an arena in which to also represent their own interests.[75] By drawing parallels between the oppression of slaves and the oppression of women, these abolitionists were able to simultaneously demand new spaces and freedoms for themselves as women. As one of the first women to discuss and criticise slavery in Brazil, Floresta's contribution to the development of a gendered attack on the institution is hugely important. A comparison of her work with the tactics employed by women abolitionists in Britain and the USA is extremely revealing in this regard.

In the British abolitionist campaign, women were active from the late eighteenth century onwards, being responsible for a quarter of all anti-slavery literature produced at that time.[76] As well as writing, British women of all classes raised money, signed petitions, abstained from slave-produced sugar and joined women's anti-slavery societies, the first of which was established in Birmingham in 1825.[77] Abolition was seen as one issue for which 'public

---

[74] See Toplin, pp. 58 and 78–9.

[75] Works such as Claire Midgley, *Women Against Slavery: The British Campaigns, 1780–1870* (London and New York: Routledge, 1995); Blanche Glassman Hersh, *The Slavery of Sex: Feminist-Abolitionists in America* (Urbana, Chicago and London: University of Illinois Press, 1978); and Jean Fagan Yellin, *Women and Sisters: The Antislavery Feminists in American Culture* (New Haven and London: Yale University Press, 1989).

[76] Midgley, p. 29.

[77] See Midgley, p. 43, and Kate Davies, 'A Moral Purchase: Femininity, Commerce and Abolition, 1788–1792', in *Women, Writing and the Public Sphere, 1700–1830*, ed. Elizabeth Eger et al. (Cambridge: Cambridge University Press, 2001), pp. 133–59 (p. 144).

interference' was proper for women because it was based on perceived feminine virtues of compassion and benevolence rather than political or economic interest, and appeals were made urging women to involve themselves in the extra-parliamentary campaign.[78] In fact, Claire Midgley suggests that 'despite their exclusion from positions of formal power in the national anti-slavery movement in Britain, [women] were an integral part of that movement and played distinctive and at times leading roles in the successive stages of the anti-slavery campaign' (pp. 3–4).

A similar situation can be found in the USA during the first half of the nineteenth century, where sentimental anti-slavery fiction, a genre which Karen Sánchez-Eppler identifies as being 'fundamentally feminine', was widespread.[79] Women's anti-slavery societies were equally popular; the state of Massachusetts alone boasted forty-one such societies in 1838. Whilst the women members of these organisations were rarely involved in the political activities of public speaking or writing pamphlets, their participation transformed traditional female, domestic activities into means of political persuasion.[80] Moreover, Garrisonian abolitionists, followers of the campaigner William Lloyd Garrison, argued that moral participation in the public sphere, rather than being contrary to womanhood, as their detractors suggested, was in fact 'an essential condition of womanhood'.[81] The Garrisonians were by no means the only group to make a link between abolitionist and feminist concerns. On both sides of the Atlantic arguments against the exploitation of slaves inevitably raised parallel questions regarding the exploitation of women. However, Hoganson stresses that although both anti-slavery and women's rights movements 'aimed to reform traditional beliefs and extend ideals of freedom', anti-slavery discourse often invoked conservative ideals of female weakness which compromised feminist notions and reinforced the view that women's position was biologically determined.[82] Both male and female anti-slavery writers made use of gendered arguments to attract female support for the cause, by emphasising women's role as guardians of morality and the particular threat to the modesty and purity of slave women.[83]

Sánchez-Eppler observes that the parallels to be found between abolitionist and feminist arguments mean 'it is hardly surprising that the figure

[78] Davies, pp. 133–4.
[79] Karen Sánchez-Eppler, 'Bodily Bonds: The Intersecting Rhetorics of Feminism and Abolition', in *The Culture of Sentiment: Race, Gender and Sentimentality in 19th Century America*, ed. Shirley Samuels (Oxford: Oxford University Press, 1992), pp. 92–114 (p. 98).
[80] Sánchez-Eppler, pp. 97–8.
[81] Kristin Hoganson, 'Garrisonian Abolitionists and the Rhetoric of Gender, 1850–1860', *American Quarterly*, 45: 4 (December 1993), 558–95 (p. 586).
[82] Hoganson, p. 560.
[83] See Midgley, p. 22, and Sánchez-Eppler, pp. 96–7.

of the female slave features prominently in both discourses'.[84] Writers were able to condemn 'the slavery of woman', fully aware of the implied double meaning, thus making abolition a question of women's rights and vice versa.[85] Likewise both slave and free women could gain from the example of the other; whilst an association with virtuous bourgeois femininity, established through a concern regarding the sexual exploitation of slaves, afforded slave women the moral value widely attributed to womanhood, the image of the labouring slave provided an example of women's strength and ability. For example, the campaigner Margaret Fuller argued that 'those who think the physical circumstances of woman would make a part in the affairs of national government unsuitable are by no means those who think it is impossible for Negresses to endure field work even during pregnancy'.[86]

Writers calling for the emancipation of women in Britain and the USA alike frequently compared the condition of women to the condition of slaves, in particular observing the parallels between slavery and marriage.[87] Likewise, those who wrote against slavery stressed the evils of the system by depicting the ways in which it destroyed the virtue of women and the sanctity of the family, stating that 'the most revolting feature of chattel slavery was the degradation of woman'.[88] Describing the British campaign, Anne Mellor observes the importance of gender in determining the nature of abolitionist discourse. Male writers stressed the theoretical 'rights of man' as espoused by Enlightenment thought and the French Revolution. Female writers, meanwhile, focused on the violation of domestic, feminine values: the separation of families and the sexual abuse of slave women at the hands of their masters.[89]

The threat slavery posed to family life was repeatedly highlighted, in particular the ways in which it obstructed the duties of motherhood, which was, of course, one of the most important indices of virtuous womanhood. Writers described the cruel punishment and over-working of pregnant slaves and their inability to look after their infants because they were forced to return to work, or because the children were sold away altogether.[90] Depic-

---

84   Sánchez-Eppler, p. 95.
85   Sánchez-Eppler, p. 109.
86   Quoted in Sánchez-Eppler, p. 96.
87   See, for example, Anne Mellor, '"Am I Not a Woman and a Sister?": Slavery, Romanticism, and Gender', in *Romanticism, Race, and Imperial Culture, 1780–1834*, ed. Alan Richardson and Sonia Hofkosh (Bloomington: Indiana University Press, 1996), pp. 311–29 (p. 311); Erlene Stetson, 'Studying Slavery: Some Literary and Pedagogical Considerations on the Black Female Slave', in *All the Women Are White, All the Blacks Are Men, But Some of Us Are Brave: Black Women's Studies*, ed. Gloria T. Hull, Patricia Bell Scott and Barbara Smith (New York: Feminist Press, 1982), pp. 61–84 (p. 76); and Sánchez-Eppler, pp. 95, 97 and 104.
88   Hoganson, p. 568; see also p. 559.
89   Mellor, p. 315.
90   Hoganson, p. 569.

tions of sexual abuse were equally common, drawing on the other great measure of femininity – modesty. In 1839 Sarah Grimké, one of the USA's most famous defenders of abolition and women's emancipation, wrote that 'in our slave states, if amid all her degradation and ignorance, a woman desires to preserve her virtue unsullied, she is either bribed or whipped into compliance'.[91] Whilst Grimké acknowledges the very different social condition of slave women, she makes it clear that she affords them the same values of modesty and virtue that were ascribed to, and expected of, white women, as well as the same right to defend that modesty from sexual aggression. Inescapably tied in with the question of sexual abuse is the issue of miscegenation. Sánchez-Eppler observes how miscegenation 'provides an essential motif of virtually all anti-slavery fiction, for even in those stories in which escape, slave rebellion, or the separation of families dominates the plot, its multiple challenges suffuse the text' (p. 103).[92]

Another common gendered motif to be found in anti-slavery writing is the description of the corrupting influence of slavery on white mistresses. Kate Davies observes the frequent depiction of the cruelty of Caribbean plantation wives in pamphlets published in Britain in the late 1700s, an image which could then be contrasted with that of compassionate and 'civilised' British women.[93] Similarly, in the USA slave-owning women were accused not only of cruelty, but also of indolence, incompetence and frivolity due to their dependence on slave labour.[94] Thus they lose their claim to true womanhood on a number of counts – not only had they lost the gentleness and compassion considered to be naturally feminine traits, they were also unable to perform a woman's domestic duty of looking after home and family.

However, it must be acknowledged, as Anne Mellor does, that despite drawing parallels, female abolitionists were also keen to confirm their difference from black slave women.[95] Women writers of anti-slavery literature included many more black characters in their work than their male contemporaries, and by giving slave men and women a voice they brought a more sympathetic dimension to the genre. However, Mellor notes that whilst they often afforded their slave characters moral authority, they continued to locate them in a position of cultural and intellectual inferiority.[96] Moreover, it must be remembered that writers imposed this 'voice' upon their slave subjects,

91   Quoted in Stetson, p. 74.
92   This statement is certainly true of *Uncle Tom's Cabin*, in which a number of Stowe's slave characters are of mixed racial descent including the novel's two most resistant and rebellious slaves, George and Cassy.
93   Davies, p. 149.
94   Hoganson, pp. 583–4.
95   Mellor, pp. 318–19.
96   Mellor, pp. 319–20 and 325.

a voice which spoke their own agenda, not, necessarily, the opinions and concerns of the slaves they claimed to speak for.

One of the most striking differences in the development of anti-slavery discourse in Brazil compared with the movement in Britain and the USA is the almost complete absence of an equivalent female participation. In fact, it was not until the 1870s that a few women began to write on the subject of emancipation and only in the 1880s, when the end of slavery was already looming on the horizon, that women began to participate in any number in abolitionist activities. Maria Lucia de Barros Mott, in her rare study of women's role in Brazilian abolition, identifies Josefina Durocher's *Idéias por Coordenar a Respeito da Emancipação* (1871) as the first female-authored essay to deal specifically with the subject of slave emancipation. This, however, is a deeply conservative and racist work which proposed a system of continuing slavery in everything but name, advocating a number of policies which were included later that year in the equally conservative and ineffectual law of the free womb.[97] Beyond this, the only woman Mott identifies as producing anti-slavery writing during the 1870s is the poet Narcisa Amália (p. 71). A few women's abolitionist societies were finally established during the 1880s, in Recife in 1884 and in Rio de Janeiro in 1885, for example.[98]

Brazil's abolition campaign never witnessed the concerted production of female-authored anti-slavery literature seen in Britain and the USA from the late eighteenth century onwards, nor the widespread participation of women in extra-parliamentary activities such as fundraising, petition-signing or public speaking. Floresta's engagement in the debate at such an early date is therefore extremely unusual and significant. However, it is immediately apparent from her work that despite being one of very few woman to write publicly about slavery in the 1850s, she makes very little engagement with female slaves in her discussions, employing few of the gendered arguments common to female abolitionist writing in Britain and the USA.

Other than Floresta, there is only one other documented example of anti-slavery literature written by a woman in Brazil in the 1850s, the novel *Úrsula*, by Maria Firmina dos Reis, which was published in Maranhão in 1859.[99] Although the novel is primarily a romantic tale of doomed love between white protagonists, it features various slave characters that are central to the narrative as well as describing and condemning the horrors of slavery. The novel is particularly unusual because the author was herself an Afro-Brazilian

---

[97] Maria Lúcia de Barros Mott, *Submissão e resistência: A mulher na luta contra a escravidão* (São Paulo: Contexto, 1988), pp. 68–70.

[98] Mott, pp. 78–9.

[99] I consulted the 1975 facsimile edition: Maria Firmina dos Reis, *Úrsula: romance original brasileiro* (Rio de Janeiro: Gráfica Olímpica Editora, 1975).

ex-slave. A comparison of this novel with Floresta's writings on slavery, in particular her work of fiction, 'Paginas', serves to further highlight Floresta's neglect of slave women. Although the central slave character in *Úrsula* is male, the novel contains a second, female slave character, Susana, who also plays an important role as spokesperson of the slaves' African heritage, recalling her idyllic former life there before being captured as a young woman. Mãe Susana, as she is affectionately called by her fellow slaves, provides the link to their own motherland, affirming their birth right to freedom and their independent identity as Africans. Moreover, although the author acknowledges no influence from Stowe's *Uncle Tom's Cabin* (as Floresta emphatically does in 'Paginas'), Susana is tortured in an attempt to discover the whereabouts of the eloping lovers and dies rather than betray them, closely echoing Uncle Tom's demise in the American novel. In fact the character of 'mãe Susana' is the female partner/parallel to Stowe's 'pai Tomás', as Uncle Tom was translated into Portuguese. Thus not only does Firmina dos Reis's character perform a final act of tacit resistance equivalent to Uncle Tom's, an option not offered to Domingos in 'Paginas', more significantly in *Úrsula* it is a woman who is given this role, whilst in Floresta's writings her female slaves never reveal the slightest resistance to their condition.

In Firmina dos Reis's novel it is also possible to identify implicit parallels between the condition of white women and the condition of slaves. The white hero Tancredo's own mother is abused by her husband and can do nothing but accept her mistreatment with patient resignation. Likewise both Úrsula, the young white heroine, and her mother are completely at the mercy of the latter's evil brother, and the brutality with which he treats his slaves echoes the callous and barbarous way in which he pursues his niece, whom he is determined to marry entirely against her wishes. This he eventually achieves, and it is a captivity from which Úrsula only escapes by her descent into madness and rapid death. In this novel the white women and the slaves are united as victims of the cruel white plantation owner, a union emphasised by the fact that the women treat their few slaves with kindness and generosity, in what is portrayed as a relationship of reciprocal devotion and solidarity. In contrast, Floresta's white men and women are united in opposition to the slave population, whether it is as abusive slaveowners in 'Paginas', or as responsible parents defending their home from the corrupting influences of slavery, as Floresta recommends in *Opúsculo*.

Whilst the very fact that female slaves have a limited presence in her work is significant, Floresta's treatment of those that do appear is particularly interesting. The first and most significant occasion in which we encounter a mention of female slaves and their experience is in *Opúsculo Humanitário* in a condemnation of the use of slave wet nurses and a discussion of the corrupting influence of close contact with household slaves in general. This subject was a source of considerable concern in Brazil in the mid-nineteenth century, as Sonia Giacomini documents in her study of female slaves. She cites a text entitled 'A substituição dos braços escravos pelos livres', published in the Rio newspaper *O Americano* in 1850: 'Como amigo dos nossos patrícios e interessados na paz das famílias da nossa terra, não devemos deixar de aconselhar-lhes que substituam, ou ao menos diminuam o número desses brutos inimigos que se nutrem em nosso seio.'[100] The choice of allegory is particularly significant here, not only because the author suggests, apparently with no sense of irony, that it is the white family that provides for the slave and is the victim of his/her greed, inverting the reality of the black woman feeding the white child, but also because the (white) Brazilian nation is clearly being constructed as a (white) nursing mother who is involuntarily suckling the 'enemy' to the detriment of her own offspring. The writer thus excludes categorically, if obliquely, the black slave family from his/her definition of 'our nation's families'.

It is clear from *Opúsculo* that Floresta shared these concerns regarding the pernicious effect of domestic slavery on the white slaveowning family and the particular threat posed by wet nurses, for she describes these slave women as 'míseras africanas' and 'desmoralizadas escravas' and their milk as impure, contaminating 'o físico e o moral' (*Opúsculo*, pp. 93–5). She shows the black slave nurse no pity in this discussion, describing them as wretched and demoralised not out of compassion for their fate, but rather out of concern for the negative influence on their charges. Floresta fails to acknowledge that many of these wet nurses would have suffered the death of their own infants or, perhaps worse, been separated from them.[101] More significantly, Floresta does not recognise the fact that these slaves were themselves mothers, with their own maternal rights and responsibilities. Two years later she briefly demonstrates a more sympathetic approach to the slave wet nurse in 'Paginas' when, in describing the horrors of family separation, she writes: 'quem não tenha visto na misera escravidão [...] a mãi a quem dilaceram a alma arrancando-lhe o filhinho para obterem d'ella maior jornal como ama de leite' ('Paginas', p. 31).

However, the only actual characterisation of a slave mother in 'Paginas' (or any other Floresta text) does not appear to maintain such a sympathetic position. Whilst acknowledging that the mother of Domingos' son has been corrupted by slavery, rather than being so by nature, it is her own degenerate physical and moral state which Floresta blames for her son's weakness and death, not the fact that she is sold away from the child. In fact Floresta confirms her belief in the potent influence of breast milk, stating that the child suffered from 'uma saude debil que o leite de uma mãi viciosa acabou por

---

100 Giacomini, p. 146.
101 See, for example, Robert Conrad, *Children of God's Fire: A Documentary History of Black Slavery in Brazil* (Princeton, NJ: Princeton University Press, 1983), p. 133.

infeccionar' (p. 55). Moreover, the woman's failure as a mother is contrasted with Domingos' 'virtudes paternaes que poderião servir de modelo ás mesmas mães' (p. 55). It is significant that the only slave mother to appear in Floresta's work should lose her child, whilst the slave nurses she condemns are not even acknowledged as mothers. This failure to highlight slave maternity is in stark contrast to American abolitionist women writers, who sought to emphasise slave women's maternal qualities as an essential part of their quest to portray slave families as fit for assimilation into free society.[102]

Beyond Floresta's discussion of slave nurses and her depiction of the mother of Domingos' son, we find only two further accounts of slave women: Maria, the object of Domingos' doomed love in 'Paginas', and the washerwomen described in 'O Brasil'. These two accounts present very different images; whilst Maria is mistreated and miserable, a state which eventually leads to her death, the washerwomen are depicted as robust and happy workers. What both descriptions appear to have in common, however, is a latent sexualisation of the slave woman. The washerwomen are described primarily in terms of there physical appearance as aesthetic objects, and Floresta points out the 'brancura deliciosa de seus curtos saiotes' ('O Brasil', p. 33), a state of dress in which a respectable white woman would never be seen, and which, described in positive terms, implies a certain natural or deliberate lack of modesty. Likewise, although Maria is portrayed as a good and moral slave, the first description the reader encounters of her is predominantly physical. She is, 'uma negra insinuante e esbelta, graciosa e intelligente' ('Paginas', p. 46). Later, when Maria is sick and dying, we are told that she has lost 'aquelle corpo gracioso e esbelto, aquella physionomia insinuante e prasenteira, a côr de veludado azeviche que lhe servia de involucro' ('Paginas', p. 47). Once again such a sensual description would be unthinkable if the object were a white woman. This sexualised portrayal of Maria seems strangely incongruous in the context of her supposed depiction as a good and virtuous companion for Domingos.

It would appear that Floresta was unable to escape the influence of prevailing contemporary perceptions of slave women as promiscuous and sexually available and/or threatening. Robert Slenes observes how many historians have continued to construct slaves as promiscuous, an image they have

> drawn from an uncritical reading of nineteenth-century accounts left by European travellers and well-to-do Brazilians [...] [who] viewed blacks through an ethnocentric and elitist prism which caused them to overlook or misrepresent the evidence regarding the intimate life and domestic arrangements of slaves. Their distortion of the experience of slave women was particularly severe.[103]

---

[102] Hoganson, p. 568.
[103] Slenes, 'Black Homes, White Homilies', p. 127.

This image was to be a persistent and deeply embedded stereotype: José Veríssimo, for example, writing after the end of slavery in 1894, describes the sexual allure and promiscuity of mulatta house slaves, accusing them of 'the ruin of our physical and moral manhood'.[104]

It is not only in the sexualised descriptions of female slaves that Floresta reveals the strong discursive influence of contemporary attitudes. Unlike British and American anti-slavery writers, Floresta never really addresses the subject of the sexual abuse of slave women, although this behaviour was equally widespread and accepted in Brazil. Conrad documents a case brought to court in 1884, only four years before abolition, of a master who had raped his approximately twelve-year-old slave girl, observing that the decision of the jury in favour of the master indicates that 'the rape or molestation of slave women by their masters was essentially *legal behaviour* for as long as slavery existed in Brazil'.[105]

We do, however, find one allusion to such encounters in 'Paginas': in an apparent attempt to justify her slave hero's morally dubious relationship with the mother of his son, whom he does not love and does not marry, Floresta explains to her reader that 'Domingos, [...] em suas passageiras relações com um ser tão inferior a si, não tinha feito mais que imitar a muitos grandes senhores' (p. 55). Whilst it is clear that Floresta does not approve of these sexual relations between master and slave, the reason for her criticism appears to be the inferiority of the slave woman, not the abuse of power exercised by the master. In fact she makes no acknowledgement of the fact that the slave women might not be willing participants in such encounters. Floresta here allocates her noble hero a position of moral superiority over white masters, whom she blames for the poor example they have set him. This is a curious reversal of the usual discourse regarding the corrupting influence of slaves, a discourse Floresta herself had previously employed in *Opúsculo*. In reality, I would suggest that this passing reference to sexual relations between master and slave is little more than a narrative necessity to explain and excuse Domingos' incongruous sexual behaviour, itself an unfortunate anomaly which, it appears, Floresta was obliged to include in order for Domingos to have a son.

However, whether she is criticising the behaviour of white masters or excusing the behaviour of Domingos, she is completely unable to engage with the women on the other side of the sexual equation. Not only does she show no perception of or sympathy for the abuse potentially involved in such an unequal relationship, she does not even refer to them as women. Instead, in an extraordinary act of degenderisation, she refers only to 'inferior beings'. I have already highlighted Floresta's portrayal of exclusively black, African

[104] Quoted in Conrad, *Children of God's Fire*, p. 223.
[105] Conrad, *Children of God's Fire*, p. 274.

slaves, in contrast to the frequent appearance of mulatto slaves in American anti-slavery literature including *Uncle Tom's Cabin*, as described above. This avoidance of the subject of miscegenation in Floresta's work goes hand in hand with her failure to address the sexual abuse of slave women, since the two issues are inexorably linked.

One gendered argument, common to British and American anti-slavery literature, which Floresta does employ to some extent, is the motif of the cruel, corrupted white mistress.[106] In a fictional context, the slave girl Maria's mistress fulfils this role in 'Paginas'. The reader is told that Maria is 'tratada com inaudito rigor por sua senhora', who is described as a 'mulher aspera e destituida dos favores da natureza, esta ostentava uma grande moralidade, á que ninguem jamais pensara attentar, espiando todos os passos da pobre escrava, empregando-a sem interrupção e com dureza em seu serviço, [...] nada a podia contentar, nem abrandar o seu genio feroz' (p. 46). One of the most noticeable aspects of the description is the way Floresta perceives this woman as unnatural, echoing the criticisms levelled against women who failed to breast-feed their children, as discussed in Chapter 1. Just as a woman's natural duty is to nurse her own children, so her natural disposition is one of gentleness and compassion. Therefore this mistress's behaviour compromises her womanhood. Whilst Floresta's portrayal of bad slave masters in 'Paginas' was intended to shame her male, slaveowning readers and highlight the negative outcome of their behaviour, this description of a cruel mistress is included to encourage her female readers to question their own treatment of their household slave women. Not only does she suggest that the poor treatment of slaves undermines white women's femininity, she also accuses Maria's mistress, and real women like her, of hypocrisy for presenting a public image of morality whilst privately indulging in an immoral and unwomanly abuse of power. This accusation echoes Floresta's frequent reference to the hypocrisy of Brazil's white male elite discussed above.

The other factor which emerges from the description of Maria's mistress is her resentment of her slave. However, although Floresta states that she watches Maria obsessively, she in fact implies that it is envy, rather than jealousy, that drives her, describing how 'a ternura com que era a sua escrava amada por Domingos', compared with 'a frieza de seu marido para com ella', exacerbates the woman's cruelty (p. 46). Contemporary observers and historians have frequently referred to the jealousy of white women towards their slave girls and the appalling acts of abuse this sometimes led to,[107] but this was a jealousy born out of the perceived sexual allure and promiscuity of slave women and the widespread and open sexual relations (consensual

---

[106] The motif of the violent mistress can also be found in many depictions of slavery in Brazil, written by Brazilians and foreign observers alike. See Giacomini, pp. 157–9.

[107] See Giacomini, pp. 155 and 159–61.

or otherwise) between master and slave.[108] In this depiction, however, there is no implication that Maria's master has, or desires to have, sexual relations with her, or even that his wife suspects as much, only that he is not particularly loving with his wife. It is possible that Floresta was here observing an actual social phenomenon, but that her apparent distaste for the subject of inter-racial sexual encounters means that she has to attribute different and somewhat implausible motivations to the white woman's rancour.

In the context of social commentary found in *Opúsculo*, Floresta makes only one brief mention of cruelty on the part of mistresses. Due to the central focus of the text on education, her criticism of such behaviour is primarily directed at the negative influence of such scenes on the white woman's daughter. In fact this concern so governs Floresta's thinking here that, although she uses strong language to criticise such cruelties, her actual recommendation is only that they should not occur in front of the children:

> é muito para desejar que certas mães de família [...] retenham perante suas filhas os freqüentes assomos de cólera que as levam a vomitar grosseiras injúrias contra eles, acompanhadas muita vez de castigos corporais que, com horror, temos visto consentirem e até excitarem suas jovens filhas a aplicar-lhes elas mesmas! (*Opúsculo*, p. 115)

Once again, women who abuse their slaves are portrayed as being deficient or incomplete women, but on this occasion their deficiency lies in their failure as mothers rather than their lack of feminine attributes. However, these two uses of the motif of the cruel mistress again reveal Floresta's overwhelming concern regarding the corrupting influence of slavery on the white slaveo-wning population. Given her constant preoccupation with (white) women's social position and her emphasis on their role as moral guardians and educators, it is of no surprise to see that she was worried about the effect of slavery on women's virtue. It is extremely significant that this should be the only specifically gendered anti-slavery argument to feature in Floresta's work; she can discuss white women's responses to slavery as distinct from white men's behaviour, but when attempting to portray the world of the slave, she is unable to engage with the very specific experiences of slave women.

Floresta's exclusion of slave women is put into even clearer perspective when we compare it with her own discussion of native Indian women. Floresta

---

[108] Jane-Marie Collins observes that whilst sexual jealousy was a common factor, and the cause widely identified by contemporary observers, there were in fact a number of other possible explanations for the abuse of slave women by their mistresses, including a desire for power, as the mistress–slave relationship was one of the few situations in which white women occupied a position of superiority ('Slavery, Subversion and Subalternity: Gender and Violent Resistance in Nineteenth-Century Bahia', in *Brazilian Feminisms*, ed. Solange Ribeiro de Oliveira and Judith Still (Nottingham: University of Nottingham, 1999), pp. 34–56).

dedicates several chapters to them in *Opúsculo*, as discussed in Chapter 4, emphasising the role they have to play in Brazilian society. She goes to considerable lengths to stress what excellent mothers they are, thereby including them in her discussions of virtuous womanhood as defined by maternity. The social status she ascribes to them in *Opúsculo* is still clearly inferior to that of educated, bourgeois white women, but she is able to acknowledge them as fellow women and citizens, and credit them with all the virtues and piety essential to her vision of a regenerated and valuable female identity, a vision she cannot or will not extend to black slave women.

A comparison of Floresta's writings on women's position in society and her discussion of black slavery reveals a number of essentially identical arguments. She stresses the moral fortitude of both women and slaves, and more importantly their potential for virtue if properly educated and treated. Leading on from this idea, she also suggests that neither should be blamed for faults which are the product of their oppressed condition. Moreover, Floresta emphasises that both the emancipation of women and the emancipation of slaves are vital to elevate Brazil's standing in the hierarchy of civilised nations, and that their oppression is incompatible with the liberal identity of the free and independent Brazilian nation. Yet, despite employing such similar rhetoric, not once does she unite these arguments or draw parallels between slavery and the condition of women in patriarchal society, parallels which, as discussed above, were frequently made in feminist and abolitionist literature in Britain and the US.

Most specifically, by not addressing the particular experiences of slave women, Floresta reveals the racial and social conditioning and bias behind her thinking, which prevented her from identifying with black slave women or including them in her vision of universal womanhood. In particular, by excluding them from her consideration of motherhood whilst emphasizing the natural bond between white mother and child, Floresta naturalises the exclusion of the black slave population from Brazilian patriotic discourse and denies black women's part in the nation-building project and their resulting claim to citizenship.

Floresta's inability to combine her 'feminism' with her 'abolitionism', undoubtedly the two discourses which have most firmly secured her status in the Brazilian canon, means that both lost out on the power that such reciprocity afforded, and which was so successful in British and American discourse. More importantly, the incompatibility of Floresta's apparent concern for the oppressed and her complicity with the racist, bourgeois patriarchy within which the Brazilian elite constructed their new nationhood, compromises her defence of the slave and her vision of woman equally. Despite accusing the white male elite of hypocrisy for sanctioning slavery after sacrificing so much to cast off their own colonial chains, Floresta in fact commits the same act of selective, elitist liberation within her own discourse on womanhood.

6

The Patriot

The primary aim of this chapter is to look at how Floresta reconciles one of the core contradictions within her own literary identity: her continual construction of herself as a devoted, patriotic Brazilian despite living in Europe for most of her adult life, and how, in fact, these two parts of her identity, the patriot and the ex-patriate, are inter-connected and mutually dependent. I will therefore be looking at how Floresta depicts both her own nation and the European nations she lives in and visits, how she manipulates these representations according to whether she is addressing a Brazilian audience or publishing in Europe, and the final construction of Brazil which emerges in her European writing. A particularly intriguing element of this construction is the question of political structure, and at the end of the chapter I will attempt to piece together Floresta's mostly brief and sporadic references to modes of governance in order to identify her own political ideals and thus test the validity of her reputation as an adherent of federal republicanism.

As I have already noted on various occasions through the course of this study, Floresta's work undergoes a noticeable change in style and approach after her first visit to Europe between 1849 and 1852. The chance to contemplate Brazil from the outside apparently enables her to conceptualise the nation for the first time. After this visit, foreign perceptions of Brazil and its status in the international arena become central to her discussion of every social phenomenon she addresses, but more importantly she also begins to address the issue of national identity itself, constructing the nation within this newly-acquired international awareness. Despite adopting the pseudonym of 'Brasileira' as early as 1832, it is only upon leaving Brazil that Floresta's patriotism is really awoken. I will therefore be looking at works written and published after 1852, in particular her most important Brazilian publication *Opúsculo Humanitário* (1853), which I will be comparing with various essays and travel journals published in Florence and Paris between 1857 and 1871.

More than anything else, the commonality in these seemingly disparate texts is patriotism, as a defining rhetoric and driving force. Floresta states her patriotic motivations baldly in *Opúsculo* (p. 45), as discussed in earlier chapters, and they are no less tangible in her European work. Despite no longer addressing a Brazilian readership she continues to use patriotism as her primary justification for writing and publishing. Moreover, she makes continual reference to her love for the 'pátria', and her profound *saudades*, observing that 'a memória da Pátria [é um] poderoso talismã que segue a todos na terra estrangeira' ('Abismo', p. 67). Apparently aware of the incongruity of this posture in the face of her continuing residence in Europe, she also consistently implies that she is not a willing traveller, but is rather obliged to remain an 'exilada sobre a terra' ('Abismo', p. 69) by some unexplained force of circumstance (e.g. also, *Itinerário*, pp. 153 and 165; *Três Anos*, pp. 86 and 98).

In truth, Floresta's life was defined by travel more than any other factor.[1] The true extent and nature of her movements in Europe is undocumented, but some details are well known and others can be glimpsed from *Fragmentos de uma Obra Inédita*, her final publication in homage to her dead brother, which contains some biographical information. What is known is that on her first visit to Europe she spent six months in Portugal as well as living mostly in France, and may also have visited England at this time. After her return in 1856 she travelled briefly in Germany and Belgium, a trip from which her first European publication, *Itinerário de uma Viagem à Alemanha*, resulted, and spent three years travelling in Italy and Greece between 1858 and 1861, residing in Florence for part of that time, where she published several works. She also states that she lived in London for a while (*Fragmentos*, p. 32), as well as visiting different parts of England on several further occasions, and she appears to have been living in Germany, probably in Berlin, in 1868, visiting Austria and Switzerland before returning to Paris (*Fragmentos*, p. 32). She was to see her 'beloved' patria only once more, returning for a little over two years between 1872 and 1875. It is extraordinary that such an evidently restless soul should claim, as Floresta does, that she can never be a true traveller, because her heart is not in it (*Itinerário*, p. 116).

It is not only Floresta's image of the nation and of herself as a patriot that is shaped by her travels, however. It is clear that she also draws immense confidence from the experience, employing her new-found identity as a traveller to establish a position of greater authority for herself as a writer, in both her Brazilian and her European work. Most significantly, she is acutely aware of her very particular and unusual identity as a Brazilian (and moreover a Brazilian woman) travelling in Europe, frequently observing the lack of compatriot travellers and twice noting with pride that she must be the first Brazilian woman (or even the first Brazilian) to perform a certain rite (*Três Anos*, pp. 61 and 348). The relish she evidently takes in her pioneering status belies her construction of herself as an unwilling traveller. Maria Frawley

---

[1]   Even before leaving Brazil she had in fact travelled extensively, covering a greater distance between Rio Grande do Norte and Rio Grande do Sul than on most of her travels between European countries.

observes that, as for Dorothy in *The Wizard of Oz*, travel was meant to reveal that there is no place like home.[2] Floresta's decision not to return 'home' simultaneously contradicts and underscores the patriotic discourse within which she constructs her writing and her actions.

Throughout this chapter I will be drawing comparisons between *Opúsculo* and Floresta's European publications to demonstrate how she manipulates the discourses of national identity and *ufanismo* to serve her differing 'patriotic' purposes, focusing primarily on her polarised construction of Brazil versus Europe, a polarity through which she highlights Brazil's failings in *Opúsculo* but elevates her nation's position in the world order when writing in Europe. However, I shall begin my discussion by looking at Floresta's reaction to and manipulation of European depictions of her homeland, specifically the popular accounts of travel in Brazil which were published throughout the nineteenth century. It is this literature, and the images and attitudes towards Brazil that it fostered, which appear to have first awoken Floresta to her own national identity and the importance of Brazil's status within a wider order. It is therefore the logical starting point for an analysis of the discursive response it provoked, as well as providing one of the clearest insights into her own patriotic positioning and her relationship with European thought.

Floresta as a reader of travel writing

Floresta's considerable use of French travel accounts of Brazil in her depictions and discussions of Brazil's social ills is undoubtedly one of the most interesting aspects of *Opúsculo*. She quotes from five different sources. Two are amongst the most famous French writers on Brazil in the nineteenth century, Ferdinand Denis,[3] and Auguste de Saint-Hilaire,[4] who were both there in the years immediately before independence and whose names would have been well-known to Floresta's readers. Two are writers whose work had been published extremely recently in Paris.[5] Together with the passage quoted from an article in the *Revue des Deux Mondes* of 1851, Floresta's use of these contemporary writers reveals the extent to which she kept abreast

---

[2]   Maria H. Frawley, *A Wider Range: Travel Writing by Women in Victorian England* (Rutherford: Fairleigh Dickinson University Press; London: Associated University Presses, 1994), p. 27.

[3]   The author of a number of famous historical and descriptive studies on Brazil, where he travelled from 1816 to 1821. He is often credited with inspiring Brazil's Romantic Indianist movement of the nineteenth century through his appeals for an original Brazilian literature.

[4]   The naturalist Saint-Hilaire also travelled in Brazil for six years from 1816 onwards, and published a number of studies of Brazilian botany and travel accounts between 1825 and 1849.

[5]   These texts are Alphonse Rendu, *Études topographiques, médicales et agronomiques sur le Brésil* (Paris: J. B. Baillière, 1848), and Francis de Castelnau, *Histoire du voyage*, vol. 1 (Paris : Chez P. Bertrand, 1850).

of new literary production regarding Brazil during her time in Europe and hints at something approaching an obsession with foreign opinion regarding her nation.

Floresta quotes from these various texts on a range of social issues including the corruption of the clergy and religious practices, and the idleness and degradation of the poor. However, she makes it clear that her interest in these travel accounts lies primarily with their depiction of women and it is her clearly stated awareness of women's under-representation in traditional national histories which leads her to turn to foreign observers for information. She writes, 'não é na história de nossa terra que iremos estudar a situação de nossas mulheres, porque infelizmente os poucos homens que têm escrito apenas esboços dela não as acharam dignas de ocupar algumas páginas de seus livros. Assim recorremos aos viajantes estrangeiros' (p. 47). Floresta here reveals herself to be far ahead of her time, not only in criticising women's exclusion from history and implicitly appealing for a new, inclusive approach, but also in her identification of travel writing as a source of historical data about women's lives. A century and a half later, historians in Latin America and elsewhere are still turning to travel accounts as valuable sources.[6] Where Floresta differs from many of today's historians is that she uses only male-authored accounts, whilst women travel writers are now widely seen as the source of more detailed depictions of women's domestic life.[7] Whilst the absence of women-authored travel accounts in *Opúsculo* might be attributed to a sense of the greater authority of male writers, it is likely that the explanation lies simply in the lack of published accounts by women. In her list of nineteenth-century women travellers to Brazil, Miriam Moreira Leite includes only six who were there before 1853 (when *Opúsculo* was published), and of those, only the journal of the English woman Maria Graham was published during this period, and then only in English, which Floresta did not read.[8]

What is most interesting, however, about Floresta's engagement with the work of these male travel writers is her response to the criticisms they make and the tension which begins to emerge between her patriotic desire to highlight Brazil's problems and thus encourage improvement, and her own deep-seated sense of national pride, which evidently baulks at hearing her nation

---

[6]   One of the first historians to draw on travel writing in Latin America was Gilberto Freyre. See June Hahner, *Women Through Women's Eyes: Latin American Women in Nineteenth-century Travel Accounts* (Wilmington, DE: SR Books, 1998), p. xxi (note 31).

[7]   See, for example, Hahner, *Women Through Women's Eyes*, p. xvi, and Miriam Lifchitz Moreira Leite, 'A dupla documentação sobre mulheres no livro das viajantes (1800–1850)', in *Vivência: História, Sexualidade e imagens femininas*, ed. Cristina Bruschini and Fúlvia Rosemberg (São Paulo: Brasiliense; Fundação Carlos Chagas, 1980), pp. 195–226.

[8]   Miriam Lifchitz Moreira Leite, 'Mulheres viajantes no século XIX', *Cadernos Pagu: gênero, ciências, história*, 15 (2000), 129–43 (p. 131).

derided. Floresta astutely acknowledges that the descriptions of Brazilian customs made by foreign observers are 'por vezes alterada[s]' (p. 47), clearly recognising the potential for cultural bias when she observes that even 'aqueles mesmos cuja simpatia pelos brasileiros é uma garantia de imparcialidade [...] referem muitos casos [...] que demonstram evidentemente o triste estado da nossa civilização' (p. 100). Floresta's problem, though, is that it is not in her interest to emphasise the prejudices which might have coloured these texts. On the contrary, it is important to stress their validity as honest and accurate accounts if she is to use them to spur her Brazilian readers into action, and for the most part she does just this, following her quotes with confirmations such as 'o viajante brasileiro [...] não poderá deixar de reconhecer o cunho da verdade nessas linhas' (p. 129) and 'esta franqueza agrada por ser a expressão da verdade' (p. 140). Floresta is also keen to stress that despite their criticisms, travellers to Brazil all give credit to the Brazilian character as 'dócil, modesto e generoso' (p. 139), and makes a point of informing the reader that she had personally heard Auguste de Saint-Hilaire in 1851 'falar dos brasileiros com a mais entusiástica afeição' (p. 100).

Whilst acknowledging that it is painful to hear these 'verdades que ferem o nosso orgulho nacional' (p. 100), Floresta stresses that they are deserved, and urges her readers not to be blinded by a false sense of patriotism: 'o mal entendido orgulho que nos faz persistir em inveterados erros' (p. 100). However, this position appears to slip a little by the end of the text, in particular with regard to the passage Floresta quotes from the *Revue des Deux Mondes*, where we see a new, more defensive stance being adopted. It is perhaps telling that this particular article describes the open flirting to be seen during church services in Rio, and adopts a noticeably ridiculing tone. As a double condemnation of middle-class women's modesty and their piety, this passage appears to have caused Floresta particular offence, for she writes with obvious chagrin: 'Lemos estas linhas em Paris, quando com mais indulgência analisávamos outras repreensíveis faltas dos franceses, mais dignas da censura desse escritor, pois que são cometidas por um velho povo que tantos séculos conta de civilização' (p. 138). Although she reluctantly admits that the account is not entirely untrue, we no longer find the earlier suggestion that such criticism is deserved, nor that it is in the nation's interest to hear it. On the contrary, she appears almost to be accusing the writer of meddling in others' business when she goes on to observe: 'Os erros da pátria são como os de nossos filhos: queremos nós mesmos censurá-los e puni-los, mas não podemos sofrer vê-los estigmatizados por estranhos a quem nada devem' (p. 138).

It is interesting to observe here the beginnings of a more critical approach to Europe and the acknowledgement that the Old World does not offer a perfect model for Brazil to follow. This subtle shift can also be seen a few pages earlier when Floresta comments on the miserable situation of many lower-class women who are reduced to prostitution in England, which she pointedly refers to as 'o país mais poderoso da idade actual' (p. 132). On both occasions Floresta reveals a particular frustration with the continued existence of social and moral degeneration in supposedly great and civilised nations which, it is implied, do not have the excuse of colonial mismanagement and should know better. Although such criticisms are drowned out by the overwhelmingly positive descriptions of European society necessary to Floresta's purpose in *Opúsculo*, these brief comments foretell the increasingly defensive and critical position which Floresta would subsequently come to adopt when writing and publishing her own work within Europe.

It is not only Floresta's depiction of Brazilian society which undergoes a radical shift in her European publications; her very approach to the European travel writers who describe Brazil also changes noticeably. In *Opúsculo* these accounts were central to her purpose in highlighting Brazil's social problems and, more importantly, in showing the reproach these problems provoked in 'civilised' Europe. Once she is writing for that European audience, however, Floresta sets out to challenge and refute the negative accounts of Brazilian society which shape overseas perceptions of her nation. This newly critical approach is most clearly voiced in the essay 'O Brasil', in which she accuses travellers to Brazil of writing 'os maiores absurdos acerca daquele vasto império' (p. 25) and 'argúcias empregadas para fazer rir os Europeus' (p. 27). As we saw previously in *Opúsculo*, it is this ridiculing tone which Floresta resents most strongly. Here she gleefully turns the tables with an example of European ignorance, observing that one contemporary traveller to Brazil, a 'divertido amontoador de palavras, a quem faremos a cortesia de calar o nome', mistook for eternal snow the mists that crown the mountains behind Rio ('O Brasil', p. 25). Floresta also reiterates with much greater force the accusation touched upon above in *Opúsculo*, that European observers are in no position to condemn Brazil's social failings, 'erros e defeitos que não precisariam cruzar o Atlântico para encontrar. Muitíssimos países da velha Europa fornecê-lhos-iam em grande quantidade' ('O Brasil', p. 37).

However, it is the widespread ignorance of travel writers regarding their subject which forms the basis of the fundamental point Floresta wishes to make in her European works. She observes that, as a huge country with widely varying peoples, customs and climate, Brazil can only be known through extensive travel and impartial observation, yet European writers who have spent only a short time in one part presume to know the whole nation. In misrepresenting Brazil to their readers, Floresta states, these travel writers commit 'duas grandes faltas: primeira, carecer de amor para com um povo por quem foram sempre bem acolhidos, e amiúde enriquecidos; segunda, trair à verdade, deixando os leitores numa completa ignorancia' ('O Brasil', p. 27). This scathing criticism, which reveals Floresta's rational response as a reader and, in its somewhat petulant accusation of ingratitude, her emotional response as a Brazilian, is a far cry from the reassurances of accuracy which accompanied her quotes from travel accounts of Brazil in *Opúsculo*.

Floresta's concern regarding these accounts extends further than mere literary inaccuracy, however. On a number of occasions throughout her European publications Floresta describes the ignorance and prejudice regarding Brazil, its population and society, which she encounters on her travels, and it soon becomes clear that she holds travel writers in large part responsible for these misconceptions. In 'O Brasil' she recalls the amazement with which an educated Brazilian woman is greeted in the Paris salons (p. 57), and observes that 'não menos que pela instrução, há expressões de surpresa também quando é visto um Brasileiro de pele assaz branca' (p. 57). She also recounts the story of an illustrious Brazilian (o doutor de Barros) travelling in northern Europe, whose hostesses rush to meet him only to be disappointed, and subsequently embarrassed by their own ignorance, when they do not find a man with 'o lábio furado, nem qualquer outro sinal característico dos nativos do Brasil' (p. 59). As discussed in Chapter 4, these last two examples reveal the degree of importance Floresta attributed specifically to foreign perceptions of Brazil's racial demography. By ridiculing European notions of the native Indian as representative she creates an image of a white Brazilian society, with its accompanying notions of civilisation, which in no way reflects the reality of a Brazilian population in which, in fact, blacks and mulattos outnumbered whites.[9]

In the journal of her travels in Italy Floresta also describes a number of incidents in which she encounters and forcefully challenges popular misconceptions about her nation (*Três Anos*, e.g. pp. 127, 352 and 362). She explicitly attributes these prejudices to travel accounts, echoing the accusations found in 'O Brasil': 'A civilização atual do Brasil, repito-o, é ainda muito pouco conhecida em grande parte da Europa, onde os escritos de alguns pretensos críticos de costumes e hábitos daquele vasto império quase não fazem senão manter os europeus em completa ignorância quanto ao seu progresso' (*Três Anos*, p. 362). In fact, it becomes apparent that Floresta is concerned with 'misinformation' about Brazil only when it presents the nation as backward and uncivilised.

When comparing the criticisms found in these European publications with her engagement with travel literature in *Opúsculo* it is clear that Floresta's representation of foreign travel accounts in the former is diametrically opposed to that which we find in the Brazilian text. These accounts have gone from being a source of accurate information on Brazilian society to being the primary source of misinformation, resulting in widespread ignorance and prejudice. However, the prejudices she now rails against were not a new experience on her return to Europe in 1856. In fact, in *Opúsculo* she recalls

---

9   See Skidmore, p. 57.

encountering the same incredulity towards educated Brazilian women during her time in France between 1849 and 1851. It is therefore quite clear that Floresta manipulates the genre of travel writing on Brazil to suit the purpose of the text, using accounts of Brazil's social failings to support her own arguments and reinforce the sense of national shame she wished to provoke in her Brazilian readers of *Opúsculo*, whilst refuting such negative accounts when publishing for a European readership, and making travel writers a specific target in her mission to enhance the popular image of Brazil in Europe.

Within the context of her European publications, her repeated criticism of the body of travel literature on Brazil questions and undermines the validity of the popular image of her nation as barbarous and uncivilised, but it also serves a second, arguably more important purpose, as a validation of her own portrayal of Brazil. By denouncing European-authored accounts primarily on the basis of the writers' lack of knowledge of Brazil's many regions and customs, she is able to present herself, with forty years of 'experience' of Brazilian culture, as an alternative, superior source of information. Moreover, Floresta is not prepared to allow this position of superiority only to emerge implicitly from her criticisms. She states it clearly, as in the following passage from 'O Brasil':

> O estudo por nós feito do Brasil, mediante as viagens que aí empreendemos em nossa juventude, examinando com severa imparcialidade os costumes, os usos, o espírito e os sentimentos do seu povo [...] faz-nos esperar que não seria obra vã a nossa de descrever, sempre que possível com a maior particularidade, o estado e os valores desta não suficientemente conhecida nação. (p. 61)

What is most curious about this statement, however, is that Floresta does not attempt to present her native experience of Brazil as being intrinsically more genuine or in any way different from that of a foreigner, instead merely emphasising that she has travelled extensively. In fact, she clearly sets out to construct herself in the mode of the ideal impartial observer, effectively denying her own identity as part of, and participant in, the society she claims to observe. It is clear that Floresta hopes to compete on an equal footing with European writers and thus mount a challenge from within the genre, to take on the narrative authority of the enlightened, rational observer. However, by implying that only extensive travel is the key to a better knowledge and understanding of Brazil, she effectively denies the authenticating and authorising value of her own Brazilian identity, and thus reveals the subtly inferior position in which she continues to locate the voice of 'the native' vis-à-vis European, 'outsider' discourse on Brazil.

Furthermore, the essay in which the above statement appears is the clearest example of *ufanismo* in her work and one of only two pieces published with the primary purpose of portraying Brazil to her European readers. Floresta's attempt to portray herself as a disinterested traveller and observer can therefore also be read as a move to pre-empt any accusations of patriotic bias which might be levelled against such an unstintingly positive depiction. Yet the effectiveness of this disclaimer is immediately sabotaged by Floresta's declaration that she has taken on the task of describing Brazil 'para gratificar a cara pátria', a task which, she writes, will have been worthwhile if 'ao cumpri-lo, pudermos de algum modo contribuir para sua futura grandeza' (p. 63).[10]

What becomes apparent, from the statement of patriotic purpose above and from the staunch defence of her nation to be found in almost all her European publications, is that Floresta quickly began to see herself in the role of ambassador for Brazil. She seizes every opportunity on her travels to emphasise Brazil's natural wealth and cultural development. On one occasion in Italy, having relieved an ageing customs official of his misconceptions regarding the inhabitants of Brazil, she presents herself literally as an allegory of the nation (or rather of the entire continent), ending the account with the ostentatious conclusion: 'E nos separamos: a velha Europa espantada com sua ignorância, e a jovem América, indulgente para com seus detratores' (*Três Anos*, p. 353). What is clear throughout is that she considers herself to be a worthy representative of her nation by virtue of her status as educated, white, and middle-class; features of the idealised, Europeanised Brazilian society which she seeks to portray.

Brazil versus Europe

Thus far we have seen how Floresta portrays a very different image of her own nation to her compatriots and her European readers. However, it is not only Brazil that is subject to this reconstruction. Significantly, her construction of Brazil is at all times juxtaposed with a construction of Europe. Addressing fellow Brazilians in *Opúsculo*, her criticisms of Brazil are contrasted with the positive example of European civilisation, but when writing for a European audience Floresta sets out to invert the paradigm of the civilised European traveller documenting the barbarous Brazilian by eulogising her homeland whilst simultaneously condemning the political and social condition of Europe. Nowhere is this inversion more overtly and knowingly expressed than in the following recollection of her own travels: 'Nós, que tivemos a bela oportunidade de percorrer e de observar a parte mais culta do antigo continente, amiúde tivemos a ocasião de aí vislumbrar bizarros tipos, e bárbaros

---

[10]   This awkward attempted juxtaposition of cool impartiality and patriotic mission is a permanent feature of Floresta's writing in Europe, and is typical of the multifaceted and constantly shifting self-representation which besets so much of her work.

costumes desconhecidos alhures [no Brasil]' ('O Brasil', p. 37). Through this double vision of the Old World and the New, Floresta seeks to reconfigure the Eurocentric colonial hierarchies of 'civilisation' and 'barbarism', culture and nature. It is this mutually dependent construction of Brazil and Europe that I will now go on to discuss, looking first at how she portrays Brazil to its own (elite) population.

Floresta is certainly not wholeheartedly critical of Brazilian society in *Opúsculo*; her own patriotism and, more importantly, the patriotic rhetoric of the text would not have allowed it. In fact, she appears to adopt one of the core justificatory discourses employed by her contemporaries to excuse the nation's failings: *lusofobia* and the curse of colonial inheritance. She suggests that Portuguese colonisation by greedy and degenerate men is to blame for society's many problems (*Opúsculo*, pp. 52–5) and states categorically that 'os povos do Norte [...] o teriam incontestavelmente melhor preparado para um mais glorioso porvir' (p. 52). However, she is not content merely to offer Portugal as a scapegoat. On the contrary she implies that Brazil's colonial heritage can no longer be used as an excuse for its own failings. Whilst acknowledging that the vices of today are nothing more than reproductions of those practised by past generations (p. 69), she goes on to write: 'Uma só coisa censuramos às atuais gerações, e muito particularmente à nossa: é o não tirarem da experiência que nos fornecem os erros de nossos antepassados o antídoto precioso para minorar os nossos' (p. 70). Thus the evils of colonisation are presented as a valuable lesson and a means to social improvement. It is the failure of the independent nation to move forward and shake off its uncivilised colonial history which lies at the heart of Floresta's criticism of Brazilian government and society. Unsurprisingly, this critical stance is contradicted in her subsequent European texts, as will become apparent below.

Alongside her accusation of human indifference we find a very different, positive engagement with Brazil's geographic identity in *Opúsculo*, which is an indication of the importance the writer, like many of her contemporaries, ascribed to Brazil's geography when imagining the nation. Throughout the text Floresta makes frequent reference to Brazil's vast natural wealth and beauty, and stresses the potential for greatness that such wealth brings with it, suggesting that a nation so blessed by providence must surely be destined to play a more significant part in the world (p. 159). However, she is not naive enough to suggest that these natural resources alone are sufficient to secure the nation's prosperity; on the contrary, she astutely recognises the corrupting influence of such endless abundance, describing 'os desvios de nosso povo, que vemos crescer, prosperar, ensorbecer-se pelos pingues dons que lhe doou a pródiga natureza, sem refletir que é o trabalho do homem, e não a riqueza natural do solo, que engrandece as nações' (p. 134). This is, in fact, a very significant statement in which Floresta effectively challenges the basis of *ufanistic* discourse, which sought to establish Brazil's greatness through its geography and natural resources. Yet she employs this same naive discourse herself when writing for a European audience.

Floresta's depiction of Brazil is overwhelmingly positive in her European writing. That is not to say that she is never critical of Brazilian society in these texts, but whilst *Opúsculo* took the form of an organised and sustained denunciation of Brazil's education system, which in turn initiated a firm criticism of a number of other social practices and attitudes, in her work published in Europe the few negative comments made appear randomly, are not followed through and are purposefully toned down with reassurances of the virtues of the people and the future greatness of the nation. A clear example of this is Floresta's references to slavery, discussed in Chapter 5.

The only other notable criticism of Brazilian society to be found in any of her European publications is the suggestion of a lack of culture or civilisation in comparison with Europe. However, it is no coincidence that these criticisms almost all appear in *Itinerário*.[11] This travel journal, which takes the form of a series of letters to her family in Brazil, was the first of Floresta's works to be published in Europe. The preface to the text, written by a French friend of Floresta, Eugénie Pelserf, assures the reader that she had not intended to make the letters public and that it was only the 'reiterada insistência' (p. 35) of this friend which led her to publish them. At the time it was common to find female-authored travel accounts in the format of letters home, and many women travel writers accompanied their accounts, be they letters or journals, with disclaimers stating their lack of intention to publish.[12] It is therefore quite possible that Floresta's *Itinerário* is merely adopting this popular rhetoric of feminine modesty. On the other hand, the noticeably more critical, and arguably more forthright tone of the text, in which Floresta finds positive and negative things to say about both Brazil and Europe, would seem to support the idea that Floresta genuinely did not record her impressions of Germany with a European reader in mind. If she did indeed pen *Itinerário* with the intention of publishing it in Europe, then the text reveals a naivety and disinterestedness which were not to last long.

Although separated by as little as a few months from *Itinerário*, in contrast her subsequent works all show a clear textual purpose and a sharp awareness of the patriotic potential of her own position as a Brazilian (and as a Brazilian writer) in Europe.[13] The criticisms expressed in *Itinerário* find only the faintest

---

[11]   For example, she describes Brazil as 'uma sociedade onde o pedantismo e as nulidades em mérito real sabem, melhor que os genios, brilhar' (*Itinerário*, p. 113). See pp. 148 and 174 for further examples.

[12]   Frawley, p. 52.

[13]   Although her next work, the collection of essays entitled *Cintilações*, was only published in 1859, two years after the publication of *Itinerário*, the earliest of the dated essays in the

of echoes in occasional comments in her subsequent works (e.g. *Três Anos*, p. 318). Instead, Floresta adopts an overwhelmingly positive, laudatory stance in her portrayal of Brazil. Central to her depiction of her nation is a focus on its extraordinary natural wealth and beauty, typical of Brazilian *ufanismo*. She writes of 'este filho predileto da natureza [...] assentado entre diamantes e ouro' ('O Brasil', p. 9), with 'imensos pavilhões de montanhas coroadas de immortal verdor; risonhas e férteis pradarias, atapetadas de multicoloridas e perfumadas flores' ('Viagem', p. 163). In her presentation of 'Viagem', Duarte observes the parallels in the text with one of the most famous examples of *ufanismo*, Gonçalves Dias's poem 'Canção do Exílio', when, for example, Floresta refers to the delights of the birdsong and the scent of the flowers in Brazil compared with those found in Europe ('Viagem', p. 167).[14]

However, still discussing the same essay, Duarte also suggests that Floresta challenges the traditions of *ufanismo* by including 'uma vigorosa denúncia social [...] para [...] corroer criticamente este mesmo ufanismo'.[15] Yet I would suggest that this interpretation reads too much into the criticisms which appear, and which in truth constitute only a small proportion of the text. In fact, Floresta criticises only two Brazilian social issues: slavery and the persecution of the native Indian, and neither critique could be described as vigorous, considering the seriousness of the subject matter. Her condemnation of slavery offers an opportunity to stress the virtues of Brazil's people and the 'liberalíssimas instituições que governam este belo país' (p. 171) (in relation to which, slavery is, of course, an aberration), whilst her already brief consideration of the Brazilian Indian includes just one sentence criticising their persecution, in a passage which otherwise smacks of idealised aesthetic objectification (p. 165).[16] Although the inclusion of any social criticism clearly breaks the rigid mould of pure *ufanismo*, none of Floresta's European texts shows the kind of conscious move to undermine or subvert this well-established discourse, as Duarte suggests. On the contrary, Floresta embraces this rhetoric as one of several tactics she employs to elevate Brazil in the European collective imagination.

Another parallel tactic is Floresta's frequent insistence on Brazil's flourishing civilisation, an assertion which often appears in tandem with descriptions of the nation's natural beauty in an apparent attempt to dispel any associations between nature and barbarity. For example, she writes: 'A essas magnificências da natureza juntam-se os prazeres de uma civilização progressiva, espalhada em

---

collection was written in 1856, shortly after, or possibly even before, her visit to Germany in the August and September of that year.

14   Constância Lima Duarte, 'Apresentação', in *Cintilações de uma Alma Brasileira* (Florianópolis: Editora Mulheres, 1997), pp. xii–xxix (p. xxv).

15   Duarte, 'Apresentação', p. xxv.

16   See Chapters 4 and 5 for a more detailed consideration of Floresta's discussion of the Brazilian Indian and slavery in her European works.

muitas de suas partes' ('O Brasil', p. 9), and 'entre inumeráveis tesouros naturais [...] vejo o engenho e as artes que dão as mãos para facilitar os modernos
progressos' ('Viagem', p. 169). She is also keen to point out the knowledge and
aptitude of Brazil's population: 'seus filhos [...] mostram-se habilíssimos em
todas as artes e ciências, que muitos deles conhecem a fundo, mais do que não
é preciso para construir-se um nome, uma reputação na Europa' ('O Brasil',
p. 53). This assurance wholeheartedly contradicts her denunciation of Brazil's
education system when writing for a native audience in *Opúsculo*. However,
these opposing positions can be seen to share the same starting point: the
importance of European comparison and opinion. In *Opúsculo* the education
systems of European nations are offered as models to be aspired to and Brazilians' lack of education is presented as a source of national shame; once she is
writing for a European readership, it is equally vital for Floresta to emphasise
her compatriots' ability to compete equally and earn respect in an international
context. Whether critical or full of praise for Brazil's social condition, Floresta
consistently constructs her nation from the outside.

A further theme to emerge in Floresta's depiction of her nation is the
innate virtue of the Brazilian people. She describes their frank, upright and
compassionate nature, the simplicity of their customs, their 'notável desinteresse [...] e principalmente, a sua proverbial hospitalidade com os forasteiros'
('O Brasil', p. 11). This generosity and friendliness to foreigners receives
particular attention from Floresta, and is an attribute that she had also repeatedly praised in *Opúsculo*. She reiterates the image later in 'O Brasil', stating
that 'essa hospitalidade e esse desinteresse são, mais ou menos, uma virtude
comum a cada pessoa' (pp. 23–5), and takes the opportunity to recall this
innate hospitality every time she encounters a warm welcome on her own
European travels (e.g. *Três Anos*, pp. 363 and 365; *Itinerário*, pp. 62 and
118). It is significant that it should be Brazilians' interaction with the rest
of the world that is singled out for attention, rather than those virtues which
might be of most benefit to Brazilian society itself. Once again Floresta
shows her overwhelming concern for foreign opinion, apparently picking
up an idea that has its source in the many travel accounts she read, emphasising in both *Opúsculo* and her European texts the fact that so many travellers to Brazil comment on this generous hospitality. However, whilst in the
former this observation appears to be included primarily in order to reassure
her Brazilian readers of the impartiality of otherwise critical accounts, in
her European texts Floresta embraces the image as a central aspect of the
Brazilian national character. In fact, by alluding to her own experiences of
Brazilian hospitality, she effectively casts herself in the role of the visitor
to Brazil, thus adopting and identifying with the foreigners' gaze and rein-
forcing the stereotype they have created.

Perhaps the most important aspect of Floresta's portrayal of Brazil,
however, is the position she claims for her nation within an international

arena. Not only does she state that Brazil is the most advanced and most important nation in South America ('O Brasil', pp. 59 and 61), she also suggests that it is able to occupy an elevated position amongst the most civilised nations. Whilst the greatest nations in Europe all envy Brazil, she suggests ('O Brasil', p. 61), 'o Brasil de hoje em dia não inveja nenhuma nação do mundo; já que [...] ele encerra todos os materiais para tornar-se uma das mais importantes entre elas' ('O Brasil', p. 53), a statement which contrasts sharply with her shrewd observation in *Opúsculo* that it is the work of men, not the richness of the soil, which makes a nation great (quoted on p. 179 above). Moreover, the suggestion that Brazil does not envy Europe is clearly wishful thinking at a time when Brazilian society slavishly imitated the customs and fashions of France and England,[17] something which she herself even criticises in her Brazilian writing (e.g. *Opúsculo*, pp. 100 and 134). Once again, Floresta is clearly constructing a very particular version of Brazilian society for the benefit of her European reader.

However, Floresta does not limit herself to pointing out Brazil's position amongst the most civilised nations. She goes so far as to suggest that Brazil will surpass the great nations of the day, employing epithets such as 'esta terra de promissão e de um tão grande futuro' (*Três Anos*, p. 312), and 'este escrínio misterioso de um grande porvir' ('O Brasil', p. 9). In fact, a reading of Floresta's European publications reveals that she began to see in the New World the source of a new and better kind of progress to challenge the civilisation of the Old World. In order to understand how Floresta constructs this often only implicit argument, it is first necessary to look at the equally fundamental shift in her attitude towards European society and the stern criticisms she makes of it once publishing in Europe.

As we have seen, *Opúsculo* is dominated by positive references to European society and its more advanced civilisation, and a certain underlying fondness for, and fascination with, the Old World can still be sensed in Floresta's European texts. She is mostly complimentary about the national character of the countries she visits, observing the kindness and sincerity of the Germans (*Itinerário*, p. 118) and the 'bons costumes' of the English (*Itinerário*, p. 149). She is particularly captivated by the history and romance of Italy, confessing to a childhood desire to visit (*Três Anos*, p. 24), and by the poignancy of its current repression, in which she sees clear parallels with Brazil's colonial domination.

It is France, however, that receives special attention in all Floresta's European publications. She frequently acknowledges her identification with the country, 'que eu sempre amara muito' (*Fragmentos*, p. 32), although she is

---

17 See, for example, E. Bradford Burns, *Nationalism in Brazil: A Historical Survey* (New York, Washington and London: Frederick A. Praeger, 1968), p. 38; and Costa, *The Brazilian Empire*, p. 51.

careful to clarify that it is only her preferred nation after Brazil (*Itinerário*, p. 40). On separate occasions Floresta refers to both France and Paris as her 'segunda pátria' (*Itinerário*, p. 71; *Fragmentos*, p. 36). Floresta first uses this phrase as early as 1856, when she had spent a total of less than two years in France, and had only returned from Brazil a few months earlier, before such a powerful attachment might be expected to develop. It therefore seems likely that, consciously or unconsciously, Floresta's identification with France reflects the influence of French Enlightenment thought and contemporary opinions on her intellectual formation, an influence which is only too apparent from the disproportionate number of French writers she names, and quotes from, in *Opúsculo*. In fact she herself acknowledges this intellectual connection, describing the allure of 'a vida intelectual de que se frui nesta Atenas moderna' (*Itinerário*, p. 37). That said, it is no coincidence that this and many of Floresta's other positive references to European society appear in her early German travel account, which, as discussed above, lacks the calculated patriotic purpose of subsequent texts.

Floresta's depiction of Europe inevitably becomes part of this textual mission, so it is no surprise that the positive descriptions found in *Opúsculo* (and also in *Itinerário*) are overshadowed by constant criticisms of contemporary 'civilised' European society in the remainder of her European publications. It is interesting to note that the fundamental accusation Floresta levels at Brazil in *Opúsculo* is the very same criticism she goes on to make of European society in the texts she published there. As discussed above, whilst blaming Portuguese colonialism for the origin of Brazil's social ills, in *Opúsculo* Floresta criticises the independent nation for not learning from its colonial past and working harder to bring about improvements. By the same token, Floresta now acknowledges that Europe's sins are not new ones, observing that she might designate the 1800s as the century of indifference and selfishness, if these 'dois abortos do espírito humano' had not been equally prevalent in ancient societies (*Três Anos*, p. 239). Once again, the failure of contemporary society, she suggests, lies in its utter inability to learn from the lessons of the past. Alongside this recycling of an argument previously used against Brazil, we inevitably find that Floresta now exempts her original target. So instead of condemning the Brazilian government for failing to instigate changes well within its capabilities, as she had done in *Opúsculo*, Floresta now states that any Brazilian shortcomings must be forgiven because the young nation has to overcome many 'preconceitos e erros grosseiros, herdados de seus antigos dominadores', whilst Europe, with the advantage of many centuries of stable government, cannot be forgiven its faults. In fact, Floresta even goes so far as to suggest that Brazil is a shining example which puts the Old World to shame: in total contrast with her frustration at the lack of progress expressed in *Opúsculo*, she now urges her (European) readers to consider how 'o progresso da civilização do Brasil foi tão rápido, quanto foi lento a se desenvolver entre os franceses' ('O Brasil', p. 53).

Considering her obvious affection for France and Paris, it seems curious at first glance to see that it is France which suffers Floresta's harshest criticisms; throughout her European publications she has hardly a good word to say about French society or France's population. On consideration, however, there is a correlation between the two discourses and their rhetorical strategies. Just as Floresta writes disparagingly about her own nation, for a native readership, in the hope of provoking action, so she condemns French society when writing for a French audience. The clearest example of her desire to influence social behaviour can be found in two of her essays, 'A Mulher' and 'O abismo sob as flores da civilização', which look at wet-nursing practices and prostitution in an explicitly French context and can be read as clear appeals for change.[18] Despite frequent reminders of her patriotic love for Brazil and the *saudades* that are her constant companions, it appears that Floresta's intellectual affinity with France leads her to a similar, displaced 'patriotic' desire to see improvements in French society.

There is, however, another way of reading this textual special relationship, as distinct from the 'real' special relationship which clearly existed with the nation Floresta chose to make her permanent home. In the Brazilian popular imagination France was the model of desirable civilisation and political structure *par excellence* and France, together with Great Britain, occupied the most powerful, elevated position in contemporary Europe. For Floresta, a condemnation of French society would therefore have been the most powerful means of undermining the established, Enlightenment hierarchy of civilisation, which, by constructing the New World as natural, maintained Brazil in a position of 'barbarous' inferiority.

This tactic can be clearly identified in much of Floresta's European writing: on a number of occasions she specifically represents Paris and London – as the supposed collective embodiment of 'progress' – as proof of the ultimate failure of modern societies (e.g. 'O Brasil', p. 37; 'Luxemburgo', p. 203, *Três Anos*, p. 246). But Floresta's attack goes far beyond a simple critique of the societies she observes. What emerges from her European publications is a complex and passionate challenge to the relative values of the nature/civilisation dichotomy, and with it the relative status of the New World versus

---

18 Curiously, neither of these essays was ever published in France, although it is quite clear that both were penned there (and undoubtedly in French), as were the other three essays that appear in *Cintilações*. Plans for their publication appear to have been permanently disrupted by Floresta's unexpectedly long sojourn in Italy between 1858 and 1861, during which time she chose instead to publish them in Italian whilst living in Florence, but I would suggest that all were originally written with a French readership in mind. Only one, 'O Brasil', was subsequently published, as *Le Brésil*, in Paris in 1871, with some small but significant additions that will be discussed later in this chapter.

the Old, thus opening a position for Brazil at the top of a new kind of hierarchy of nations. Rarely does Floresta construct her argument with calculated purpose, but from the disjointed, often emotional, responses which characterise much of her later writing, certain distinct themes are revealed.

Firstly, she repeatedly draws attention to the misery and corruption which lies beneath the supposed wonders of modern progress, observing, for example, that human misery is viewed with indifference whilst vast amounts of talent, energy and wealth are spent 'em exibir aos olhos do mundo as pompas e os resultados faustosos do progresso material' (*Três Anos*, p. 138). In a clear accusation of their failure to learn from the past, she pours scorn on the gullibility and blindness of contemporary European societies and the 'ingénua crença em que estão quase todos, pensando caminhar na senda do verdadeiro progresso, só porque reproduzem com mais elegância e menos solidez as obras dos antigos e aperfeiçoam, com certo refinamento, a arte de seduzir pelas aparências' (*Três Anos*, p. 239). Europe prides itself on its modern discoveries, 'quase idolatrados', whilst all around 'ainda geme a raça humana nas calamidades que não fizeram senão mudar de aspecto e nome, desde seis mil anos até agora' ('A Mulher', p. 111). In other words, Floresta argues that 'progress' has entailed no meaningful progress whatsoever. True progress, she writes, is nothing more than 'a prosperidade dos povos' ('A Mulher', p. 113), by which she means moral and spiritual, over and above material, prosperity.

When an acquaintance in Rome comments that they are no longer in the 'tempos de barbárie', Floresta responds, 'e eu penso na ruína dos povos! Quando os bárbaros desaparecerão da terra?' (*Três Anos*, p. 91). Civilisation, she implies, is a veneer, which masks the barbarity at the heart of European society. Nature, on the other hand, is presented as a counter to this corrupt and valueless civilisation: 'sempre se disse e se repetiu, que tudo é bem feito na harmonia da natureza; [...] mas não se dá o mesmo na sociedade!' ('A Mulher', p. 109). Nature also works as a powerful restorative force, most radiant where death and destruction have been (*Três Anos*, p. 206). Men, in the march of 'civilisation', build and destroy and all their pretensions come to nothing; but nature, Floresta writes, is an 'invariável poder' (*Itinerário*, pp. 100–1).

Brazil, Floresta claims, has avoided the many pitfalls of modern progress, maintaining a healthy and virtuous balance between nature and civilisation. She describes how 'a mão do homem tocou esta terra sem desfigurar a imperiosa obra da natureza!' ('Viagem', p. 163). She also suggests that her nation 'conserva hoje em dia em meio à civilização e ao luxo uma esplêndida liberdade que não se encontra mais na Europa' ('O Brasil', p. 59), and she praises Brazilian society's 'primitivos costumes patriarcais, de que os Europeus parecem ter perdido até de memória' ('O Brasil', p. 11), identifying patriarchalism as a natural, and thus a harmonious, system. With stridently patriotic rhetoric she writes: 'salve, ó povo, que com a aquisição de tua civilidade, manténs ainda em toda a sua inteireza a santa religião do coração!' ('Viagem', p. 167).[19]

Floresta is keen to stress the superiority of Brazil's nature over Europe's culture, observing, for example, that all the splendour of the art she sees in Italy pales beside the beauty of Brazilian nature (*Três Anos*, p. 33). More significantly, though, she appears to specifically attribute the purity of Brazilian society in the face of progress to the purity of its natural surroundings. She writes: 'Pelo horror que te inspira o refinado progresso dos outros povos, teu coração inda não aprendeu a ciência calculista; e a tua poesia permanece virgem como as mais remotas florestas de tuas paragens encantadoras' ('Viagem', pp. 167–9). She also seeks to establish a direct relationship between nature and the most elevated emotional and intellectual pursuits of culture. Thus music and poetry are innate in all Brazilians, due to the beauty of the nature that surrounds them ('O Brasil', p. 55). It is this positive natural context that enables the Brazilian man to operate without sacrificing to material interests 'os mais sagrados sentimentos da natureza', and the Brazilian woman to maintain her first and most attractive quality – modesty; a quality which, Floresta now implies, is lacking in European women ('Viagem', p. 169).

Throughout this re-evaluation of the Old and New Worlds, Floresta's message is clear: Europe's time is passing. Moreover, it is from the purity and greatness of its natural geography that America earns its future role in the world once it has shaken off its colonial residues. In a particularly curious passage in *Três Anos*, Floresta recounts a dream she has in which she sees a great tree, representing the new era, which is being slowly eaten away by insects. Her guide in the dream, the Roman patriot Cincinnatus, says to her, 'ó filha do Novo Mundo, de vasto e límpido horizonte! De lá surgirá o radioso astro do progresso, ainda envolto em algo como um espesso nevoeiro, pelo egoísmo mesquinho de nossas velhas gerações esgotadas!' (p. 59). Central to this refashioning of traditional hierarchies is, of course, Brazilian independence, and Floresta celebrates this shift in the balance of power with aplomb when she writes that Brazil's sons have liberated the nation from 'o jugo da Europa, que não poderá, nunca mais, quaisquer que sejam suas pretensões futuras, fazer inclinar-se diante de sua decrepitude disfarçada, a jovem, a vigorosa cabeça da vasta América' (*Três Anos*, p. 389). It is interesting to note that an idea which begins the sentence as Brazil, ends it as America, widening out to draw a definitive line between Europe and the Americas, Old World and New.

---

[19] It should be noted that in the original Italian the word used is 'civiltà', which, in *Cintilações*, is more usually translated as 'civilização'. The use of the word 'civilidade' in this instance is a distinction drawn by the translator.

As the various passages quoted above reveal, Floresta's criticisms of European civilisation and her construction of the New World as an alternative model of 'true progress' appear sporadically through her texts and do not amount to a focused argument. As with so much of Floresta's writing, this lack of focus and her impulsive, unstructured patriotism often lead her to contradict herself and undermine her own argument. Thus, whilst on the one hand she stresses Brazil's resistance to the pernicious influences of modern civilisation and suggests that the ostentatious material assets of progress do not bring happiness, she simultaneously embraces an entirely Eurocentric notion of progress in order to stake Brazil's claim to a place in the league of civilised nations. When describing with pride the roads, rail networks and steam ships which unite the vast provinces of Brazil ('Viagem', p. 169), she is clearly competing in a very conventional, material vision of progress. More than any other factor, it is the deep-seatedness of these western, Enlightenment values in her own social and intellectual formation that prevents Floresta from mounting a more sustained challenge to European civilisation and the status quo of eurocentric world hierarchies.

Only once do we catch a glimpse of the power that Floresta's anti-Europe argument could have had and this one organised and persistent contrast of progress in the Old and New Worlds appears unexpectedly in the short essay 'Um Passeio no Jardim de Luxemburgo'. This text is primarily concerned with the importance of education, for both sexes and specifically for women, in order to bring about the regeneration of society, and is Floresta's only work to state her support for Positivism explicitly. For most of the piece Floresta does not distinguish between nations or societies, merely recounting the 'projeto de universal melhoramento' (p. 187), which the three Brazilian friends discuss during their walk. However, at the close of the essay a very different, aggressively patriotic tone emerges in which Europe's most celebrated civilisations are singled out for damning criticism. Floresta notes that these three Brazilian observers (one of whom is, of course, the writer herself) have not been blinded by the superficial ostentation of Paris and London, as so many foreigners are (p. 201). Commenting with irony that she has perhaps mistranslated the word 'progress', Floresta then describes the complete absence of the liberty, prosperity, virtue and happiness which she had expected to find in these 'duas grandes nações tão progressistas' (p. 203). Then, in an abrupt shift, Floresta turns her back on the degeneracy of these long-established societies to gaze upon 'a terra natal [...] jovem, fresca, forte e generosa'. She concludes the essay, and the collection, with a clear declaration, not only of her credentials as impartial observer and of her own Brazilian identity (a juxtaposition which is inevitably unconvincing), but also of her nation's superiority in the future world she envisaged:

E após um bem ponderado e imparcial exame das vantagens da civilização falaciosa do velho mundo, e daquela que surge fúlgida e espontânea no vasto horizonte do novo mundo, seus corações exultavam em si mesmos por terem sido formados sob o belo céu da mais bela parte da América. (p. 203)[20]

Despite the fact that this argument never again attains the coherent, fervent structure we briefly see in 'Luxemburgo', by repeatedly drawing attention to the corruption and misery beneath the much lauded civilisation of western Europe and re-evaluating nature as a positive, purifying influence to counter the degenerative effect of conventional progress, Floresta still manages to launch an audacious attack on the accepted, European social and intellectual values of her day. Inevitably, though, discrepancies and contradictions abound as she struggles to shake off the profound influence of a value system imposed by the Old World, unable to reconcile the need to do away with the conventional hierarchies of European cultural 'civilisation' versus New World natural 'barbarism' that maintain Brazil in a position of inferiority, with her instinctive desire to prove her nation's worth within the very system she seeks to question.

Perhaps it is not surprising that Floresta's growing sense of patriotic purpose should culminate in a direct and overt appeal for the benefits of life in Brazil. Already in the essentially *ufanistic* essay 'Viagem' her suggestion that the 'manifestas vantagens oferecidas pelo governo e pelos opulentos agricultores deste fértil continente, atrairão laboriosos colonos, que abandonando uma pátria exaurida, conseguirão após breves esforços uma completa prosperidade' (p. 171) might be read as a sales pitch to attract would-be migrants. However, at this point such a vision is expressed as a hope for the future, and Floresta does not explicitly state that these colonists might be European, nor does she make clear what 'pátria exaurida' she has in mind. No such ambiguity or hesitancy is to be detected in the 1871 French re-edition of the essay 'O Brasil'. Floresta adds several paragraphs which include an undisguised advertisement for emigration to Brazil, suggesting that 'les classes laborieuses de l'Europe' will see 'leur travail mieux récompensé' in Brazil (*Le Brésil*, p. 45). This updated essay appeared at a time when the Brazilian government and in particular the state of São Paulo, was just beginning to take serious steps to promote European immigration,[21] revealing Floresta's ongoing engagement with Brazilian current affairs, despite her long-term absence.[22] The additional paragraphs emphasise the vastness of the country, the richness of the land, and its flourishing civilisation and modernity. They also contain high praise for

[20] It is certainly possible to see the influence of Comte's thinking in this passage in Floresta's loaded use of the word 'progress'. Once again, though, we see her manipulating this discourse to suit her own very specific, patriotic purpose.

[21] See, for example, Boris Fausto, *A Concise History of Brazil* (Cambridge: Cambridge University Press, 1999), p. 118.

[22] In fact Floresta comments specifically that effective measures are now being taken by the Brazilian government to facilitate immigration.

Brazil's Emperor, and a discussion of the recent victory in the Paraguayan War, which is presented as a triumph over tyranny and thus proof of Brazil's liberal, humanitarian political system (*Le Brésil*, pp. 44–9).

Although Floresta is arguably a little off target in publishing this text in Paris, given that France was to be one of the European countries that furnished Brazil with the fewest immigrants,[23] what we see here is Floresta very deliberately seeking to contribute to a highly politicised, patriotic discursive process. Presumably without solicitation (although we cannot be absolutely certain of this since her brother appears to have been a well-respected and connected figure in Rio who, at the time of his death in 1875, held a position of responsibility in the Ministry of Agriculture[24]), Floresta takes up the message of the Brazilian establishment and in a very tangible way wields her pen for what she clearly believes to be the good of her nation.

Political theory versus patriotic practice

Noticeably absent from Floresta's depiction of Brazil considered so far is any discussion of political ideals and government of the nation. To some extent the purpose and nature of the various texts does not allow for an analysis of political processes. In particular the travelogue genre permits only a superficial, tourist's gaze, whilst in *Opúsculo*, all issues are addressed within the limiting framework of her appeal for women's education. However, that is not to say that Floresta entirely neglects the subject of political rule, either in the specific context of Brazil, or in a wider theoretical context. From her scattered, often unstructured references to government on both sides of the Atlantic it is possible to draw valuable conclusions about her own political positioning and her employment of political discourse to further the image of Brazil which she sought to construct.

Traditionally, Floresta's biographers have always identified her as a republican and a federalist,[25] a reputation based primarily on her ardent defence of the Praieira Revolt in *A Lágrima de um Caheté*, discussed in detail in Chapter 4, and the undocumented 1842 meetings in which she is said to have expressed her support for republicanism and 'a federação das províncias'.[26] *Lágrima* is unquestionably the most overtly political of Floresta's works and the only text in which the writer sets out the political ideals with which she has come to be wholeheartedly associated. In the poem, she makes it quite

---

[23]   See, for example, E. Bradford Burns, *A History of Brazil*, 3rd edn (New York: Columbia University Press, 1993), p. 217.

[24]   *Fragmentos*, pp. 78–9.

[25]   Although biographers have not made as much of Floresta's political ideals as they have of her supposed feminism and abolitionism, Seidl, for example, writes that she is a 'republicana de convicções firmes' (p. 43).

[26]   Sabino, p. 172.

clear that she believes federal republicanism to be necessary for the good of not only Pernambuco, but all Brazil, as we see in the following verse, which pays homage to the fallen hero Nunes Machado:

> A causa, que defendia,
> Por quem ardia,
> Era causa da nação! ...
> Mais tarde o Brasil dará,
> Affirmará
> A prova desta asserção. (p. 27)

Yet this position certainly does not find confirmation in Floresta's other early texts. Most significant is the case of the short piece of didactic fiction *Fany* (1847), discussed in Chapter 2. Constância Lima Duarte observes how the setting of the action during the Farroupilha War and the fact that the heroine's father fights on the side of the revolutionaries have led many scholars to interpret the text as pro-Farrapo.[27] However, Duarte convincingly demonstrates that this interpretation is inaccurate, identifying instead 'um posicionamento nacionalista [...] pouco afeito a tendências separatistas que colocariam em risco a soberania e unidade nacional'.[28]

Back in Rio after her first visit to Europe, *Opúsculo* is Floresta's only other Brazilian text to even touch upon questions of national governance, but a number of references can be found in her European texts. Although at times she adopts quite markedly different positions to suit the purpose of *Opúsculo* and her subsequent European works, from 1852 onwards her treatment of Brazil's political structure and her engagement with the wider issues of monarchy and republicanism, oligarchy and democracy are at all times ambiguous, unfocused and contradictory, revealing a powerful tension between her emotive representation of the nation as a unified entity and her concept of the state as a functioning political system, between her acutely felt public mission as a writer and her own personal, theoretical political ideals.

Floresta's position regarding the Brazilian monarchy in *Opúsculo* is not clearly set out. On the one hand she has high praise for Pedro I, whom she refers to as 'um príncipe herói [...] em cujo coração superabundavam amor e entusiasmo pelas grandes e difíceis empresas' (pp. 73–4) and quotes at some length from the *Manifesto* he pronounced a month prior to his declaration of independence in 1822 (p. 54). Despite this enthusiasm for Brazil's first

---

[27] Duarte, *Vida e Obra*, pp. 234–5.

[28] Duarte, *Vida e Obra*, p. 240. Curiously, Duarte does not acknowledge or address the fundamental contradiction between this nationalist position and the appearance two years later of *Lágrima*, a contradiction that, I would suggest, lies primarily with Floresta's personal acquaintance with the hero of the Praieira Revolt and her strong identification with Pernambuco as well as the didactic purpose of *Fany*, published in Rio.

Emperor, she also observes that a truly national government was only gained with his abdication in 1831, effectively condoning the monarchy under Pedro II. In adopting this position, Floresta is echoing a common aspect of *nativistic* national identity discourse, in which the power struggles between the political elite and Pedro I, which brought about his abdication, were constructed as the triumph of Brazilian interests over a Portuguese ruler.[29]

The explanation for Floresta's predominantly unchallenging, pro-establishment rhetoric in *Opúsculo* may in part lie with the purpose of the text and her own previous publishing history. *Lágrima* was the last work she had published in Rio before her initial departure for Europe and it is probable that the publication of this text, with its overtly anti-monarchist tone and subsequent censorship, contributed to the writer's decision to travel to Europe. Such an anti-establishment text would not have been entirely forgotten by the time she returned two years later. It therefore seems possible that she was keen to re-establish her reputation amongst the readership of Rio, and *Opúsculo*'s uncritical approach to the monarchy, and its frequent assertions regarding Brazil's natural wealth and potential future greatness, together with the constant reiteration of the text's patriotic purpose, could be seen as an attempt by Floresta to publicly distance herself from the more radical political positionings of her earlier work and make peace with the capital's elite. This suggestion is supported by the presence of a significant passage in *Opúsculo* in which Floresta forcefully condemns divisive regionalist sentiments, suggesting instead that Brazil's power lies in its great size and therefore also in its unity. In what can only be read as a denunciation of the ambitions of separatist uprisings like the Praieira Revolt, which she had celebrated in *Lágrima*, she writes: 'Nunca nos assomaram os epidêmicos delírios de mal entendido orgulho provincial, funesto germe fomentado outrora entre nós por disfarçados inimigos da prosperidade desta grandiosa e rica peça' (p. 129).

In the light of this apparent disclaimer, it seems surprising that Floresta in fact quotes from *Lágrima* on several occasions in the text. However, none of the passages quoted include any allusion to the Praieira Revolt or contemporary politics, instead focusing primarily on the barbarity of Portuguese colonisation, an issue which complements the patriotic tone of *Opúsculo*, and thus perhaps serves to remodel the writer's earlier poem as a less confrontational, more conventionally patriotic text. As well as a desire to appease, and appeal to the establishment, Floresta's apparent abandonment of her federalist ideals also reflects a shift in Brazil's national politics, perhaps indicating that she recog-

---

[29]   Whilst Pedro's persistent favouring of the Portuguese-born *reinóis* did nothing for his popularity, his nationality was by no means the primary factor in the first Emperor's demise. See Barman, p. 131; Costa, *The Brazilian Empire*, p. xix; and Miriam Lifchitz Moreira Leite, 'Uma construção enviesada: A mulher e o nacionalismo', in *A Mulher na Literatura*, ed. Nádia Battella Gotlib, vol. 3 (Belo Horizonte: Imprensa da UFMG, 1990), pp. 56–66 (p. 57).

nised the fundamental defeat of such hopes at that particular time in the nation's political development. Historians recognise the suppression of the Praieira Revolt as a turning point for Brazilian national identity, when the old *nativist* loyalties of the 'pátria' as region were finally laid to rest and a new concept of a unified Brazilian 'pátria' took hold, ushering in a period of national unity and harmony which would last for several decades.[30] In sharp contrast to *Lágrima*, Floresta now makes it clear that Brazilians from every corner of the nation are brothers, united by a common interest (p. 130). In one of the most emphatic statements of her own patriotism to be found in any of her works, she declares: 'Amamos com religioso entusiasmo a nossa pátria, isto é, toda a vasta terra de Santa Cruz' (p. 130). A reading of *Opúsculo* certainly seems to cast doubt on the strength of the republican and federalist sentiments with which Floresta has traditionally been associated. It must be remembered, however, that her agenda for writing *Opúsculo* was an improvement in women's education and that in order to see her work read and taken seriously by the establishment it was not in her interests to challenge or fundamentally criticise the system on which that establishment was founded.

In Floresta's European works her patriotic purpose continues to shape her discussion of political theory and practice, in Brazil and in Europe. She makes very little mention of Brazil's government and its Emperor throughout her European texts, and what few references we find are predominantly positive, though at times surprisingly unenthusiastic. In her account of independence in 'O Brasil', the nation's first Emperor receives only a passing and almost begrudging mention (p. 17). Pedro I appears just once more in her European work, in *Três Anos*, where he is described as 'o grande príncipe que proclamou a independência' (p. 107), in a brief passage recounting his challenge, on behalf of his daughter Maria, to the Portuguese throne after his abdication in 1831. Significantly, no information is given about the circumstances of his abdication and Floresta is clearly not interested in discussing Brazil's political history. In fact the subject only arises because she happens to meet the daughter of Dom Miguel, the ousted king of Portugal and brother of Pedro I.

Brazil's current Emperor also receives relatively little mention, but, unlike her somewhat cold and formulaic glorification of his father, Pedro II's leadership abilities receive a clear endorsement. In fact she celebrates the benefits that his rule brings to the nation:

> Apenas atingindo a adolescência, dotado de excelentes qualidade [*sic*] e de um gosto particular pelos estudos sérios, ele propicia que se augure ao jovem e vasto Império um grande desenvolvimento de progresso tanto

---

30 Roderick Barman, for example, writes that 'the one final challenge to the system, the Praieira Revolt [...], would serve only to confirm and consolidate the supremacy of the nation' (p. 216).

moral quanto material, que deverá marcar, nos fatos de sua história, uma
época de felicidade e glória. (*Três Anos*, p. 313)

As she had done previously in *Opúsculo*, Floresta also notes here that Pedro
II is the first Brazilian Emperor of Brazilian birth, making her exaltation of
his virtues doubly meaningful as he is cast as both shaper and product of
Brazil. This praise for Brazil's ruler is forcefully reiterated in the additions
to be found in *Le Brésil*, where he is described as wise, liberal and humanitarian, and 'un homme providentiel' for Brazil. She also stresses his status as
a constitutional monarch and his moderate, conciliatory approach (p. 46).

It comes as no surprise that Floresta appears equally, if not more interested
in the female members of the Brazilian royal family. She includes a reference to four, and on every occasion is keen to stress their virtues, using these
royal women as powerful representatives and symbols of the virtuous family,
which she saw as the model of nationhood (see *Três Anos*, pp. 107 and 196;
and *Itinerário*, p. 171). On one occasion in Florence, Floresta sees the Grand
Duke of Tuscany and his family and is reminded of Brazil's current Empress,
D. Pedro II's wife, who is the sister of the Grand Duchess. She recalls at
length the scenes of celebration on 4 September 1843 when the new Empress
arrived in Rio, in a passage which sounds anything but anti-monarchist. Most
significant, however, is her description of the Empress as 'a mais feliz esposa
das cabeças coroadas' (*Três Anos*, pp. 311–12).

This comment, which effectively states Pedro II's virtues as a husband,
also offers a valuable insight into Floresta's lack of enthusiasm for Pedro I,
despite his central role in achieving a peaceful transition to independence.
Unlike her daughter-in-law, Brazil's first Empress Leopoldina certainly could
not have been described as a happy wife, as she had to tolerate her husband,
Pedro I's extremely public affairs.[31] This lack of private virtue, so central
to Floresta's vision of a reformed society, probably contributes significantly
to her terse references to Brazil's first Emperor. In contrast, she is able to
present Pedro II as an erudite and progressive young monarch and a virtuous
husband, that is to say, a model leader and a model man. Thus her depiction
of Brazil's ruler reflects her depiction of the nation as a model of flourishing
civilisation and progress built on the good character of the Brazilian people
and the solid social virtues of patriarchy and family. In *Três Anos*, Floresta
also contrasts this positive portrayal of Brazil's monarch with references to
the despotism of Italy's various rulers (e.g. pp. 197 and 283), reminding her
readers of Brazil's superior political condition.

It would be no exaggeration to state that something of a fascination with

---

[31] This was most famously the case with Domitila (or Domitília) de Castro, whom the
Emperor made Marquesa de Santos and who wielded considerable influence. See, for example,
Cavaliero, p. 171 for a discussion of this painful and scandalous ménage-à-trois.

royalty in general emerges from her European travel accounts. She describes at length no fewer than four different European royal families that she encounters on her travels and mentions several other royal figures in passing. Moreover, although she claims to like observing rulers in order to 'ler os sentimentos que o fazem agir para com os homens que governa' (*Três Anos*, p. 195), the details about family relationships and physical appearances to be found, particularly in the less calculated and therefore more candid account of her travels in Germany, suggest a less noble and high-minded interest.[32]

Whilst Floresta denounces the despotism of Ferdinando II of the two Sicilies and of the heir to the Grand Duchy of Tuscany, she is very impressed by both the King of Belgium and the King of Wurttemburg and has high praise for both. About the latter she writes, 'pudemos observer [...] essa elegante simplicidade régia, que tanto valoriza o chefe de uma nação, aos olhos daqueles que não julgam o mérito de uma cabeça coroada segundo o enxame de borboletas douradas que a cercam constantemente' (*Itinerário*, p. 176). Her endorsement of the former is even more resounding. Describing him as 'o digno rei de um povo livre', she concludes: 'Todas as cabeças coroadas atrairiam minha profunda simpatia, se fossem como a de Leopoldo I da Bélgica' (*Itinerário*, pp. 46–7). Such comments certainly appear to present a challenge to the notion that Floresta was a supporter of republicanism. However, the Belgian monarchy, which had only been established in 1831, was a constitutional, parliamentary monarchy which functioned under the principle of ministerial, rather than monarchical, responsibility. Floresta may well have been drawn to such a political system as an effective middle ground in which the radical, often violent connotations of republicanism were disarmed by the conservative image of monarchy. If this is the case, however, she misses the opportunity to advocate such a system or even to highlight the relatively democratic nature of Belgium's political administration to her readers, instead limiting herself to superficial and prosaic details.

The only one of Floresta's European publications in which she gives voice to republican and federalist ideals is the essay 'O Brasil', and even then a note of caution and reluctance can be detected in her writing. The title of this essay could almost be considered a misnomer; it might be more appropriately entitled 'Pernambuco', so redolent is it with Floresta's love for the province she considered her own. Page after page is filled with descriptions of Pernambuco's virtuous people and natural beauty, the 'límpido céu' and 'risonho solo' which its natives 'em vão procuram alhures' (p. 33). According

---

[32] Amusingly, when Floresta and her daughter get out of their carriage to better observe the Belgian royal family, the writer is careful to state that she stops the carriage 'para agradar a nossa Lívia' (*Itinerário*, p. 46), implying that she does not share her daughter's idle curiosity, but promptly goes on to comment on the attractiveness of the Princess Charlotte in comparison with her overweight sister-in-law.

to Floresta, however, the most important defining feature of the province, which sets it apart from the others and gives it 'uma verdadeira marca de poesia e de grandeza', is the spirit of liberty which has shaped its history (p. 33). This powerfully regionalist rhetoric stands in sharp contrast to Floresta's argument in *Opúsculo* that Brazil's importance comes from its size and unity, where she asks: 'Que importa termos visto pela primeira vez a luz nesta ou noutra de suas províncias, se é o mesmo céu brasileiro que nos cobre, o nosso verdejante solo que pisamos?' (*Opúsculo*, p. 130). Here, free from the constraints of a conservative Brazilian readership and the need to back-track from the polemic of *Lágrima*, it would appear that Brazil's unifying sky and soil have been fractured and reallocated.

When Floresta is not singing the praises of the province, she is quoting the German writer and painter Johann Moritz Rugendas on the same subject.[33] In fact she quotes more than twenty paragraphs of text, affording Rugendas unprecedented space and attention which no other writer receives in her work. In quoting so extensively from Rugendas' work in 'O Brasil', it is clear that Floresta seeks to borrow his male, European authority to support her Pernambucan bias, and to voice, through him, her own endorsement of Brazil's federalist republican movements. Referring to the uprisings of 1817 and 1824, he writes that it would be a grave error to deny that the spirit of federalism, spreading across the Americas, had gained considerable ground amongst the people of Pernambuco. Floresta interrupts her quotation of the German writer to note that:

> O digno autor expunha estas considerações, antes que o dito espírito tivesse tomado vulto na nobre província do Rio Grande do Sul, onde o partido republicano resistiu por dez anos aos esforços da monarquia, e não depôs as armas senão sob condições favorabilíssimos para ele, condições essas que ele requereu, e obteve, do Governo central. (p. 49)

Interestingly, she makes no mention of the Praieira Revolt, perhaps because that uprising was unequivocally suppressed, meaning that Pernambuco did not see the concessions Floresta implies were enjoyed by the *Farrapos*. This apparent expression of support for a republican, federalist uprising starkly contradicts the condemnation of such 'epidêmicos delírios de mal entendido orgulho provincial' made for the benefit of her Brazilian readers in *Opúsculo* (p. 129).

Moreover, when discussing Italy's political condition in *Três Anos*, she laments the fragmentation of a previously great nation, 'hoje tão dividida e tão desunida' (p. 317), and indicates that this division lies at the heart of

---

[33] From his work *Voyage Pittoresque dans le Brésil*, trans. M. de Golbéry (Paris: Engelman, 1835).

Italy's continuing oppression, suggesting on several occasions that these regional divisions have been deliberately imposed by those in power to maintain the status quo (e.g., pp. 176 and 317). It is impossible not to read such clear appeals for national unity against Floresta's discussion of the Brazilian nation, and the arguments she employs regarding Italy closely echo the ideas she expressed earlier in *Opúsculo* on the importance of a single national identity and the power which lies in unity for her own nation. Even the notion that division is a tactic of oppression is found first in *Opúsculo*, where she states that regional loyalties are fostered by 'disfarçados inimigos' of national prosperity (*Opúsculo*, p. 129). Yet the reiteration of these ideas in *Três Anos* is curiously at odds with the regionalist, federalist sentiments she expresses in 'O Brasil'. Such contrasting positions, adopted within Floresta's European writing, once again hint at the unresolved conflicts of political affiliation which so often complexify her engagement with the discourse of political organisation, be it theoretical or specific to Brazil.

Even Floresta's treatment of republican or federalist ideals within 'O Brasil' is by no means consistent and it is only in her reference to the Farroupilha Revolt that she herself appears to support the republican endeavour, not so much by noting the 'condições favorabilíssimos' secured by the Farrapos, but by inserting her comment within Rugendas' undeniably positive portrayal of republican uprisings and his criticism of the nascent Brazilian government (pp. 49–51). Elsewhere in the essay Floresta's concern for European opinion reasserts itself and the inevitable contradictions begin to appear. When recounting the process of independence, Floresta observes that there were some difficulties as elements loyal to the old government fostered a hatred for all those who supported the liberal ideas of the new Emperor, whilst others, 'ofuscados pela gloriosa perspectiva a eles aberta pela nascente e livre monarquia, nela vislumbravam o único expediente capaz de alçar a sua pátria ao auge da prosperidade' (p. 17). This statement can certainly be read as an observation on the existence of different forms of monarchy, or even of a viable alternative to monarchy, but it is far from being an expression of anti-monarchism, and she leaves the idea hanging. This would have been complicated ground for Floresta because the leading proponent of the monarchy, and the man who did most by far to see Pedro I securely in place, was José Bonifácio de Andrada e Silva, whom she hails as a genius and the patriarch of independence later in the essay and elsewhere.

In 'O Brasil' Floresta finds herself in the difficult position of opposing the fundamental political ideology of the nation whilst seeking to portray the current government in the best possible light to her readers. This dilemma is painfully apparent in the final paragraphs of the essay when Floresta describes Brazil's elevated status in South America. She writes:

É a única daquele vasto continente que tem um governo monárquico; e a despeito disto, posta em confronto com todas as suas outras co-irmãs, governadas de modo democrático, goza de uma plena liberdade à sombra de sábias leis, conformíssimas à índole humanitária de seus cidadãos. (p. 61)

This passage is extremely important in an evaluation of Floresta's political ideals: she clearly, though understatedly, indicates her preference for republicanism. In fact, looking beyond the inconvenient presence of a monarch, it is as if Floresta seeks to refashion her nation as an idealised republic. Liberty she claims with ease; equality, an impossible claim in the face of continuing slavery, is substituted by humanity; and with the closing lines of the essay Floresta completes the holy trinity of the French Revolution when she adds that Brazil is also 'a mais fraternalmente governada' (p. 63).

By the time Floresta decided to republish this essay in Paris, in 1871, her primary interest lay elsewhere. Although the changes she made to the pre-existing text were very minor, the substantial new section she added at the end certainly does not confirm her preference for republicanism. As indicated earlier, she praises Pedro II emphatically, and stresses the moderation, and conciliatory approach that characterise his reign (*Le Brésil*, p. 46). A hint of wistfulness might be detected in Floresta's comment that 'ce vaste empire comptait un grand nombre de démocrates', which precedes her reiteration of the fact that the Republicans of Rio Grande do Sul were able to hold the imperial forces at bay for a decade, although this information is stated quite neutrally now. She concludes that 'aujourd'hui, républicains, démocrates ne sont plus que des partis évanouis; et depuis vingt ans les Farapillos du Sud, comme les républicains du Nord, se sont soumis au gouvernement' (p. 47) It is not easy at first to deduce whether Floresta considers the demise of these parties to be a cause for celebration or dismay. However, she immediately goes on to refer, somewhat opaquely, to two occasions when 'les provocations les plus téméraires et les plus coupables' have forced the Emperor to take up his sword, struggles in which, we are assured, he was able to defeat the rebels and tyrants with the help of interested neighbours. One of these occasions is clearly the Paraguayan War, which Floresta goes on to discuss for the second time in three pages. The other remains unidentified, but coming hot on the heels of two references to the Farroupilha Revolt, this highly critical tone cannot but cast her previous comments in a more nuanced light.

Floresta's motive here becomes clearer, I think, when we consider the context in which she is writing. Only a few months earlier she and all of France had witnessed the chaotic rise and bloody fall of the Paris Commune (18 March to 28 May 1871).[34] In fact Floresta lived through both the siege of

---

[34]   See, for example, Alfred Cobban, *A History of Modern France. Volume 2: 1799–1871* (London: Penguin Books, 1991), pp. 199–215.

Paris by the victorious Prussian army and the establishment of the Commune, and she describes the horrors vividly in *Fragmentos* (pp. 32–6), referring to the latter as 'a mais horrorosa das insurreições' (p. 33). This people's uprising, with its revolutionary republican ideals and its haphazard and violent methods represented the perfect example of the threat posed by political ideals, or more precisely political power, in the hands of the masses. Indeed, given the very specific purpose of these additional paragraphs – to advertise Brazil as a destination for migrants – it is quite evident that highlighting Brazil's stable, solid political base, from which all threat of the revolutionary left has been eliminated, in contrast to France's political instability and consequent social vulnerability at that time, would have been a very effective selling point.

Looking at *Opúsculo* and her European publications together, it seems clear that political idealism was not convenient to Floresta's purpose and was thus largely discarded as a topic for logical or sustained discussion. In the former she would not have wanted to risk alienating her readers, and since she sought action in part from the government with regard to her appeals for improved education, as discussed in Chapter 2, she could not afford to condemn its very foundation, instead limiting herself to a criticism of certain legislative failings. In her European work, she probably recognised that Brazil's constitutional monarchy aligned it with the majority of western European nations and thus did nothing to damage its credibility; if anything, it is likely to have made Brazil more familiar and less threatening to her readers than South America's unstable republics. Moreover, by emphasising the strong links of blood and marriage between the Brazilian royal family and European monarchies, as well as the happiness or esteem European empresses enjoyed in Brazil, Floresta effectively draws her own nation closer to Europe, literally incorporating it into the European family of nations. In fact, in her mission to portray Brazil as a politically and socially mature nation, a critique of its monarchy would have been utterly counterproductive. However, it seems that Floresta is unable to totally exorcise an intellectual preference for republicanism. In the essay 'O Brasil' we see the writer's one attempt to express her political ideals, and in doing so she discovers their incompatibility with her patriotic purpose. The difficulties she so clearly encounters in juggling these two irreconcilable positions may well explain why she never attempts it again.

A comparative reading of Floresta's Brazilian and European publications after her first stay in Paris and Lisbon between 1849 and 1852 reveals a wholly new sense of her own national identity and of Brazil as a political and cultural entity. It also tells of an overwhelming concern with foreign opinion and perceptions of her nation, which leads her to constantly envisage and construct Brazil from the outside and in juxtaposition with Europe. Floresta's position reflects a far wider identity crisis facing Brazil at this time, as the new nation struggled to carve a discrete, American identity out of a society that had always looked to Europe for inspiration and looked through European values at itself. Although Brazilian intellectuals 'resented the influence Europe exerted over the psychological formation of their nation', they did not embrace the task of identifying alternative, national values, and Brazilian nationalism was in large part constructed by a concerted process of Europeanization, or by reaction to foreign events and attitudes.[35] In fact, like Floresta, Brazil's elites had a very ambiguous relationship with Europe. Bradford Burns observes the paradox by which the xenophobic rhetoric of *nativism* was to be found alongside an obsession with pleasing the foreigner. 'Mouthing anti-foreign phrases, the Brazilians [...] slavishly copied European styles, words, customs, and tastes, especially those of France and England.'[36] In his famous study of Brazil's cultural origins, published in 1936, Sérgio Buarque de Holanda noted how the nation's efforts to develop in fact contributed to a system that belonged to another world, a system which had rendered Brazilians 'desterrados' in their own land.[37]

Despite Floresta's problematic and often subservient interaction with European perceptions, however, her patriotic purpose is overt and she eventually proves herself to be in no way complicit in the construction of European superiority. Rather, with the express purpose of highlighting Brazil's greatness and potential, and thus fulfilling her 'duty' to her nation, she systematically portrays the Old World as just that – decrepit and spiritually moribund, in contrast to Brazil's youthful vigour. However, it becomes apparent that Floresta is obliged to override her own intellectual and ideological preferences in order to maintain this construction. Most visibly, her decision to remain in Europe, and her enthusiastic participation in the cultural and intellectual activities it offered, belie her condemnation of Western society's moral degeneration and the powerful *saudades* she claims to suffer. Floresta truly is a 'desterrada', caught between two worlds and two identities. Hers, perhaps, is the inevitable fate of the voluntary ex-patriate: to constantly mythologise the homeland whilst knowing full well that life is better in exile.

Floresta certainly employs the rhetoric of patriotism to her advantage throughout much of her writing, to add strength and influence to her arguments, to mask her more liberal, challenging appeals, and to justify and give purpose to her intellectual activities in Brazil and Europe. Needless to say, it is this same patriotic focus that also limits and defines the extent and nature of her engagement with social and political discourses, as I have demonstrated in this chapter and throughout this study.

---

[35] Burns, *Nationalism in Brazil*, pp. 31 and 46. See also Leite, 'Uma Construção Enviesada', p. 56.

[36] Burns, *Nationalism in Brazil*, pp. 37–8.

[37] Sérgio Buarque de Holanda, *Raízes do Brasil*, 21st edn (Rio de Janeiro: José Olympio, 1989), p. 3.

Conclusion

Through the course of this study I have highlighted and challenged some of the more mythical, idealised and monolithic constructions of Nísia Floresta and her work which still abound in Brazilian studies of the writer, particularly as regards her recuperation by liberal feminist scholars over the last two decades. Floresta's reputation and her position within the canon is inevitably founded first and foremost on her writings about women and her considerable contribution to the emergence of feminist discourse in Brazil. The starting point for any re-evaluation of that position can therefore only be her first publication, *Direitos*, and its exposure as a direct translation of Sophia's *Woman Not Inferior to Man*. As I have discussed, it is the early date and, more importantly, the radical content of this text that have done most to earn Floresta her reputation as Brazil's first feminist, and the fact that it is not the 'free translation' it was thought to be means that Floresta can no longer be credited with the arguments found in *Direitos*, nor can her name be linked with the powerful feminist associations of Mary Wollstonecraft. However, Floresta's translation offers a valuable insight into her thinking at that early time, and it remains an extremely significant moment in the development of Brazilian feminism. If no longer its 'texto fundante', it is undoubtedly its rallying cry, and we can be almost certain that it had a considerable influence on de Barandas's writing, and perhaps on other women writers in the years that followed.

The importance of *Direitos* in an analysis of Floresta's own feminist credentials now lies in a comparison of this text with her own work, which is markedly more conservative, focusing increasingly on the value of patriotic feminine virtue and women's exclusively domestic role as wives and mothers. It is easy to see how this shift away from the tone of *Direitos* might have been a practical necessity when Floresta needed to court a conservative readership in order to support herself. However, the fact that she does not attempt to advocate women's operation in the public sphere once she is financially independent and living in Europe reveals the fundamentally constraining effect of Catholic patriarchalism, nation-building discourse and Enlightenment constructions of the family on her own intellectual formation, coupled with the influence of Positivism. In the end, the radical tone and content of *Direitos* cannot be claimed for Floresta's own work, and her feminism must be viewed within the context of conservative, nineteenth-century representations of women's domestic and relational identity and value. Though less challenging in her defence of women's rights, where Floresta clearly stands out from Barandas and other Brazilian contemporaries, however, is that she continued to write and publish extensively on the subject of women's condition, their right to better education and to a higher regard in society, throughout her life. It is in this sustained concern for and contribution to the discussion of women's position in society that Floresta's influential place in Brazil's feminist canon is secured.

It is arguably in her life, as much as in her work, that Floresta can be identified as a feminist. Her own extraordinary erudition and constant quest for knowledge and experience; her ability to support herself and her family alone after the death of her husband; her lengthy writing career, in which she wrote and published openly on essentially male, public discourses;[1] her extensive travels; her voluntary decision to distance herself from her male family members; and her interaction with the intellectual elite of mid-nineteenth-century Europe reveals a profound conviction of her own equality as an independent, public being and a citizen of the world. Yet these life choices and identities do not reverberate in the image of womanhood she constructs in her work. This dichotomy is particularly tangible in her engagement with women's education. Whilst her writing focuses increasingly on moral and religious instruction as a preparation for women's domestic duties, the broad curriculum she taught in her school tells a different story. It is perhaps as a kind of 'feminist-educator' that Floresta in fact earns her most powerful liberal feminist credentials: with the practical work done in the Collegio Augusto, educating girls to an unprecedented intellectual level and simultaneously confronting and combating parental and social prejudices, Floresta showed herself to be operating far ahead of her time and in the face of considerable cultural and practical constraints.

However, Floresta's right to enjoy an important historical reputation by no means rests only on her discussion of women's education and wider condition. It is in her engagement with a range of other social and literary discourses that we find some of the writer's most interesting and challenging positionings, which highlight the unconventional stance she was taking as a woman writer simply by engaging in public, political debates, and moreover often espousing polemical causes. Undoubtedly her Indianist poem *Lágrima* numbers amongst her most important works in its political audacity and ingenious manipulation of a nationalist, establishment discourse for very different ends, demonstrating an impressive degree of literary intuition. This unique

---

[1]   It must be remembered that she did not adopt her lifelong pseudonym as a means to anonymity.

text certainly warrants a mention in studies of Indianist literature, not only to redress the exclusion of women writers from such works, but more importantly because it provides a revealing counterpoint to the political ideologies traditionally associated with the movement. It is ironic that, although *Lágrima* has received limited attention in most studies of Floresta's writing, no doubt largely due to the fact that it does not address the subject of women, in this instance her own gender appears to have opened new spaces for her. It is in part the very fact that she was a woman, and thus excluded from the authorial conventions of the state-endorsed nation-building programme that fuelled the Indianist movement, which allowed her to write this truly radical and subversive text on its margins.

A focus on Floresta's concern for the oppressed, her supposed 'missão humanitária',[2] leads Constância Lima Duarte to look for a very different significance in *Lágrima*, but the fact that I do not believe the poem reveals a genuine concern for the Brazilian Indian, as Duarte suggests, in no way detracts from its significance. In fact, I would suggest that *Lágrima*, seen as an Indianist text, albeit a fundamentally unconventional one, needs to be ascribed greater value in an analysis of Floresta's work. Moreover, the title of 'Indianist', an aspect of her literary identity that is often lost behind the façade of feminism and abolitionism, deserves to feature more prominently in her definition as a writer and her position in the canon.

Floresta's reputation as an abolitionist, fostered by Brazilian positivists at the end of the nineteenth century, in fact pre-dates the focus on her writings on women and education, which now dominate discussions of her work. However, as I have demonstrated, this abolitionist definition is monolinear and reductive, and in fact hides a complex and shifting engagement with the slavery debate. In particular, her only work to focus exclusively on the subject, 'Paginas', is a problematic and ambiguous text which clearly reveals the influence of the prevalent pro-slavery attitudes and discourses of the time, alongside its anti-slavery elements. However, as possibly the earliest work of fiction criticising the conditions of slavery, written at a time when public and political opinion was still overwhelmingly in favour of the institution, 'Paginas' remains a significant early contribution to the development of anti-slavery discourse in Brazil.

Floresta's later writing reveals a more overtly anti-slavery and emancipatory message, but even in her final texts her patriotic concern for her nation's international reputation still overrides her concern for the slave. Furthermore, in her European texts the image she seeks to construct of Brazil as essentially white and civilised continues to stymie her appeals for the end of slavery and to prevent her from engaging with the rights of the black slave, as it does also in her brief depictions of the indigenous population. What is perhaps

---

2   Duarte, *Vida e Obra*, p. 329.

most significant in an evaluation of Floresta's 'abolitionism', however, is the fact that she does not draw parallels between the oppression of women and the state of slavery, instead treating the two issues in isolation, or even as opposing factors. Nor does she engage with the specific conditions of black slave women, and she in fact excludes them from her vision of 'universal' womanhood. In the end this inability, or unwillingness, to unite her attack on the oppression of women and her condemnation of slavery acts as a powerful ideological brake on the intellectual development of both discourses.

More than any other, I would therefore suggest, it is the title of 'abolitionist' that must be reassessed. It is far too uniform and general a label for such a complex engagement with the subject. However, that is not to say that Floresta's writings on slavery should not be afforded considerable importance. As the earliest female voice to be raised in a discursive process marked by the conspicuous absence of female participation, her contribution to the long and difficult path to abolition is certainly significant.

The final discourse by which Floresta is consistently defined is, of course, that of liberal political ideology in the form of federalism and republicanism, and once again this label is by no means consistently endorsed in an analysis of her work as a whole. Although *Lágrima* is unquestionably pro-federalist and pro-republican in its support for the Praieira Revolt, other texts written only a few years either side of this poem are critical of such divisive politics, and Floresta's personal loyalty to Nunes Machado makes an objective analysis of her ideals difficult in a reading of *Lágrima*. In *Opúsculo* Floresta clearly expresses her belief in the immense value of Brazilian unity, and subsequent European texts do not adopt a consistent position with regard to modes of national governance and political systems. What is most apparent is that Floresta's increasingly patriotic motivation is incompatible with in-depth political discussion, and it is the former that takes precedence.

In fact, careful reading of Floresta's work consistently reveals that alongside, and at times even more than, gender, it is patriotism that shapes the majority of her writing and her construction of herself. If we are to continue ascribing labels to this writer whose work resists such easy definitions, the title of 'patriot' should certainly count amongst them. Yet this is a discursive foundation which is largely neglected by those who have studied her work.

This study is based on the premise that while the recent liberal feminist recuperation of Floresta's work in Brazil has been a valuable intellectual move, a more politically objective and attentive reading of Floresta's writings is now called for in terms of her contribution as a woman to the key national debates of the nineteenth century. In this way, a picture emerges of the complexities and inconsistencies that shaped her views on the controversial big topics of post-independence Brazil: slavery, republicanism, national identity, education and literary Indianism, and it is then possible to see how her shifting constructions of gender, race and class interact and shape one another depending on the social and geographical context. These shifting discourses make it increasingly difficult to reduce Floresta's identity to any fixed political or discursive label.

It need hardly be said that there is still much more to be thought, said and written about Floresta and her work. Her own writings are so extensive, so broad in their scope, and so complex in their positionings that more detailed studies could, and should, be dedicated to particular aspects of her work. With this book I hope to have countered some of the more hagiographic constructions of the woman and her writing which have allowed certain myths and misinformation to pass unchallenged in Brazil's literary historiography. I have questioned and re-evaluated some of the prevailing definitions of Floresta as a writer upon which her place in the Brazilian canon has been established, and highlighted the complexity of the textual reality behind these labels. And yet, despite the many constraints and contradictions that beset her work, the fact remains that Floresta was a woman participating in the (male) social, political and literary discourses that were central to the construction of the Brazilian nation after independence. In this she is one of a tiny number of women writers, and is probably unique in tackling such a broad range of issues. For this reason, her contribution to Brazilian letters and the history of women's writing in Brazil is outstanding. It is therefore all the more important that her work be objectively re-evaluated, and that all aspects of her multifaceted literary career be given the consideration they deserve, in order that her status can be defended fairly, without obfuscation by the mythology that continues to surround her.

BIBLIOGRAPHY

Works by Nísia Floresta

Discurso que as suas educandas dirigio N. F. B. Augusta, em 18 de dezembro de 1847 (Rio de Janeiro: Typographia Imparcial de F. de Paula Brito, 1847)

A Lágrima de um Caheté, por Tellesilla (Rio de Janeiro: Typ. de L. A. F. de Menezes, 1849)

'Páginas de uma vida obscura', *O Brasil Ilustrado*, Rio de Janeiro, 14 & 31 March, 15 & 30 April, 15 & 31 May, 15 & 30 June 1855

'Passeio ao Aqueducto da Carioca', *O Brasil Ilustrado*, Rio de Janeiro, 15 July 1855

'O Pranto Filial', *O Brasil Ilustrado*, Rio de Janeiro, 31 March 1856

Trois Ans en Italie, Suivis d'un Voyage en Grèce, vol. 2 (Paris: E. Dentu Libraire-Éditeur et Jeffes, Libraire A. Londres, 1871)

Le Brésil (Paris: Libraire André Sagnier, 1871)

Itinerário de uma Viagem à Alemanha, trans. Francisco das Chagas Pereira (Natal: Editora Universitária, 1982)

Direitos das Mulheres e Injustiça dos Homens, 4th edn?, introduction and notes by Constância Lima Duarte (São Paulo: Cortez Editora, 1989)

Opúsculo Humanitário, 2nd edn, introduction and notes by Peggy Sharpe Valadares (São Paulo: Cortez Editora, 1989)

'Conselhos a minha filha', in *Nísia Floresta: Vida e Obra*, Constância Lima Duarte (doctoral thesis, Universidade de São Paulo, 1991), vol. III anexos, pp. 33–64

'Fany, ou o modelo das donzelas', in *Nísia Floresta: Vida e Obra*, Constância Lima Duarte (doctoral thesis, Universidade de São Paulo, 1991), vol. III anexos, pp. 65–73

'O Brasil', in *Cintilações de uma Alma Brasileira*, trans. Michele A. Vartulli (Florianópolis: Editora Mulheres, 1997), pp. 7–63

'O abismo sob as flores da civilização', in *Cintilações de uma Alma Brasileira*, trans. Michele A. Vartulli (Florianópolis: Editora Mulheres, 1997), pp. 65–81

'A Mulher', in *Cintilações de uma Alma Brasileira*, trans. Michele A. Vartulli (Florianópolis: Editora Mulheres, 1997), pp. 83–159

'Viagem Magnética', in *Cintilações de uma Alma Brasileira*, trans. Michele A. Vartulli (Florianópolis: Editora Mulheres, 1997), pp. 161–81

'Um passeio no jardim de Luxemburgo', in *Cintilações de uma Alma Brasileira*, trans. Michele A Vartulli (Florianópolis: Editora Mulheres, 1997), pp. 183-203

Três anos na Itália seguidos de uma viagem à Grécia, vol. 1, trans. Francisco das Chagas Pereira (Natal: EDUFRN, 1998)

Fragmentos de uma Obra Inédita: Notas Biográficas, trans. Nathalie Bernardo da Câmara (Brasília: Editora da UnB, 2001)

General Bibliography

Agulhon, Maurice, *Marianne into Battle: Republican Imagery and Symbolism in France, 1789–1890*, trans. Janet Lloyd (Cambridge: Cambridge University Press, 1981)

Alencar, José de, *Iracema* (São Paulo: Editora Moderna, 1984)

Aron, Raymond, *Main Currents in Sociological Thought* (New York: Doubleday, 1968)

Azevedo, Célia Maria Marinho de, *Onda Negra, Medo Branco: O negro no imaginário das elites – Século XIX* (Rio de Janeiro and São Paulo: Editora Paz e Terra, 1987)

Barandas, Ana Euridice Eufrosina de, *O Ramalhete, ou flores escolhidas no jardim da imaginação*, 2nd edn (Porto Alegre: Nova Dimensão, 1990)

Barman, Roderick J., *Brazil: The Forging of a Nation, 1798–1852* (Stanford, CA: Stanford University Press, 1988)

Barre, François Poulain de la, *The Equality of the Sexes*, trans. Desmond M. Clarke (Manchester and New York: Manchester University Press, 1990)

Barreto, J. J., 'Precursora da emancipação feminina no Brasil: Nísia Floresta – (1885–1985)', *O Poti*, Natal, 26 May 1985

Bethell, Leslie, *The Abolition of the Brazilian Slave Trade: Britain, Brazil and the Slave Trade Question, 1809–1869* (Cambridge: Cambridge University Press, 1970)

Brazil, Érico Vital, and Schuma Schumaher (eds), *Dicionário Mulheres do Brasil* (Rio de Janeiro: Jorge Zahar, 2000)

Brook, L., *Books and Book-Collecting* (Aldershot: Gower, 1982)

Brookshaw, David, *Paradise Betrayed: Brazilian Literature of the Indian* (Amsterdam: CEDLA, 1988)

Burns, E. Bradford, *A History of Brazil*, 3rd edn (New York: Columbia University Press, 1993)

—, *Nationalism in Brazil: A Historical Survey* (New York, Washington and London: Frederick A. Praeger, 1968)

Câmara, Adauto da, *História de Nísia Floresta*, 2nd edn (Natal: Departamento Estadual de Imprensa, 1997)

Câmara, Nathalie Bernardo da, *Da Aurora ao Crepúsculo* (Natal: Fundação José Augusto, 1997)

Castro, Ana Luísa de Azevedo, *D. Narcisa de Villar*, 3rd edn (Florianópolis: Editora Mulheres, 1997)

Cavaliero, Roderick, *The Independence of Brazil* (London: British Academic, 1993)

Clarke, Desmond M., 'Introduction', in *The Equality of the Sexes*, François Poulain de la Barre, trans. Desmond M. Clarke (Manchester and New York: Manchester University Press, 1990), pp. 1–39

Cobban, Alfred, *A History of Modern France. Volume 2: 1799–1871* (London: Penguin Books, 1991)

Collins, Jane-Marie, 'Slavery, Subversion and Subalternity: Gender and Violent Resistance in Nineteenth-Century Bahia', in *Brazilian Feminisms*, ed. Solange Ribeiro de Oliveira and Judith Still (Nottingham: University of Nottingham, 1999), pp. 34–56

Conrad, Robert, *Children of God's Fire: A Documentary History of Black Slavery in Brazil* (Princeton: Princeton University Press, 1983)

—, *The Destruction of Brazilian Slavery, 1850–1888*, 2nd edn (Malabar, FA: Krieger Publishing, 1993)

Coole, Diana H., *Women in Political Theory: fromAancient Misogyny to Contemporary Feminism* (Brighton: Wheatsheaf, 1988)

Costa, Emilia Viotti da, *The Brazilian Empire: Myths and Histories* (London: University of Chicago Press, 1985)

—, 'Patriarchalism and the Myth of the Helpless Woman', in *The Brazilian Empire: Myths and Histories*, revised edn (London: University of North Carolina Press, 2000), pp. 247–65

Coutinho, Jose Lino, *Cartas sobre a educação de Cora, seguidas de um cathecismo moral, politico e religioso* (Bahia: Typ. de Carlos Poggetti, 1849)

Davies, Kate, 'A moral Purchase: Femininity, Commerce and Abolition, 1788–1792', in M*Women, Writing and the Public Sphere, 1700–1830*, ed. Elizabeth Eger et al. (Cambridge: Cambridge University Press, 2001), pp. 133–59

Davis, Darién, *Avoiding the Dark: Race and the Forging of National Culture in Modern Brazil* (Aldershot: Ashgate, 1999)

Dépêche, Marie France, 'As traduções subversivas feministas ontem e hoje', *Labrys, Estudos Feministas*, 1–2 (2002), n. pag. <http://vsites.unb.br/ih/his/gefem/labrys1_2/mfd1.html> [accessed 29 July 2010]

Dias, Gonçalves, *Poesia Indianista* (São Paulo: Martins Fontes, 2002)

Douglas, Ann, 'Introduction: The Art of Controversy', in *Uncle Tom's Cabin or, Life Among the Lowly*, Harriet Beecher Stowe (London: Penguin, 1986), pp. 7–34

Duarte, Constância Lima, 'Apresentação', in *Cintilações de uma Alma Brasileira*, Nísia Floresta Brasileira Augusta, trans. Michele A. Vartulli (Florianópolis: Editora Mulheres, 1997), pp. xii–xxix

—, 'Nísia Floresta: Incompreensão em relação à sua Genialidade', *Ciência e Trópico*, 26 (July/Dec. 1998), 253–60

—, *Nísia Floresta: a primeira feminista do Brasil* (Florianópolis: Editora Mulheres; EDUNISC, 2005)

—, 'Posfácio: Nos primórdios do feminismo brasileiro', in *Direitos das Mulheres e Injustiça dos Homens*, Nísia Floresta Brasileira Augusta, 4th edn? (São Paulo: Editora Cortez, 1989), pp. 97–134

—, *Nísia Floresta: Vida e Obra* (Natal: EDUFRN, 1995)

Durão, José de Santa Rita, 'Caramuru', in *Épicos Brasileiros*, ed. F. A. de Varnhagen, 2nd edn (Lisbon: Imprensa Nacional, 1845)

Espelho das Brasileiras, Recife, 8 April 1831

Fausto, Boris, *A Concise History of Brazil* (Cambridge: Cambridge University Press, 1999)

Finkelstein, David and Alistair McCleery, *An Introduction to Book History* (New York and London: Routledge, 2005)

Flores, Hilda Agnes Hübner, 'Ana Euridice Eufrosina de Barandas: Vida e Obra', in *O Ramalhete, ou flores escolhidas no jardim da imaginação*, Ana de Barandas (Porto Alegre: Nova Dimensão, 1990), pp. 11–50

—, 'Nísia Floresta Brasileira Augusta', *Letras de Hoje*, 89 (Sept. 1992), 101–13

Frawley, Maria H., *A Wider Range: Travel Writing by Women in Victorian England* (Rutherford: Fairleigh Dickinson University Press; London: Associated University Presses, 1994)

Frehse, Fraya, 'Review of *Nísia Floresta, O Carapuceiro e outros ensaios de traduçao cultural*, by Maria Lúcia Pallares-Burke', *Revista da Antropologia*, 40: 2 (1997), 235–45. http://www.scielo.br/scielo.php?script=sci_arttext&pid=S0034-77011997000200008&lng=en&nrm=iso <doi: 10.1590/S0034-77011997000200008> [accessed 29 July 2010]

Gama, Basílio da, 'O Uraguay', in *Épicos Brasileiros*, ed. F. A. de Varnhagen, 2nd edn (Lisbon: Imprensa Nacional, 1845)

Garnier, C., ' "La Femme n'est pas inférieure à l'homme" (1750): oeuvre de Madeleine Darsant de Puisieux ou simple traduction française?', *Revue d'Histoire Littéraire de la France*, 4 (1987), 709–13

Giacomini, Sonia M., 'Ser escrava no Brasil', *Estudos Afro-Asiáticos*, 15 (1988), 145–69

Grillo, Joaquim de Meiroz, 'Conferencia proferida na então vila de Goianinha, em 1924', appendix to João Medeiros Filho, *Nísia Floresta*, Separata do livro em preparo *Um advogado na Academia de Letras* (Natal: [n. pub.], 1981)

Hahner, June, *Emancipating the Female Sex: The Struggle for Women's Rights in Brazil, 1850–1940* (Durham, NC and London: Duke University Press, 1990)

—, *Women Through Women's Eyes: Latin American Women in Nineteenth-century Travel Accounts* (Wilmington, DE: SR Books, 1998)

Hallewell, Laurence, *Books in Brazil: a History of the Publishing Trade* (Metuchen, NJ and London: Scarecrow, 1982)

Hemming, John, 'Indians and the Frontier', in *Colonial Brazil*, ed. Leslie Bethell (Cambridge: Cambridge University Press, 1991), pp. 145–89

Hersh, Blanche Glassman, *The Slavery of Sex: Feminist-Abolitionists in America* (Urbana, Chicago and London: University of Illinois Press, 1978)

Hofkosh, Sonia, 'Tradition and *The Interesting Narrative*: Capitalism, Abolition and the Romantic Individual', in *Romanticism, Race, and Imperial Culture, 1780–1834*, ed. Alan Richardson and Sonia Hofkosh (Bloomington: Indiana University Press, 1996), pp. 330–43

Hoganson, Kristin, 'Garrisonian Abolitionists and the Rhetoric of Gender, 1850–1860', *American Quarterly*, 45 (December 1993), 558–95

Holanda, Sérgio Buarque de, *Raízes do Brasil*, 21st edn (Rio de Janeiro: José Olympio, 1989)

Johnson, H. B., 'Portuguese Settlement, 1500–1580', in *Colonial Brazil*, ed. Leslie Bethell (Cambridge: Cambridge University Press, 1991), pp. 1–38

Jornal do Commercio, Rio de Janeiro, 31 January 1838 and 18 December 1846

Le Triomphe des Dames. Traduit de l'Anglois de Miledi P**** (Paris: [n. pub.], 1751)

Leite, Miriam Lifchitz Moreira, 'A dupla documentação sobre mulheres no livro das viajantes (1800–1850)', in *Vivência: História, Sexualidade e imagens femininas*, ed. Cristina Bruschini and Fúlvia Rosemberg (São Paulo: Brasiliense; Fundação Carlos Chagas, 1980), pp. 195–226

—, 'Mulheres viajantes no século XIX', *Cadernos Pagu: gênero, ciências, história*, 15 (2000), 129–43

—, 'Uma Construção Enviesada: A mulher e o nacionalismo', in *A Mulher na Literatura*, ed. Nádia Battella Gotlib, vol. 3 (Belo Horizonte: Imprensa da UFMG, 1990), pp. 56–66

Liddell, Charlotte, 'Nature, Nurture and Nation: Nísia Floresta's Engagement in the Breast-feeding Debate in Brazil and France', *Feminist Review*, 79 (2005), 69–82

Lima, Oliveira, 'Nísia Floresta: discurso pronunciado na Escola Doméstica do Natal', manuscript, 1919

Loomba, Ania, *Colonialism/Postcolonialism* (London: Routledge, 1998)

Lopes, Eliane Marta Santos Teixeira, 'A educação da mulher: A feminização do magistério', *Teoria & Educação*, 4 (1991), 22–40

Louro, Guacira Lopes, 'Mulheres na sala de aula', in *História das mulheres no Brasil*, ed. Mary del Priore, 2nd edn (São Paulo: Contexto, 1997), pp. 443–81

McClintock, Anne, *Imperial Leather: Race, Gender and Sexuality in the Colonial Contest* (London: Routledge, 1995)

Macedo, Joaquim Manuel de, *A Moreninha*, 34th edn (São Paulo: Editora Ática, 2001)

Maia, Emilio Joaquim da Silva, *Ensaio sobre os perigos à que estão sujeitos os meninos, quando não são amamentados por suas proprias mãis* (Rio de Janeiro: Typ. de R. Ogier, 1834)

Martins, Wilson, 'Cidade das Mulheres', *Jornal de Poesia/O Globo On Line – Prosa e Verso*, 20 November 1999. <http://www.revista.agulha.nom.br/wilsonmartins071.html> [accessed 29 July 2010]

Matthews, Charlotte Hammond, 'Between "Founding Text" and "Literary Prank": Reasoning the Roots of Nísia Floresta's *Direitos das Mulheres e Injustiça dos Homens*', *Ellipsis*, 8 (2010), 9–36

Medeiros, José Henrique de, *A mamentação materna é quase sempre possivel*, medical thesis (Rio de Janeiro: Typ. Imparcial de Francisco de Paula Brito, 1848)

Mellor, Anne, '"Am I Not a Woman and a Sister?": Slavery, Romanticism, and Gender', in *Romanticism, Race, and Imperial Culture, 1780–1834*, ed. Alan Richardson and Sonia Hofkosh (Bloomington: Indiana University Press, 1996), pp. 311–29

Mendonça, Maria Helena, 'Nísia Floresta: romantismo e consciência reformadora', in *Desafiando o Cânone (2): ecos de vozes femininas na literature brasileira do século XIX*, ed. Helena Parente Cunha (Rio de Janeiro: Faculdade de Letras da UFRJ, 2001), pp. 27–40

Midgley, Claire, *Women Against Slavery: The British Campaigns, 1780–1870* (London and New York: Routledge, 1995)

Mott, Maria Lúcia de Barros, *Submissão e resistência: A mulher na luta contra a escravidão* (São Paulo: Contexto, 1988)

Mulher Brasileira – Bibliografia Anotada, vol. 2 (São Paulo: Fundação Carlos Chagas; Brasiliense, 1981)

O Jornal das Senhoras, Rio de Janeiro, January 1852 to December 1855

O Mercantil, Rio de Janeiro, 2 & 17 January 1847

Offen, Karen, 'Contextualizing the Theory and Practice of Feminism in Nineteenth-Century Europe (1789–1914)', in *Becoming Visible: Women in European History*, ed. Renate Bridenthal, Susan Stuard and Merry Wiesner, 3rd edn (Boston and New York: Houghton Mifflin, 1998), pp. 327–55

Owen, Hilary, 'Gender and Revolution in Southern Brazil: Restitching the Farroupilha Revolt in the Works of Delfina Benigna da Cunha and Ana de Barandas', in *Latin American Independence: Gender, Politics, Text*, Catherine Davies, Claire Brewster and Hilary Owen (Liverpool: Liverpool University Press, 2006), pp. 210–40

Pallares-Burke, Maria Lúcia Gárcia, 'A Mary Wollstonecraft que o Brasil conheceu, ou a travessura literária de Nísia Floresta', in *Nísia Floresta, O Carapuceiro e outros ensaios de traduçao cultural* (São Paulo: Editora HUCITEC, 1996), pp. 167–92

—, 'A Spectator in the Tropics: A Case Study of Production and Reproduction of Culture', *Comparative Studies in Society and History*, 36: 4 (1994), 676–701

Pateman, Carole, *The Disorder of Women* (Cambridge: Polity Press, 1995)

Quintas, Amaro, *O Sentido social da Revolução Praieira*, 6th edn (Recife: Editora Massangana, 1982)

Ramalho, Christina, 'Um Indianismo transgressor: Nísia Floresta', in *Elas escrevem o épico* (Florianópolis: Editora Mulheres; EDUNISC, 2005), pp. 55–67

Reis, Maria Firmina dos, *Úrsula: romance original brasileiro*, facsimile edn (Rio de Janeiro: Gráfica Olímpica Editora, 1975)

Rousseau, Jean-Jacques, *Discourse on Political Economy and The Social Contract*, trans. Christopher Betts (Oxford and New York: Oxford University Press, 1994)

—, *Émile*, trans. Barbara Foxley (London: J. M. Dent & Sons, 1911)

Sabino, Ignez, *Mulheres Illustres do Brazil* (Rio de Janeiro and Paris: H Garnier, 1899)

Saffioti, Heleieth I. B., *Women in Class Society*, trans. Michael Vale (New York and London: Monthly Review Press, 1978)

Sánchez-Eppler, Karen, 'Bodily Bonds: The Intersecting Rhetorics of Feminism and Abolition', in *The Culture of Sentiment: Race, Gender and Sentimentality in 19th Century America*, ed. Shirley Samuels (Oxford: Oxford University Press, 1992), pp. 92–114

Seidl, Roberto, *Nisia Floresta, 1810–1885* (Rio de Janeiro: [n. pub.], 1933)

Sharpe, Peggy, 'Brazilian Women and Social Reform in Nísia Floresta's *Opús-*

culo Humanitário', *Brazil: A Journal of Brazilian Literature*, 1 (1988), 17–29

—, 'Reading Nísia Floresta: A Feminist Perspective', *Linea Plural*, 1: 2 (Spring 1988), 28–32

Silva, Innocencio Francisco da, *Diccionario Bibliographico Portuguez*, Tomo 6 (Lisbon: Imprensa Nacional, 1862)

Silva, José Bonifácio de Andrada e, *Representação á Assemblea Geral Constituinte e Legislativa do Imperio do Brasil sobre a Escravatura* (Paris: Typ. De Firmin Didot, 1825)

Skidmore, Thomas E., *Brazil: Five Centuries of Change* (Oxford: Oxford University Press, 1999)

Slenes, Robert Wayne, 'Black Homes, White Homilies: Perceptions of the Slave Family and of Slave women in Nineteenth-Century Brazil', in *More than Chattel: Black Women and Slavery in the Americas*, ed. David Barry Gasper and Darlene Clark Hine (Bloomington, IN: Indiana University Press, 1996), pp. 126–46

Sophia, A Person of Quality, *Woman Not Inferior to Man: or, A short and modest Vindication of the Natural Right of the Fair-Sex to a Perfect Equality of Power, Dignity and Esteem, with the Men*, facsimile edn (London: Brentham Press, 1975)

Sousa, António Gonçalves Teixeira e, *Os Três Dias de um Noivado* (Rio de Janeiro: Typ. Imparcial de Paula Brito, 1844)

Stetson, Erlene, 'Studying Slavery: Some Literary and Pedagogical Considerations on the Black Female Slave', in *All the Women Are White, All the Blacks Are Men, But Some of Us Are Brave: Black Women's Studies*, ed. Gloria T. Hull, Patricia Bell Scott and Barbara Smith (New York: Feminist Press, 1982), pp. 61–84

Stowe, Harriet Beecher, *Uncle Tom's Cabin or, Life Among the Lowly* (London: Penguin, 1986)

Sussman, George D, *Selling Mother's Milk: the Wet-nursing Business in France, 1715–1914* (Urbana, Chicago and London: University of Illinois Press, 1982)

Todd, Janet, 'Introduction and Notes', in *A Vindication of the Rights of Woman*, Mary Wollstonecraft (Oxford: Oxford University Press, 1999), pp. vii–xxxvi

Toplin, Robert Brent, *The Abolition of Slavery in Brazil* (New York: Atheneum, 1972)

Treece, David, *Exiles, Allies, Rebels: Brazil's Indianist Movement, Indigenist Politics, and the Imperial Nation-State* (London: Greenwood Press, 2000)

Vliet, Rietje van, 'Print and Public in Europe 1600–1800', in *A Companion to the History of the Book*, ed. Simon Eliot and Jonathon Rose (Oxford: Blackwell, 2007), pp. 247–58

Warner, Marina, *Monuments and Maidens: The Allegory of the Female Form* (London: Butler & Tanner, 1985)

Wernick, Andrew, *Auguste Comte and the Religion of Humanity: The Post-Theistic Program of French Social Theory* (Cambridge: Cambridge University Press, 2001)

Wollstonecraft, Mary, *A Vindication of the Rights of Woman* (Oxford: Oxford University Press, 1999)

Yellin, Jean Fagan, *Women and Sisters: The Antislavery Feminists in American Culture* (New Haven and London: Yale University Press, 1989)

Zaira Americana Mostra as Imensas Vantagens que a Sociedade inteira obtém da Ilustração, Virtudes e Perfeita Educação da Mulher, como Mãe e Esposa do Homem (Rio de Janeiro: Typ. Dois de Dezembro de Paula Brito, 1853)

INDEX